CULTURAL DIVERSITY
AND ISLAM

Edited by
Abdul Aziz Said
Meena Sharify-Funk

University Press of America,® Inc.
Lanham · New York · Oxford

Copyright © 2003 by
University Press of America,® Inc.
4501 Forbes Boulevard
Suite 200
Lanham, Maryland 20706
UPA Acquisitions Department (301) 459-3366

PO Box 317
Oxford
OX2 9RU, UK

ISBN 0-7618-2522-3 (clothbound : alk. ppr.)
ISBN 0-7618-2523-1 (paperback : alk. ppr.)

⊖™ The paper used in this publication meets the minimum
requirements of American National Standard for Information
Sciences—Permanence of Paper for Printed Library Materials,
ANSI Z39.48—1984

Contents

Acknowledgments

Acknowledgments

This edited volume would not have been possible without the support of many individuals. We thank them for their patience, generosity, and support. We offer our gratitude to all the participants of the international conference on "Cultural Diversity and Islam," including those who were not able to submit their papers. Several special thanks need to be expressed towards the American University's (AU) Center for Global Peace and the Mohammed Said Farsi Chair of Islamic Peace at American University. We are grateful to Mohammed Said Farsi and Hani Farsi, his son, for their vision, kindness and devotion. Their vision, inspired with a devotion to peace, enables them to see that East and West can meet—that the East can remain faithful to its cultural heritage while accepting the best that the West can offer, and, moreover, that the East can offer its own cultural riches to the West.

We would also like to give special thanks to Betty Sitka and Rachel Pentlarge of the AU Center for Global Peace who both provided invaluable assistance and encouragement throughout this project. Also our appreciation goes out to Nicole Forbes of the Mohammed Said Farsi Chair who contributed her time and effort in proofreading the manuscript. And lastly, we would like to thank Nathan C. Funk for his continual technical and emotional support of this project.

INTRODUCTION

A Summary of Papers

Abdul Aziz Said
and Meena Sharify-Funk

Islam is perhaps the most misunderstood religion today, among both non-Muslims and Muslims. The Prophet Muhammad's saying appears to have been realized: "Islam began as a stranger (*gharib*, i.e. exiled and unrecognized), and it will revert again to the condition of being a stranger. Blessed are the strangers." What accounts for the West's feeling of estrangement from Islam and Muslims' feeling of estrangement from the ideals of their own religion?

Islam is not only a theological doctrine, but it is also a historical dynamic that involves today's Muslims as well as abstract Islam. We need to understand Islam, Muslims, and the diversity of Muslim societies. The history of Islam is a one of tension between the ideals of the Qur'an and the ability of Muslims to realize them. The ideals of Islam are not static but constantly evolving. Every historical period and cultural milieu has fostered a different synthesis of Islamic Command, from rigid Wahhabism to the more flexible Sufism.

In addition to its social and cultural role, Islam serves a political function, providing a transcendental order to which rulers can be held accountable and a religious standard to which the oppressed can appeal. In the face of corruption and repression, Islam offers a vocabulary of resistance and of hope for a cultural future. This Islamic vocabulary is the way that Muslims express their political identity. Hence, everybody links Islam to his or her own political concerns.

Just as there has always been a stamp of Calvinism on American culture, so, too, there is a stamp of Islam on in those countries in which it is the predominant religion. Modernization theory and scholarship on democracy have been somewhat misleading in the projection of cultural change in the West. Religion has not been simply left behind or rendered obsolete by modernization; even when traditional religion has been bypassed, there have emerged new modes of cultural edification: nationalism, the free-market economy, and cultural triumphalism.

The cultural roots Islam shares with the West are too often forgotten. Although recently voiced (and frequently ill-conceived) opinions regarding a "clash of civilizations" argue that Islam falls outside the Islam's Hellenism was mediated primarily through Eastern Christian intellectual circles, and the important streams of Muslim philosophical and scientific thought remain an understudied link between late antiquity and the Renaissance. Islamic contributions went far beyond mere preservation of the classical legacy, exemplified by the efforts that Abd ar-Rahman Ibn Khaldun made to tutor an Andalusian prince after the model of Plato's *Republic* or by the Heliocentric planetary theories that Copernicus read in Arabic during his studies at the library of Padua. Thus, Islam, as a civilizational force and religious tradition, is an integral part of the Western tradition.

Unfortunately, because of the tragic events of September 11, 2001, a "clash of symbols" is being waged between Islam and the West. This is not a clash of civilizations. Westerners are now repelled by headscarves, turbans, and other symbols of Islam, just as fundamentalist Muslims have seen bluejeans and other manifestations of Western culture as explicitly anti-Islamic. Belief systems are becoming simplified into images to be either rejected or absorbed in their entirety.

Cultural contact between Islam and the West has been marred by a historical inequality of power relations that has rendered the West arrogant and insensitive and the Muslim world defensive and insecure. The West and Islam are caught in a twin cycle of arrogance that breeds contempt, fanaticism, and paranoia. Western cultural triumphalism is sustained through the use of mass media, educational systems, and control over the symbols of legitimacy and status. The "with us or against us" simplification is the latest expression of Western cultural triumphalism, backed up on this occasion by overwhelming military force.

The West and the Islamic world are out of touch with each other: the West is uncertain whether the Muslim world understands its belief that it is not waging a holy war against Islam, while Muslims remain uncertain that the US is not embarking on a Crusade. This degree of mutual estrangement also suggests the antidote: before the West can effectively convey its intentions, it must understand what is going on in the Arab and Muslim world today. This understanding involves active listening to the voices from the region and active engagement with them in sustained dialogue.

In this volume, we examine Islam as a deeply embedded discourse, an enduring system of meanings, and the basis for a harmonious social order for Muslims with universal prescriptions for social justice, human dignity, and cultural pluralism. Over three years ago, on November 20-21, 1998, fifteen internationally known scholars on Islam gathered and presented papers at the conference, "Cultural Diversity and Islam," at American University in Washington, DC. Organized under the auspices of the Mohammed Said Farsi Chair of Islamic Peace and American University's Center for Global Peace, this two-day conference examined the role of diversity and cultural coexistence in Islam. This volume is a compilation of papers by the participating scholars, presented with commentary. These papers address Islamic concepts of conflict resolution and cultural diversity as a counterpoint to the West's standard, liberal position of neutrality and tolerance toward cultural differences. Cultural diversity in Islam parallels political pluralism in the Western liberal tradition. While the latter receives ample acknowledgment, Islamic contributions in the area of cultural diversity deserve more of our attention, particularly as we enter a new world in the wake of the events of September 11, 2001.

In the first section, "Cultural Diversity in a Civilizational Perspective," the precepts and practices of cultural diversity and religious tolerance within Islamic and Western civilizations are explored and compared. Particular attention is given to the ways in which religious precepts and values have coalesced with cultural realities and intellectual developments to produce broad patterns of historical practice. The chapters also concentrate on notions of unity and diversity within Islamic culture and examine how cultural traditions are interpreted and practiced in a modern context.

Although each author in this section approaches the subject from different perspectives -- philosophy, social values, metaphysical understanding, and identity -- there are nonetheless overlapping themes, including the transcendent foundation of diversity, the cultural strength that diversity contributes to Islam, the flawed emulation of

European nationalism, and the confusion of monotheism with monolithism.

In contrast to classical or premodern ideas of an integrative force of unity amid the providential necessity of diversity, many Islamic scholars are lamenting new trends toward a monolithic, flat Islamic discourse and the marginalization of minorities. Scholars also lament the translation of Islam into a state system, a shift from *dawlah* (state government) to the nationalistic discourse. This notion of regression within Islamic societies, found within the current populist discourse, is unsophisticated; in the search for authentic identity and political ideas, Islamic thinkers have neglected much of the historical development of Islam. Nonetheless, there are some signs of a restoration process and of a deeper recognition of internal pluralism.

The former Ibn Khaldun Professor of Islamic Studies at American University, Serif Mardin, has often stated that one of the saving graces of classical Islamic societies is the ability to "live with more than one face." Unfortunately, this ability is at odds with a currently prevailing spirit of nationalism. The constant expansion of Islam from Arabia has become a nationalization of Islam. This Islam encountered a number of pre-Islamic, well-established, non-Arab cultures, each with its own characteristics that were integrated into Islam. Marshall Hodgson has labeled this integration as the rise of "Islamicate" culture. Not all Arab thinkers were sanguine about these developments, but the idea of an Islamic community overcame fears that this integration was still incomplete. This saving grace is also undermined in much contemporary Islamic discourse, which is essentially preoccupied with the Islamization of modernity.

Modern developments and the nature of modernity have brought back elements of dissociation in the *Ummah* (Islamic community). Modernity, insofar as it promoted wide-ranging education for all, relied on a spread of literacy that depended on national languages such as Arabic, Farsi, and Turkish. The propagation of Islamic culture thus reached many of the classes that had been left out of the elite Islamic discourse, but only by widening the gap between cultures. Not much has been written about this nationalization of Islam, which is an element Islam has to be taken into account.

It is this exchange between the classical and modern models for diversity that has the capacity to accommodate and integrate reciprocal exchange among parts of the whole. Several authors, however, point out how this unifying, integrating form of diversity is unraveling in the face of nationalism, the modern nation-state, the Western concept of the self, and the form of diversity embraced by contemporary Western society. The dominant economic and even mass cultural pattern expanding around the world leads to conflict. Without integrative unity, pluralism and diversity result in conflict, not integration.

In the opening keynote address and first chapter, Seyyed Hossein Nasr reminds us that the essential Islamic doctrine of *tawhid* (unity) involves both uniformity and integration of multiplicity into unity, which consequently stems from the Divine. Unity. This attempt to inject a distinction between contemporary diversity and this Islamic vision of unity and diversity is a major theme throughout most of the papers. That Islam embraces so many cultures yet functions as a unified civilization is indicative of this phenomenon.

In "Unity and Diversity in Islam and Islamic Civilization," Nasr establishes the relation between unity and diversity in Islam as both religion and civilization. He addresses the common misconception that because Islam is based on unity, it is opposed to diversity. He examines the first principles and metaphysical understanding of unity within Islam, providing a solid foundation from which to view Islamic history, culture, and civilization. Unity, he explains, is not uniformity but encompasses multiplicity. This concept of unity in multiplicity has preserved the diversity of Islamicized cultures through history while at the same time unifying them through the bond of Islam and the principle of faith in the One.

Nasr also presents various types of multiplicity and diversity that existed within traditional Islam and contributed to the vitality of Islamic civilization: schools of law, thought, and culture. Diversity that models itself on modern European nationalism does not help the cause of pluralism in the Islamic world. Nasr explains that it has helped destroy to a "notable extent the traditional Islamic world in which pluralism was accepted without the surrender of unity and its integrating power." The challenge for Muslims today is to preserve the message of unity without trying to reduce Islam to a force for uniformity.

Authentic pluralism has a moral basis, affirmed by Nasr's insistence on its connection to a divine, transcendent principle. This principle, he continues, has an integrating power to stabilize a proper unity in diversity, enjoining coexistence among differing worldviews.

Sulayman Nyang, in his chapter, "Continuities and Discontinuities in Islamic Perspectives on Cultural Diversity," eloquently asserts that the homogenizing cultural forces of the globalizing economy and mass communications have also shaken the foundations of Muslim societies. The domination of the mass media combines with the "dumbing down" of Muslim discourse, creating a tendency to ignore the subtlety and flexibility of classical Islamic traditions in favor of the current literalism.

Nyang's insight makes an important contribution by affirming internal pluralism as a means of upholding the principle of self-critique: Muslims need to empower themselves by looking within their own traditions and to refrain from concentrating on outward forces impinging on Islam. Nyang also points out that the original Muslim formulation of the nature of human identity has changed, not only because of lapses in Muslim judgment and behavior, but also because of Muslim attempts at emulating other cultural forms and patterns around the globe. In particular, he explores the influence of the European attitude toward cultural diversity after the fifteenth century, when Europe broke the Muslim monopoly of global trade. Attitudes fostered during the expansion into the Americas, he explains, established a model for the colonization of Muslim lands as well as the cultural and philosophical shifts toward diversity among Muslim intellectuals in the colonial and postcolonial periods.

Nyang also looks at the radical changes in the human view of physical space and the philosophy of ownership raised by the relatively recent events of the Industrial Revolution and the rise of nationalism. In addition to exploring the conflation of color, creed, and culture into one metaphysical category, he discusses the polarization of Muslims in the processing of identity in relation to others and self. The rise of Communism, the Cold War, and the Iranian Revolution provide illustrations of challenges to the Muslim self-definition of pluralism.

The discussions by Nasr and Nyang on Islam and cultural diversity serve as a backdrop for Richard Khuri's chosen emphasis on pluralism. In "'True' and 'False' Pluralism in Relation to the West and Islam," he argues that although the problem has arisen from opposite historical directions in both the Arab Muslim and Western worlds, it is nevertheless the same: the restoration of (true) pluralism. What really matters, however, is not pluralism itself, but its transcendent foundation. Pluralism and cultural diversity are not ends in themselves but, at their best, signs of something more profound. As Khuri notes, part of the challenge is to differentiate authentic pluralism from superficial pluralism.

Khuri first examines pluralism and diversity in the United States, where these values find their strongest expression and thus provide a model—for better or for worse—for some Muslim theorists. He addresses the changing concept of pluralism in the public voice. True pluralism, he explains, is the coexistence between profoundly different worldviews. It no longer thrives in the usual domains in the United

States, however. In higher education, political systems, and the media, for example, true pluralism has been replaced by uniformity and false pluralism or monolithism, which has global implications. In conclusion, he addresses challenges faced by Muslims as they return to a morality-based true pluralism within Islam.

The second section, "Islamic Perspectives on Cultural Diversity," includes the work of three scholars addressing the ways in which Muslims have handled cultural diversity and the notion of coexistence among different ethnic and religious groups within the Islamic world. Through an examination of the essential expressions of cultural diversity within the Qur'an and the Prophet's Moral Conduct (the Sunnah), these authors propose that much of the strength of Islam has been derived from its accommodation of cultural diversity and promotion of coexistence.

The first chapter in this section, by Wadad al-Qadi, is entitled, "The Conceptual Foundation of Cultural Diversity in Pre-Modern Islamic Civilization." In this detailed study, al-Qadi explores the Qur'anic text for Islamic concepts of diversity and authority in order to compare and contrast their relation towards the Islamic concepts of *tawhid* (unity), universalism, and *fitnah* (civil discord). She also comments on the interaction between Islam as a faith and historical events before and after the Prophet's death.

Al-Qadi then looks at the movement of Shu'ubiyya, national self-expression, as a source of cultural diversity within premodern Muslim society. Although this movement has led to many clashes and differences within and between Muslim societies, she contends that it is a source of strength, allowing a society of openness and acceptance of diversity. Emphasizing the benefits of this diversity, al-Qadi frames the tensions associated with national self-expression within a larger process of consensus-building. Though Islam supports diversity, al-Qadi points out that even in the Qur'anic discourse there is a limitation, especially within the context of a single community facing *fitnah* (strife) and its tendency to split into groups. *Fitnah* is deemed a moral and political defect.

Sachiko Murata, in the following chapter of this section, "The Islamic Encounter with the Chinese Intellectual Tradition," reflects on the history of Islam and Muslim thought in China. Her main argument is that the Chinese Islamic tradition, which consists both of Islamic texts that have been translated into Chinese and of indigenous Chinese Muslim scholarship, approaches Islam by means of the neoconfucian tradition. In examining these texts, one can see that Islam has taken on a distinct but nonetheless recognizable form in China. It moves from being explained from an Arabic point of view to being explained from a Chinese point of view in a Chinese context. In order to understand the history of Islam in China, we must recognize both the unique and general features of Chinese Muslim experience: how Chinese Muslims see themselves in Chinese civilization, the nature of Islamic thinking in China, and similarities between Islamic thinking inside of China and Islamic thinking outside of China.

Murata first concentrates on the Chinese *ulama*, the Islamic scholars. Citing two main Chinese Muslim scholars, she makes the case that Islamic texts, when translated into Chinese, focus more on the nature and origin of Islam than on technical Islamic practices. They re-express basic Islamic perspectives in the context of the intellectual tradition of the day. In this, we see the idea that the concepts behind Islam are more fundamental than the structure of Islam, a theme that may also be found in other instances where Islam has spread into non-Arabic cultures. Murata also points out the difficulties of translating from Arabic to Chinese. The Chinese words chosen by the translators usually connote different meanings than were intended in the original Arabic version; these connotations gave a distinctive character to the message in order to express it in Chinese terms.

There are inherent similarities between Islam and the Chinese tradition, such as the concept of unity (*tawhid* in Islam) and a belief in the sacredness of the natural world. She concludes with a provocative quotation showing the shared vision of Islam and the Chinese traditions.

Islam poses a powerful enigma for all those who seek to understand it and write something sensible about it. The very word, "Islam" immediately suggests a set of values and practices that can be understood in terms of its defining texts (the Qur'an), the practice of exemplary individuals (*sunna*), or collective (*Ummah*) or institutional expression (Islamic state, *shari'a* and caliphate). Since the seventh century, scholars have seized upon one or more of these expressions as the primary source for understanding and practicing Islam. These expressions have grown into a rich tapestry of historical experiences that exemplify the diversity and tolerance of Islamic civilization. As contemporary scholars study this rich tapestry, employing the most modern conceptual and epistemological tools, more nuanced and elaborate frameworks for understanding Islam have gradually emerged.

In the third chapter of this section, "Pluralism and Islamic Perspectives on Cultural Diversity," John Voll examines the different precepts and practices within Islam that can serve as means of understanding and dealing with cultural diversity in an Islamic paradigm. He begins with a brief summary of the development of international perspectives on cultural diversity and their impact within Muslim societies. He points out a gradual shift from the view that cultural diversity is a problem demanding a solution toward the view that cultural diversity can be a source of strength and a resource. From the latter viewpoint we come to appreciate our diversity by discovering our similarities and celebrating our differences.

In addition, Voll points out that traditional approaches to diversity have perceived plurality as an obstacle to unity, resulting in the miscasting of unity as uniformity. In response, Voll suggests a new definition of pluralism: "glocalization"--an interaction of the forces of globalization and local assertions of identity.

This sets the stage for Voll's analysis of pluralism in Islam. As the world once again confronts pluralism, the Muslim world also faces this issue and attempts to wrestle out a definition. A new analysis is emerging in which both the theological foundations as well as the historical experiences of the *Ummah* (Islamic community) are being reexamined. Voll points out that there are many conceptual resources within Islam that support an acceptance of pluralism and that there is a growing body of Muslim scholarship defending the argument that God would not have permitted pluralism had it not been beneficial to humanity; this view has led to a popular contention that pluralism is a divine benefaction.

After addressing the theological foundations of pluralism in Islam, Voll then focuses on a reexamination of the historical experiences of pluralism in Islamic traditions and practices. He notes evidence of pluralism in Islam in the four different schools of law and in the different devotional paths. However, he does not address the fact that although these historical examples contain elements of diversity, they have also been the basis of many conflicts. Furthermore, he raises the possibility that these examples of diversity are intended for intra-Muslim relations as opposed to relations between Muslims and followers of other religions.

The third section, entitled "Crisis in Islamic State and Society," critically examines the ways in which modernization, nationalism, and state formation have altered Muslim approaches to coexistence among cultural and religious groups and have affected the lives of Muslim and non-Muslim minorities. The authors of this section offer relevant and timely illustrations of contemporary scholarly approaches to the understanding and misunderstanding of Islam. All three are helpful insofar as they decipher the rich tapestry of values, practices, institutions, and societies that make up Islam and its flexibility of Islam in responding to the challenges of globalization.

In the first chapter of this section, "Islamists as Modernists?," Robert D. Lee, is less concerned with the correct conceptual categories for understanding Islam than with explaining why social groups and institutions appropriate the word *Islam* to respond to different contingencies posed by modernization and globalization. Lee suggests that the revival of Islam is due to the antithetical processes of sacralization and secularization. While Muslim societies become more secular in response to the contingencies of modernization, the counter reaction,"sacralization," is evident in the Islamization of state policies and institutions. This practice legitimizes secular institutions wary of being outflanked by social groups that take up the mantle of Islam in opposing state policy and institutions.

In his analysis of the "sacralization" of society and the secularization of religion, Lee interprets these trends as objectifications of Islam involving an increasingly broad popular discourse that reflects the context of the nation-state. On an optimistic note, Lee detects among Islamist movements and thinkers an increased propensity for democratization and an appreciation of the need to realize a prosperous, harmonious, unified, and just society. He points out that tolerance and the acceptance of plural viewpoints has become a necessity, articulated both in modern, Western terms and in the popular discourse of Islamic groups.

In Reza Sheikholeslami's chapter, "The Transformation of Iranian Political Culture: From Collectivism to Individualism," he addresses a crucial internal question that every Islamic community, society, and state is facing: what is the relationship between Islam as a religion and the domains of the state and the individual? It is a debate between the national, democratic, and Islamic identities of individuals and groups. Sheikholeslami succinctly traces the major development in the relationship between these three major powers during the immediate pre- and postrevolutionary period in Iran. In explaining the fall and deligitimization of the Shah (Western democratic and capitalist ideology), *Tuda* (Iranian communist party), he examines the seeds of change in the Iranian political culture. The liberal or democratic Islamist ideology is emerging and gaining power and legitimacy. The clues and indicators for the democratic Islamist influence and growth provided by Sheikholeslami are extremely important: for example, the publication of new journals, the type of best-selling novels being read by Iranians, and the election of President Khatami. Sheikholeslami cautions those who enthusiastically rallied for Khatami by categorizing him as a mainstream and pragmatic president. Khatami's silence about the violation of human rights and the fierce attacks on his ministers and followers, along with his lack of access to the state communication system, have shown that Khatami alone cannot bring about the desired reforms, that Iranians are not ready for another revolution, and that two revolutions do not take place in one generation. Sheikholeslami also captures the most fundamental change in Iranian political culture since the revolution: the increasing legitimacy of diverse political ideologies and the reconciling of Iranian national identity and pride within an Islamic context.

Political diversity and coexistence among the various ideologies within Islamic state or society is a survival issue for many Muslims. The Iranian experience in the creation of a new Islamic democratic system is among the most promising political and social experiments that the rest of the Islamic world will be watching with hope.

Both authors point out the rich tapestry of values and practices of historical and contemporary Islam; in so doing they seek to counter the reductionist accounts of Islam found in some scholarship, the media, and in Western policy-making circles. The pluralist couterpoint to Western reductionism is an especially critical component of the response to globalization, especially in view of the misconception abroad among some Westerners that the resurgence of Islam poses an implicit threat to Western political interests.

In the final section, "Alternative Models of Coexistence," the four authors explore ways of implementing and applying Islamic teachings on cultural diversity in the contemporary world-historical context, drawing on examples from three countries: South Africa, Lebanon, and Thailand. Each of these chapters assumes that coexistence is not only compatible with Islam but also that it has a strong foundation in Islamic religion and tradition. The specific topics included are the essential dialogue between East and West, constructive responses to communal conflicts in the Muslim world, ways of restoring the integrative capacity of Islam, and the relevance of alternative models for social organization and human development in the contemporary Islamic world.

Sociologists and political scientists have identified assimilation and pluralism as two competing models for interethnic coexistence and peace-building. These remain the tools used to maintain and develop a consciousness of coexistence in diverse religious and ideological communities. Diversity, according to this approach, preserves values such as equality and justice and the cultural, religious, or national identity of the interdependent groups. These three papers investigate the Islamic principles, values, and dynamics that support the development of a peaceful coexistence in an Islamic pluralist community.

In "Religio-Cultural Diversity: For What and With Whom? Muslim Reflections from a Post-Apartheid South Africa in the Throes of Globalization," Farid Esack raises the many challenges facing Muslims today in a convincing and cogent explanation of the self-critical Muslim's dilemma. Some of the ideas on self-critique and pluralism within society bring us back to the notion of identity.

In his depiction of South African Muslim community, Esack addresses Islam in the unique context of a community of Muslims out of touch with the greater Muslim world for centuries. With the advent of post-apartheid freedom, Muslim identity in South Africa faces fresh challenges. There is a natural tendency toward division in peace; this idea harks back to the philosophy that nothing unites different people like a common enemy. Changes in the political system have led to a crisis in Muslim identity in South Africa, just as changes in the world system are leading to changes in Muslim identity in general. In *dar al-Harb* (the abode of war) and *dar al-Islam* (abode of Islam), Muslims are confronting issues of diversity and tolerance that they have never confronted before. In understanding these issues, Esack takes a postmodern stance in looking at four different factors in identity formation and unity.

The first factor is the unstable nature of identity; Muslims are not a uniform group of people. Second, he addresses the idea of the *Ummah* as a potentially uniting force for Muslims. Third, he raises the issue of religious diversity. Muslims, Christians, and Jews have not only worked with one another but also have come to understand one another in their right to mutual coexistence. Finally, he points out that freedom brings moral diversity.

This link between freedom and diversity leads to the paper's final stage, which outlines the challenges of diversity, itself. Muslims must face these challenges as the world becomes more diverse. Esack sees two different kinds of challenges facing Muslims: theological and political. In his conclusion, Esack points to the market's leveling of the uniqueness of Muslim identity.

In "Personal Reflections on Intellectual Diversity and Islam: The Example of Lebanon," Su'ad al-Hakim, reminds us that every individual carries multiple identities at different levels of his or her being. This point leads to a discussion of the problem of communal identity and an investigation of the differences between two Arabic words: *ta'adud* (multiplicity) and *tanawu'* (diversity). In certain

Islamic countries or states where Muslims are a minority, communal identity is a highly charged topic that leads to conflict. There is a need, then, for self-discovery and reexamination of what Islam means in terms of one's personal identity and one's communal existence.

In this chapter al-Hakim addresses and illustrates the current Lebanese ethnic and religious model of coexistence. Different religious groups in Lebanon have an arrangement of multiplicity rather than diversity. Each group jealously preserves and protects its boundaries. The groups live by one another and not with one another. The rule of power balance and proportionality governs the relationship between the different religious and ethnic groups. There is no genuine coexistence; instead, there is a mere multiplicity of groups. Historically, the different Lebanese groups sought outside protection and affiliation (both from East and West) and neglected their commonality. Thus, in public, individuals use terminology of unity but maintain and nurture their differences in private.

In seeking a genuine sense of diversity rather than multiplicity, al-Hakim denounces the new sense of secularist identity being developed by some Lebanese, arguing that secularists are adding another dimension to the problem rather than resolving it. She suggests that the Qur'an and the Prophet's tradition are important sources for promoting diversity among all Lebanese, including non-Muslims. Based on the teaching of Sultan Ben Duroudie Mohammed Ben Duroudie, al-Hakim suggests four principles for a new sense of diversity in Lebanon: (1) a unifying Lebanon, not for some but for all; (2) creating guardians for the unified Lebanese entity; (3) creating shared heroes and symbols; (4) promoting a collective Lebanese identity based on commonality rather than the individualism.

The final chapter of the manuscript, "Muslim Communal Nonviolent Actions: Exemplar of Minorities' Coexistence in a Non-Muslim Society" by Chaiwat Satha-Anand, provides much-needed reporting and research on the experience of Muslims employing nonviolent strategies on a community level. The three community cases from Thailand illustrate how Muslim minorities can develop nonviolent strategies to pursue their rights and fight against injustice. The Apache Village's case is that of a small community fighting drug dealers and reclaiming their village's streets. Organized community actions and local resources for self-empowerment are the two primary tools used by this community. Ban Krua is the second Muslim community that struggled successfully against the development of an expressway, which threatened to destroy their houses and historic sense of collective community. Through nonviolent community mobilization methods such as protests, press conferences, cultural tours, and prayers, the community persuaded the government to change its plans. The case of Muslim fishermen from Phangnga area is the third example of nonviolent community resistance. Through protest, volunteer recruitment, fundraising, boycotting, and blockades, the fishermen managed to protect their only source of living.

Satha-Anand identifies strong community organization, use of local cultural and religious resources, various degrees of commitment to nonviolence, collective leadership, and the belief in a just cause as important factors in the success of nonviolence within those Muslim communities.

Satha-Anand does not explicitly define the terms of coexistence between Muslims and non-Muslims living in the same diverse society. From these three case studies, however, one may infer the values of justice, self-empowerment, freedom to practice one's own faith, and a strong sense of collective religious identity. Satha-Anand presents an important lesson that illustrates the possible use of Islamic religious values and cultural practices to preserve coexistence between Muslims and non-Muslims. He does not define the nature of coexistence according to Islamic values but suggests that Muslims use nonviolent actions to resolve their conflicts with non-Muslims. The paper focuses on Muslims as a minority but perhaps his ideas will stimulate those in the majority of their society to ask the same questions regarding methods of resisting injustice.

Each author in this volume addresses important issues that bring us back to the key insight of Farid Esack: we must question the questions themselves when we talk about identity and diversity, asking, "For what?" and "With whom?" These questions also relate to Seyyed Hossein Nasr's notion that the implications of Islamic diversity are integrative. We have to discover how the vision of Islam--making one out of many without imposing an artificial uniformity--can accommodate the particular, the local, and the unique while maintaining a sense of universal human solidarity.

SECTION ONE

Cultural Diversity
in Civilizational Perspectives

CHAPTER 1

Dynamics of Cultural Diversity and Tolerance in Islam

Abdul Aziz Said
and Meena Sharify-Funk

In the first rays of the dawning twenty-first century some communitarian theorists claimed to discern the lineaments of the first truly global community, notwithstanding the roiling thunderclouds of international war that threaten to eclipse those fragile beams of hope.

Whatever the uncertainties of this post–9/11 world, the centrifugal, particularist pull of clashing cultures and nation-states faces a powerful centripetal counterforce in the integrating mechanisms of global markets and political institutions like the European Union and the United Nations. With the boundaries between domestic and international politics rapidly blurring, we have witnessed a number of social movements which manifest a shift in world views from separateness to connectedness. With the fragments moving towards a collective whole, a universal vision of an interconnected humanity seems a tangible possibility rather than merely a wispy ideal.

Western cultural hegemony in the international arena has been challenged by the vigorous assertion of alternative values and worldviews by the world's non-Western majority. The new states arrived in the system with a point of view different from that of the older states, and they apply different criteria of judgment and evaluation. The result is a pluralistic global order with a limited but vital form of international democracy that contrasts with aristocratic state system it is superseding. In this context the term "democracy" applies equally to relations among states and to trends in internal political arrangements as emerging global players challenge the ossified hierarchies of the old order with a new egalitarian spirit.

Since World War II the supremacy of the nation-state has been challenged in several ways, especially through regional economic ties and a limited integration of global security the United Nations Security Council. Yet this challenge to the old order is potentially as divisive as unifying—the growing disenchantment from "below" with the political institutions of the nation-state has unleashed often clashing movements of ethnic, cultural, and political assertion. These new trends demand fresh explanations to the interactions of nation-states in which it must be recognized that ethnic nations play key roles.

The twilight of the post–World War II political order is dissolving faster than visions of a new order to replace it are being developed. For all its perils, the bipolar Cold War at least offered the predictability and stability of a tense stand-off for half a century. The recession of that framework can be followed by a new, more peaceful stability or a regression to the instability of pre-1914 Europe, with an attendant Balkanization driven by fear and violence among nations, competing with and fearing each other. The new concentration of power on the world level—in the form of corporate globalization—can either be the prelude of a new era of harmony and creativity or one of accelerating strife.

The inadequacy of nation-states in the face of the ethnic challenge invites a reexamination of the traditional conceptual scheme of "statehood" and "states rights" to one of "peoplehood" and "rights of peoples." The growing acknowledgment of cultural difference demands corresponding political structures rooted in local geographical authorities that are attuned to a region's unique social and religious realities.

We need new visions of pluralistic societies that transcend the structures of the nation-state and supranationalism. The rapid changes and disturbance of the emerging world order underscore the value of pluralism—tolerance of the other—and diversity–valuing the other's identity, as an individual and as part of a group. The increasing complexity of identity politics impels a theoretical and practical reckoning with the antinomies of the global "one" and the cultural "many."

PLURALISM AND DIVERSITY:
A SEARCH FOR UNITY

At first glance "pluralism" and "diversity" appear to be interchangeable terms. Yet, the fields of social sciences and religious studies reveal differences within the theoretical formulations of pluralism and diversity (i.e., political, cultural, religious), and within theoretical formulations there are various levels of pluralistic thinking regarding the issues of inclusivity and unity. We will attempt to tease out some precise notions from the semantic tangle.

1. *Pluralism as a Problem.* In the view of Samuel Huntington and likeminded scholars, unity entails uniformity since pluralism can pose dangers to the security of a polity, especially a democratic one.[1] This argument is implicit in Samuel Huntington's book "The Clash of Civilizations", which argues that a deficiency of authority and uniformity in a culture conduces to insecurity. This model manifests widespread cultural-triumphalist assumptions which stipulate that the whole world needs to conform to only Western norms and values to ensure a secure, orderly and stable world. If "others" fail to comply, then problems and/or clashes are inevitable. This outlook presupposes a division of the global community into "high" cultures and "low culture" and prescribes the subjugation of the latter to the former to avoid international anarchy.

2. *Political Pluralism.* Political pluralism emphasizes the crucial role of a set of authoritative rules, accepted by the politically active members of society. Thomas Hobbes's *Leviathan*, though preoccupied primarily with the problem of authority, represents an important work in the evolution of this tradition. Hobbes sought to stop the anarchy of civil war by persuading the people that it was in their own self-interest to relinquish their power to the sovereign. John Locke's "social contract theory" envisioned a more benign civil society to balance that of the state. While his conceptions greatly influenced subsequent thinking about Western liberal democracy,[2] his conception of civil society was limited to the elite class of male property owners. Antonio Gramsci differed from Locke in opposing social inequality and in advocating mass mobilization for social justice. Emile Durkheim, as a structural functionalist, wanted to preserve social solidarity in order to further the progress of rational social change, yet approached diversity in the manner of a technocrat--with a higher priority on social management than human needs. Max Weber investigated such factors as culture and identity in his political sociology; unfortunately, his investigation was only a beginning.

The objective of balancing the state and society to ensure peaceful coexistence within a pluralistic society has elicited a variety of interpretive and theoretical approaches. Each of these theorists enhanced the discussion of pluralism in their own way; their ideas accentuated the structural aspects of politics, largely disregarding cultural and psychological factors. These theorists believed that the best means of unifying humanity was through a more perfect political system, without delving into the intricacies of cultural and ethnic difference.

3. *Social and Cultural Pluralism.* The gradual emergence of a global community has fostered an increased awareness of the importance of social and cultural pluralism. This new global order, buttressed in part by the creation of institutions like the United Nations, is breaking new legal ground by creating norms and laws that promote tolerance. Identity issues such as race, gender, religion, and ethnicity occupy an increasingly prominent place in international discourse. The rise of multicultural discourse in the United States is another example of this trend. Whereas political pluralism pursues legal equality within civil society.[3] multiculturalism connects the discourse on liberal pluralism to the individual right to communal participation in one's native culture.

This participatory perspective can add new dimensions to the concept of freedom, expanding it beyond the dominant Western liberal paradigm, that celebrates individualistic freedom as the meaning of life or as the goal of society. In this enhanced conception, by contrast, freedom is equated with universal human creativity—the ability, skills, and security (both inward and outward) to express oneself (as an individual and as a member of a group) affirmatively and creatively. It implies community, because to create is to communicate, and every artist must have respect and understanding for co-participants in his or her creation. Dignity means love and respect for oneself and others as creative, free persons; the fruit of such dignity being the ability to allow all other human beings the same dignity. In the words of Raimon Panikkar, "The pluralistic attitude accepts the stance that reality may be of such a nature that nobody, no single human group to be sure can coherently claim to exhaust the universal range of the human experience."[4]

Critics claim that such an egalitarian, community-oriented approach will curb some of the essential characteristics of freedom. And it is true that belonging to a community consciously demands discipline and self-sacrifice. But perhaps individualistic liberalism is a luxury that cannot be provided for all human beings, at least for ecological reasons.

Pluralist cultural communities, each one enhancing creativity (individual and group), need to be "developed" in the sense of becoming more humanistic and open. There are many roads to humanistic, cultural pluralism; there are many potential systems of communitarian, free, creative life. What such societies might share is a communitarian value system in which cultural creation is directed toward other human beings in a spirit of co-participation. Second, such a culture would be at least as much oral-aural as literary. That is, it would promote open, concrete communication among individuals without merely enshrining cultural values on paper for the collectivity. Third, it is always contemporary, though always respectful and willing to borrow from the past. Fourth, this culture would be always particular as well as always humanist. Fifth, while delighting in pluralism and variety, it would seek to discover the human in everything and would seek to maintain communication with all other varieties of cultural expression that affirm freedom and dignity.

Freedom of thought, expression, and communication are absolutely necessary to achieve the highest level of self-renewing creativity and dignity, as are social, economic, and political equality of opportunity. In this sense, freedom is defined as belonging to the people; it is their own cultural creation.

4. *Religious Pluralism*. Authentic cultural pluralism opens the door to a religious pluralism grounded in an ecumenical, interfaith communion. This age of interfaith consciousness, where religions are meeting face to face, can open up dialogue that eschews dogmatic hegemonism in favor of empathy for the "other," even a celebration of the richness of diversity. John Hick, inspired by the vision of Immanuel Kant, believes humanity is currently experiencing a Copernican revolution in which "we must reject categorically all parochial conceptions of the centrality of our own native faith and instead recognize the radical transcendence and centrality of God alone in the universe of faiths."[5] Raimon Panikkar, a contemporary scholar of pluralism and religion, goes a step further: True pluralism struggles against absolutism not by an (equally absolute) anti-absolutism, but by relativizing all absolutisms by means of searching for their contextuality."[6] Both authors recognize that an active and dynamic pluralistic attitude is essential for human coexistence. They believe that all paradigms, whether religious, political, or cultural, have a center but that no one framework is the absolute center. In other words, each reflects aspects of the truth, yet each is limited.[7]

5. *Diversity: Beyond Tolerance*. So far we have briefly explored the faces of pluralism wherein tolerance and coexistence are paramount.

True *diversity*, however, entails moving beyond mere tolerance into a realm of valuing and appreciating the differences and similarities of the "other."

Tolerance implies acceptance of a person or people notwithstanding cultural or religious differences; but it still rejects the *content of character* within the "other."[8] The vision of diversity views difference as a source of strength and variety, as a network of interconnections rather than divisions. Hence, while we need pluralistic thinking as basis of tolerance—to familiarize and form a foundation for deeper acceptance—we also need to develop beyond just tolerating the other toward *esteeming the value of the other's identity*, whether religious, cultural, political, and so on. In other words, we open our experiences and our frames of reference toward the "other" and begin to value the other's attributes.

When we come to celebrate diversity, we become accountable to the responsibility that diversity demands of us. Diversity requires us to see the big picture. It is having a large enough view of the world, wherein cultural and political systems are seen as resources. Therefore, in diversity we not only create laws and doctrines to protect the rights of the many and the other, but we also adapt those laws to ever-changing circumstances.

Diversity is an awareness that makes us attentive to basic differences in worldview among peoples. It protects us from the fallacy of believing that "they" think precisely as "we" do. It enables each person to become more individually authentic yet simultaneously recognize the genuine uniqueness of others. It means the ability to enter the private perceptual world of others while feeling at home.

Diversity means cultural diversity. There are many roads to cultural diversity, many potential systems of communitarian, free, creative life, and many potential forms of language, art, music, drama, and literature that would issue from it. Every community needs some kind of "cultural revolution" to shed inhibitions to human development: the American Civil War and the French Revolution are cases in point. However, only with the developing primacy of the cultural community as the principal source of human realization will creativity and cooperation have a chance to replace conformity and competition.

Diversity also calls for a commitment to a system of education founded upon human solidarity and the wholeness of human life. First, Second, and Third worlds are transformed into one world. The oppressor and the oppressed change into people equally subject to life's vicissitudes. With reason and intuition seen as faces of the truth, planning and spontaneity become a reality, the flowering hedge in the courtyard. Civilization and barbarism change into culture, propositional knowledge and anecdotal knowledge into the root of knowledge.

The battle today, both nationally and globally, focuses on the issues of redefining identity and purpose. Diversity consciousness breeds a strong sense of one's own identity. If we accept diversity, we value the relationship with the other. A relationship demands responsibility—not merely accepting differences but finding "patterns which connect".[9] We must come to see enrichment of self through the other.

ISLAM AND PLURALISM:
PRECEPT AND PRACTICE

"To you your religion and to me mine."[10]

How do these levels of pluralism relate to Islam? Karen Armstrong, an influential Christian scholar of Islam, has stated that pluralism, especially religious and cultural pluralism, has been upheld and significantly practiced more in Islam than in any other Abrahamic tradition.[11] This framework of religious and cultural pluralism (freedom of ethnicity), is particularly seen in the Qur'anic commands to respect the People of the Book (as in the above verse, (2:256). In addition to the stories of the Prophet, who himself was very open towards other religions,[12] the display of such respect is depicted in the story of the second Caliph, Umar ibn al-Khattab: Umar asked to see the Christian shrines in Jerusalem and, while he was in the Church of the Holy Sepulchre, the time for Muslim prayer came around. Courteously the Patriarch invited him to pray where he was but Umar as courteously refused. If he knelt to pray in the church, he explained, the Muslims would want to commemorate the event by building a mosque there, and that would mean that they would demolish the Holy Sepulchre. This must not happen, because the Christian shrines must be preserved. Instead Omar went to pray at a little distance from the church and, sure enough, directly opposite the Holy Sepulchre there is still a small mosque dedicated to the Caliph Umar.[13]

The concept of *dhimmi*, non-Muslim protected peoples, arose from this Qur'anic command of tolerance. Influenced by the Prophet's own attitude, the law of the *dhimmi* was a recognition of monotheists (Jews, Christians, Sabians, Zoroastrians, and, in some cases, Hindus) that granted them autonomy of institutions and protection under Islam. Even though the *dhimmi* concept allocated some benefits of protection under Islamic law in the areas of rights, finance, and international law, there have been many scholarly debates on the degree of that protection. On the one hand, these non-Muslims were given the title and recognition of a "protected people"; on the other hand, they were also subjected to various degrees of humiliation and discrimination such as regulated dress (wearing the *zunnar* belt), the prohibition of various exclusively elite material items (such as fine cloth and noble steeds), and the allocation of impoverished living quarters.[14]

These social restrictions and tolerance levels varied according to time and place: for example, under the Fatimids, *dhimmis* were not only forced to live in segregated areas of Jerusalem but were also harshly persecuted; under the Almoravids, *dhimmis* were prevented from obtaining administrative positions and other social elite occupations; and under Hanafi jurisprudence in the Ottoman Caliphate, *dhimmis* were seen as second-class citizens whose blood was worth one-half to two-thirds that of a Muslim. Moreover, a *dhimmi* man was forbidden to marry a Muslim woman, but a Muslim man could marry a *dhimmi* woman.[15]

Even though one could debate about the actual levels of tolerance stemming from the *dhimmi* concept, the relationship with the *dhimmis* was orginally based on the precepts of tolerance and respect. Because of the shift from traditional forms of government to secular, nationalistic ones, the laws towards *dhimmi* communities have altogether disappeared.[16] In the time of *dhimmi* communities, coexistence was sharply defined by religious boundaries. Today, however, ethnicity seems to be the dividing factor. For example, a Persian would first be known as a Muslim or non-Muslim rather than as a Persian. This change in focus leaves more room for ambiguity, especially within secular Western societies.

The *dhimmi* concept raises a critical question: when and why did pluralism fail? The most important initial failure was the onset of the *fitnah* wars within Islam.[17] As rightfully stated by the Prophet Muhammad, "Islam began as a stranger and will become once again a stranger, blessed are the strangers." After 'Uthman b. 'Affan, the third Caliph, the fear of *fitnah* spread as fast as of the Islamic empire. Democratic precepts were sacrificed to the fear of anarchy; influential jurists frequently recited the aphorism, "Tyranny and impiety are better than anarchy."[18] Fear of *fitnah* darkened the views of many jurists and leaders concerning the integrity of the *Ummah* (Islamic Community) and the rights of the individual. The consent of the ruled became obligatory rather than voluntary, and authoritarian power prevailed, mirroring the *Leviathan* of Thomas Hobbes.[19] Society became dependent upon the state, which commanded unquestioning obedience. This uniformity eclipsed the possibility of an Islamic humanism that could build peace among Muslims and their neighbors. This failure echoes still in contemporary discourse on nationalism and Islam.

Islam has been greatly influenced by nationalism which, unfortunately, has in practice if not in theory often culminated in autocracy and ethnic chauvinism. Although there are signs of democratic elements in countries like Iran, Malaysia, and Indonesia, where there are free elections (however marred by regulatory constraints), democracy still faces an uphill struggle in most of the Islamic world.

Much of the current debate on democracy assumes that in spite of differences which characterize the diversity of cultures, political systems can be validated only by criteria derived from Western scholars and practitioners, and that the Muslim world is therefore not ready for democracy. This is a perspective that sees democracy as only a form. For many years, Western scholars have equated Western institutional forms of democracy with the substance of democracy.

The substance of democracy is a human society that has a sense of common goals, a sense of community, a process of participation in making decisions, and protective safeguards for dissenters. The form of democracy on the other hand, is cast in the mold of the culture of a people. Democracy is built upon participation, not institutions. This is not to say that democracy, Western or Islamic, is practiced in most of the present Muslim world.

In Islamic conceptions of democracy the accent is on the community, whereas Western democratic theory privileges the individual. Islamic democracy is guided by Islamic law, while Western liberal democracy represents centuries of development of human political thought and action. The principles of democracy in Islam serve as a foundation for the establishment of a stable community, while in the West, democracy is taken as a political a priori. Freedom, an end in itself in Western democratic theory, is a means to the welfare of the community in Islamic conceptions of democracy.

Yet, there is nothing in Islam that precludes common goals, community participation, and protective safeguards. To be sure, the American form of democracy, with its provisions for political parties, interest groups, and an electoral system, is alien to Islamic tradition. But the absence of democracy in the Islamic world is more a matter of lack of preparation than a lack of religious and cultural foundations. There are democratic precepts in Islam as there are in other religions. There are also Islamic traditions, as there have been in other religions, that are inimical to democratic ideals; indeed, democratic traditions in Islam have been more commonly abused than used.

It is not theory but the press of vital currents in the real world that is obliging today's Muslims to make the connection between of democracy, modernization, and Islam. "Modern and democratic" can also mean Muslim, but not if these characteristics are patterned after existing models that prevail in the West today. Presently, there is no available model for "modern, democratic, and Muslim" advanced by modern Muslim thinkers either. At the close of the nineteenth century in Egypt, when liberal thinkers began to talk about these concepts, they accepted the Western norm as reality. In so doing, they began to hang an Islamic garb on these concepts. It did not work then, and it is doubtful that it will work now. Especially today, when people in the West are trying to rethink the meaning of modernization, Muslims need to reexamine and reconstruct their ideas of modernity and Islam.

Neither Muslim fundamentalists nor Muslim secularists represent a genuine revival of Islamic civilization; they seem, rather, to dwell in negativism and preoccuptaion with the "enemy." What is required is a Muslim alternative that is neither a superficial compromise nor a schizophrenic reaction, but a response based on Islamic values, one that reflects the historical development of Islam and responds to the challenges of contemporary life. Mainstream Islam should regain the moral high ground and emotional momentum from fundamentalism. This can be done when Muslims gain self-respect as full-fledged citizens of the modern world.

In the long run, it is better for the Islamic world to develop through its own Islamic traditions. Otherwise the people of the region will continue to suffer the contradiction between traditionalism and secularism, between fundamentalism and Westernism. Change that grows out of the soil of tradition is more secure and lasting than change that comes from an abrupt uprooting of all traditions. Islamic traditions are deep-rooted as mass culture and mass behavior; Western secular ideologies, on the other hand, often seem an alien transplant onto the cultural soil of Islam.

Probably the most dramatic example is the still awakening "Islamic Revival," which combines a rediscovery of the vitality of the Islamic experience with a determination not to submit any longer to the cultural humiliation of judging oneself by Western standards. Such cultural renaissances are not only a form of rebellion against the vestiges of cultural imperialism, but also a basis for movement back into dialogue with other cultures and subcultures.

AN ISLAMIC VISION OF DIVERSITY

O Mankind! We created
You from a single (pair)
Of a male and a female,
And made you into
Peoples (nations) and tribes that,
You may come to know one another.
Verily the most honoured of you
In the sight of Allah
Is (he who is) the most
Righteous of you. (Qur'an 49:13)

Even though classical Islamic civilization was a compound of Arab, Biblical, and Hellenic cultures, it cast an even wider net by integrating Persian, Central Asian, as well as Indian and Chinese components within its cultural synthesis. Scholars have long differed on how the Abrahamic religions approach, interpret, and practice tolerance towards others and among themselves. For instance, even though Islam is seen as an Abrahamic religion, Western scholarship has tended to classify it outside the boundaries of the Judeo-Christian cultural tradition. Preoccupation with such images and ideas as the "Islamic bomb," "jihad," and "clash of civilizations" has led many to construe Islam as an alien ideology driven by violence, intolerance, and irrationality. These harmful stereotypes undermine pluralistic practices, for they deny any prospect of coexistence.

Since is earliest days, Islam has served as a bridge between West and East. As stated by Karen Armstrong, "On the one hand Arabs were seeking to learn from the ancient cultures that had preceded them, and on the other hand the new Muslims sought to integrate these cultural traditions with their own religion."[20] For example, Islam's Hellenism was mediated primarily through Eastern Christian intellectual circles, and the important streams of Muslim philosophical and scientific thought linked Late Antiquity with the Renaissance. Islamic contributions went far beyond mere preservation of the classical legacy. For example, Abd ar-Rahman Ibn Khaldun made efforts to tutor an Andalusian prince after the model of Plato's *Republic*; Copernicus read Heliocentric planetary theories in Arabic during his studies at the library of Padua. There is even evidence that Dante Aligieri drew inspiration from Muhyiddin Ibn 'Arabi in his moral, religious, and cosmological paradigm.[21] Also, St. Thomas Aquinas had read from Averroes, Avicenna, and many other well-known Muslim philosophers.

So one may confidently assert that Islam, as both a religious and cultural force, falls well within the boundaries of the Western tradition. Simply stated, Islamic knowledge has made significant albeit often unacknowledged contributions to European philosophy and science.

Islam is not named after a people or a prophet. This is clearly evoked in the above-quoted Qur'anic verse, 49:13.   At first glance, the revelation contained in this simple but powerful statement may appear somewhat paradoxical: that the reality of ethnicity and cultural diversity is an expression of the Divine Will, while at the same time, humankind is directed to embrace the notion of the unity of humanity through the expression of human solidarity. This simple but powerful revelation is an expression of the universality of the original message of Islam.   For at the heart of the message of universalistic Islam is a respect for cultural pluralism that is inextricably linked to a recognition of the connectedness of all human beings.

The Qur'an also states that "to every people has been sent a Messenger" (Qur'an 10:47 and 16:36), which demonstrates that Islam upholds the legitimacy of other religions. One might infer from this verse that Islam accepts that truth has many centers, that all people have been chosen and none forgotten.

A tolerant unity can foster cultural diversity and coexistence. Muslims, whether Indian, African, Persian, Southeast Asian, Arab, or Asian, have retained their culture within Islam. This is reflected in the Qur'anic verse, 5:48:

> To each among you
> Have We prescribed a Law
> And an Open Way.
> If Allah had so willed,
> He would have made you
> A single People, but (His
> Plan is) to test you in what
> He hath given you; so strive
> As in a race in all virtues.

Muslims are capable of practicing cultural diversity as demonstrated by the concept of *tawhid*, unity. *Tawhid* refers us to the overall harmony and patterning of the universe. It expresses the necessity to live the unity of existence. Muslims surrender the illusion of separation for the truth of unity. *Tawhid* is a means of implementing cultural diversity. It is a means of making sense of the diversity in the world around you, as well as finding your place in that world. Gradually one sees more and more deeply into the great diversity of forms. The human essence is clarified and strengthened. There can be no barriers between the individual and unity. *Tawhid* allows one individual to approach the other in the spirit of mutual solicitude rather than mutual acrimony.

In precept and in practice, Islam is capable of accommodating a broad range of views, attitudes, and interpretations. One Westerner who recognized this inclusive character was Johann Wolfgang von Goethe, who offered the following exclamation:

How strange that in every special case
One praises one's own way!
If Islam means "surrender into God's will"
It's in Islam that we all live and die.[22]

Tawhid, Unity of God, of Humanity, of the Universe and of Truth itself, declares that the material and the spiritual are in reality one, that one cannot claim to be spiritual if one is unable to make a good thing of *this* life. Conversely, one cannot truly make a good thing of this life unless one is able to order one's spiritual life properly.

Tawhid is a conception whose reality enters into human life at many levels. Beyond the doctrinal and ideological planes, where the oneness of humanity is stressed, *tawhid* mediates one's personal relation to the Absolute, and the maintenance of harmony with the universe. It is a kind of ecology of the spirit that reconciles the apparent multiplicity of created things with the unity of existence. It is what the "Greatest Shaykh" (*Shaykh al-akbar*, the Latin *doctor maximus*) Ibn 'Arabi referred to as "the breath of the Merciful" (*nafas ar-Rahman*), the depiction of the manifestation of created multiplicity and its reabsorption into primordial singularity as the Divine Being's drawing a breath. More precisely, God comes to self-knowledge in us.

Islamic teaching reminds us that a person must cultivate in the self the character traits of God (*takhalluq bi-akhlaq Allah*). In the daily life of the veritable practitioners of Islam, there is a practical demonstration of how to cherish social and ethical values leading men and women to the good life. Islam offers the stimulus and strength for performing deeds that are distinctively human in the deepest sense: to bring the human being nearer to God and to respecting the sanctity of human relationships, which should mirror the attributes of the divine. In harmony with the world's other great spiritual traditions, Islam offers a model for integrating the impassioned mind and the informed heart which can together call forth the energy to move the planet towards realization.

CHAPTER 2

Unity and Diversity in Islam
and Islamic Civilization

Seyyed Hossein Nasr

Contemporary Islam sits on the horns of a theoretical and practical dilemma: unity vs. diversity. Many contemporary Westerners and modern Muslims alike misperceive Islam as a monolith that precludes diversity. Dispelling this misconception requires a consideration of the immanent meaning of the term *unity* (*al-tawhid*) in the Islamic tradition and then an examination of the relevant aspects of Islamic history, culture, and civilization.

The Arabic term *al-tawhid*, which is usually translated in English as "unity," has, in fact, two meanings: "the state of unity or oneness," and "the act of making one or integration." In the first sense unity in its absolute sense belongs to God alone, who in the Qur'an calls Himself by the Names *al-Ahad* and *al-Wahid*, the One and the Unique, to emphasize that *al-tawhid* as the state of Unity belongs ultimately and in its absolute sense to Him and to Him alone. All that is other than God *(ma siwa 'Llah)* participates in multiplicity. To exist in this world is to live in the domain of diversity and often opposition. In the words of the famous Persian Sufi poet of the 8th/14th century, Shaykh Mahmud Shabistari,

Zuhur-i jumla-yi ashya bi diddast
Wali Haqq ra na manadu na niddast

The manifestation of all things is through their opposite,
But the Divine Reality has no like and no equal.

Only God, the One, is absoluteness, is beyond all like, similitude, and opposition. In the world of multiplicity, however, it is metaphysically absurd to expect to realize the unity that transcends all multiplicity, unless one is able to overcome multiplicity through an inward journey while remaining bodily situated in the physicality of the manifold.

Islam as a religion has always been keenly aware of the transcendent significance of this Divine Unity to which the central testimony of Islam, *La ilaha illa 'Llah* (There is no divinity but God/Allah), bears clear witness. For that very reason traditional Islam has never confused that unity with uniformity. At the level of multiplicity and the diversity of human life, it has understood *al-tawhid* in its second meaning of integration and never uniformity, which it views, in fact, as a reduction to a least common denominator, a parody of unity.

It is true that some modernist and so-called fundamentalist movements in the Islamic world have confused unity and uniformity, but such was never the case of traditional Islam and the civilization it created. Wherever Islam went, it brought first of all the message of unity whose base sought to integrate both the individual and society without destroying cultural and ethnic differences. The coming of Islam never had a leveling effect. Rather, it revived and reformulated preexisting cultures in the context of Islamic civilization and according to Islamic values.

Classical Islamic civilization provides many examples of this principle of unity-through-difference. For example, wherever Islam spread in Africa, local cultures such as those of Nigeria and Senegal were both Islamized and preserved so successfully that in the nineteenth century many Christian missionaries would write back home complaining that Muslims were having success because they were accepting many local cultural practices of the Africans, such as reverence for nature or polygamy, which were intolerable to the Western missionaries.

What are the sources of unity in the Islamic world, and what role has it played in the unfolding of Islamic civilization? The existence of such a unity can hardly be denied even on the level of external experience, despite the claims of certain Orientalists. If one were to take a Korean or Japanese who had never experienced a world outside his own and guide him through cities and towns ranging from those of Sumatra and Bangladesh to sites in Morocco and Mauritania, he would attest to the presence of a unity, albeit elusive at first, in these vastly separated areas despite differences of climate, language, cultural habits, race, and so on. No matter how much some try to emphasize only the diversity of the traditional Islamic world, its unity remains a vibrant strength that has thrived through diversity, not uniformity.

On what then is this unity based? Theologically, it harks back to the principle of Unity of God. What unites the Islamic world most of all is faith in the One, the presence of the Transcendent One in all aspects of life and the acceptance of the message that has issued from the One. There is therefore, the Qur'an, the central theophany of Islam, accepted by all Muslims as a major unifying force. There is also the being of the Prophet of Islam, his life (*sirah*), words (*sunnah*) and sayings (*hadith*), which together make him the ultimate role model for all Muslims.

The *Shariah*, or Islamic Law, based on the Qur'an and *Hadith* is another important unifying force, notwithstanding the varying interpretations of it throughout the community (*al-ummah*). There are the unifying rites promulgated by the *Shariah*, especially those of canonical prayers (*al-salah*), fasting (*al-sawm*), and the pilgrimage to Mecca (*al-hajj*). Sufism, the inner dimension of Islam, has also been a major unifying element throughout most of Islamic history.

The basic tenets of Shariah are one, yet there are schools of interpretation, the *madhahib* of Sunni and Shi'ite Islam. Even in the daily prayers (*salah*), the central rite of Islam in which all Muslims are unified, there are certain minor differences among the various schools of law. There is but one goal of Sufism: self-purification and proximity to the One, yet there are many Sufi orders with varied litanies and forms of meditation. These examples reveal that unity in its absolute sense belongs to God alone and that in the spatio-temporal world, diversity pervades even the unifying spiritual impulse of Islam. Islam's refusal to reduce this unity-in-diversity to mere uniformity, far from weakening the faith, has been a major cause of its strength through the ages.

There are pervasive cultural as well as theological expressions of unity in global Islam: calligraphy, geometric patterns, arabesques, concepts of architectural space, and so on, which are related to the inner dimension or *haqiqah* of the Noble Qur'an. The sacred and traditional arts of Islam are no less steeped in this tradition of unity through diversity. It is an undercurrent that springs from deep wells of history. Although Islam was a unitary civilization in its earliest phase, as it spread it spawned variants that led to a bipolar civilization. The two cultural zones of this civilization have been called by classical Western historians Arabic and Iranic Arabic and Persianate. Classical Islamic historians such as Ibn Khaldun referred to them *'arabi* and *'ajami.*

The classical medieval Christian civilization of the West was unipolar, with a single, centralized Church and a unifying formal language, Latin, which was used for both the liturgy and intellectual discourse. The vernacular languages such as Provencal, Catalan, and Spanish were not widespread in the Middle Ages and thus had a limited cultural and intellectual impact. In contrast, in the Islamic world, while Arabic remained the sole sacred language, Persian as well as Arabic became classical languages used for both scholarly and daily discourse. While Arabic was used as a literary language throughout the Arab world and among many Muslims of Black Africa, Persian was used not only in Persia, present-day Afghanistan, and Central Asia, but also to a large extent in Muslim India and among the learned classes of Ottoman society in Turkey.

In the later period of Islamic history, from the fourteenth century onward, a third pole of Islamic civilization emerges, the Turkish and Ottoman, which had cultural affinities to the the Persian world, and religious (in following Sunni Islam) and political affinities to the Arab world, much of which it incorporated into its dominion. Other distinct zones emerged as well: the Malay, Chinese, and Black African joined an Islamic cultural domain that encompassed a diverse array—Arabic, Persian, the Black African, the Turkic, the Indian, Malay and Chinese—each with its own language and culture yet all distinctly Islamic and part of the one Islamic civilization. Moreover, languages that appeared later, after the Mongol invasion—even major ones such as Turkish, Urdu, and Swahili--never gained the classical status of Arabic and Persian, which have remained the main vehicles of Islamic thought and culture.

Applying the term "culture"—a nineteenth-century European coinage—to the domain of Islam requires some care. The currently preferred terms in Islamic languages, such as *thaqafah* in Arabic and *farhang* in Persian, are modern inventions that meld older terms with a new connotation adapted from an alien civilization. But the term *culture* has now become so prevalent that it is not possible to avoid it when writing about Islamic civilization in a European language or even in contemporary Arabic or Persian.

What we call Muslim culture today, which includes the arts and all that was known in classical Islamic civilization as *adab*, was born in the traditional context from the wedding between the form of revelation and the "matter" of the ethnic and psychological substance of the people who accept that revelation. When Europeans accepted Christianity, the wedding the soul of the Latin people to the form of doctrinal revelation, there emerged a Latin Christian culture with distinct features such as Romanesque art and architecture. Likewise, from the acceptance of the same religion by the Germanic people there came into being Germanic Christian culture again with its own characteristics, such as Gothic art.

These examples drawn from European civilization are akin to the multiplicity of Islamic cultures within the unity of Islamic civilization. Islam faced greater ethnic diversity than medieval Western Christianity. Yet it, too, spawned distinctive cultures born of the wedding between the archetypal reality and form of Islam on the one hand and the ethnic genius of the people who embraced the religion on the other. Each of these mergers of the spiritual and temporal has fostered a unique variant of Islamic culture an example of unity-in-multiplicity, like the Chinese, Persian, and African mosques of Mali. One can speak of a single Islamic culture, but it is more precise to speak of several Islamic cultures within a civilization that encompasses all of them.

To understand more fully how Islam created a unitary civilization that has thrived through diversity, we must look at its different cultural zones. In the vast expanse of *Dar al-Islam* (the Abode of Islam), there is first of all the Arab world or the zone of Arabic culture. This zone has itself been divided since the early Islamic period into the eastern *mashriq* and the Western *maghrib* regions, each with particular characteristics. Even within those regions there are distinct areas such as the Yemen and the areas around it stretching to the Persian Gulf as well as in the east and the "Far West," or *al-maghrib al-aqsa* (that incorporates Western Algeria, Morocco, Mauritania and for many centuries al-Andalus). The Arabic zone is dominated by the Arabic language but incorporates several ethnic types. Moreover, within the Arab world there are a number of other languages such as Berber spoken by distinct groups living in the Arabic cultural zone.

The Persian zone stretches from the eastern boundaries of the Arab world to Central Asia and present day Pakistan. Here again one finds many ethnic groups, mostly of Iranian stock; the predominant Persian language is complemented by a number of local tongues, including Kurdish, Luri, Adhari, Baluchi, and Pashtu.

The Black African zone, the most diverse in language and tribal distinctions, is another distinct cultural zone within Islamic civilization. Stretching from East to West Africa and from North Africa to Central Africa, this zone incorporates ethnic, tribal, and linguistic groups as diverse as the Hausa and Fulani in West Africa to the Somali in the East (Swahili is the dominant tongue).

The Turkish zone stretches over an even wider region, from Eastern Europe to Vladivostok, with many groups of Turkish origin using different languages and dialects of the Altaic family such as Turkish, Azari, Uzbek, and Uighur. The Turkish and Persian zones overlap in parts of Central Asia.

The zone of Indian Islamic culture is the most populous today but is one of the most homogeneous. Stretching from Bangladesh to Pakistan and Nepal to Sri Lanka, this zone encompasses a broad array of languages: Kashmiri, Sindhi, Gujrati, and Tamil. For many centuries, until the advent of British imperial rule in this region, Persian was the dominant literary language of this world. Today the most prevalent Islamic language of this zone is Urdu, followed by Bengali.

The Malay world is much more homogeneous ethnically and linguistically than the other zones; in fact, Bhasa Indonesian and Bhasa Malay are really the same language separately denominated for political reasons. Covering much of Southeast Asia, the Malay zone includes other languages, including a once-important literary language, Javi. Finally, the zone of Chinese Islamic culture embraces those of both Turkish and Chinese ethnic background and encompasses both the Chinese and Uighur languages.

Throughout this vast Islamic domain—which also includes smaller communities of Bosnians and Albanians in Europe and small communities in Burma, Thailand, and elsewhere—all the believers read the Qur'an in Arabic; turn to Mecca for their prayers; venerate and emulate the same "supreme model" (*uswah hasanah*) of the Prophet; sing praises sung to God and His Prophet, in numerous tongues; follow the tenets of the *Shariah*, in varying interpretations; learn the same basic principles of self-purification and surrender to and love and knowledge of God from Sufi masters; witness divine unity in the form of *La ilaha illa 'Llah,* which echoes from minarets and rooftops five times a day; and features the same patterns of Islamic art that cast the image of beauty upon diverse objects.

This sprawling domain encompasses ethnic and cultural groups as different as Persians and Sudanese, Chinese and Senegalese. Its sacred architecture has flowered in forms as various as the mosques in Sumatra, Cairo, and Timbouctou. Yet the unity of these diverse peoples is evident as they all circle the Ka'bah, recite the Qur'an, or perform the Friday prayers. Classical Islamic civilization bore witness to an overwhelming unity that prevailed over division. To be sure, there were squabbles and wars, but always the abiding affinities as well.

As the modern European nation-state permeated the Islamic world, a more contentious diversity emerged among Muslims, challenging the principle of unity and the very foundation of Islamic civilization. On the intellectual level, there had always been contentious debates among various Islamic schools of jurisprudence such as Sunni and Shi'ite, and diverse schools of theology, philosophy, and so on. But the Islamic principle of unity held all such acrimony within a common cultural and civilizational framework. Now, however, Islam had to grapple with new European secular philosophies and ideologies that shared no common principles with the various schools of Islamic thought and also often contradicted each other as well.

The whole citadel of Islamic intellectual life was under siege, with many Muslims simply shedding their Islamic heritage and others adopting a caricatured, intolerant version of that tradition that weakened the intellectual resources of Islam.

The attendant rise of nationalism fostered the segmentation of the Islamic world and its peoples. Before modern times, intra-Islamic battles—such as those between the Ottomans and the Safavids—were not those of modern nationalistic states (even if, in this case, the key point of division Sunnism vs. Shi'ism). Despite the enmity there was ample opportunity for a fruitful commerce in culture, of goods, and ideas and the possibility of travel. In fact, one of the remarkable features of traditional Islamic civilization was the ease of communication from one end of the Islamic world to the other.

Modern nationalism sharply curtailed these contacts and forms of exchange; despite all the modern means of communication, there is probably less intellectual and cultural awareness and exchange between Morocco and Muslim India today than when Ibn Battutah set out from Tangiers and became judge in Dehli.

It is tragic indeed to ponder that all the bitter acrimony among contemporary Muslims is over a common cultural and intellectual heritage. An al-Farabi or an Ibn Sina, who hailed from Central Asia and Persia, respectively, is pulled in several directions to be made a national Arab, Persian, or Turkish hero. And even those who were the most eloquent heralds of the message of unity, such as Jalal al-Din Rumi, the reknowned Persian poet of the thirteenth century, are now flashpoints of controversy rather than healing prophets of healing among Iranian and Turkish nationalists. Modern waves of nationalism, far from helping the cause of pluralism in the Islamic world, have rendered it an endangered political and cultural species.

This recent fragmentation is a sobering reminder of the metaphysical understanding of unity and diversity with which we began, and our distinction between the diversity that abides with unity and that which repels it. Duality can be complementary, as in Taoist correlates of yin and yang. But it can also be sheer opposition in which one polarity precludes rather than includes the other: light and darkness, good and evil, or existence and nonexistence. If there is a unifying principle, the parts of the manifold can become integrated and unified. But if there is no such principle, then there can be nothing but contention, opposition, and finally destruction. Such is the danger facing contemporary Islam.

Islam's vocation has always been to integrate this diversity and multiplicity into unity both within each human and in the society, culture, and civilization in which he or she lives. For nearly a millennium and a half, Islam succeeded in this noble task of bearing witness to divine unity and its manifestations in human life, thought, and art. Islam did not create only one school of law, one political theory, one theology, one philosophy, or one style of art. While the Arabic Qur'an has remained a single and unique theophany for all Muslims, they have used diverse languages to appropriate and interpret this sacred text.

Today the great challenge for Muslims is to preserve the message of unity without turning it into a caricature, a simplistic uniformity. These days pluralism has become a favorite term for cultural and political discourse. Islam has had a millennium of experience in pluralism in many different contexts from which the necessary lessons must be drawn for the present. How to harmonize our sense of the absolute in Islam religion with the presence of other religions? How to bring accord between a love for one's land, language, people, and culture with the same feelings harbored by non-Muslims? These are important questions to which both the doctrinal expositors and historical experience of Islam in lands as different as Spain, Bosnia, Turkey and Kashmir, just to cite a few examples, provide the instructive answers.

In the face of the contemporary challenge of pluralism and diversity, it is of the utmost importance for Muslims to remain steadfast and fully conscious of the *raison d'etre* of Islam as the harbinger of unity and the integrating principle of the type of diversity that lends itself to unity. To preserve its identity today the Islamic world must revivify those teachings that, over the centuries, have allowed it to rule over the hearts of men and women in worlds of bewildering diversity; to live for the most part at peace with followers of other religions; and to create diverse schools of law, thought, and culture, which, while outwardly different, have hearkened to a common unifying theme: acceptance of the message of the One who is the alpha and omega of all life.

CHAPTER 3

Continuities and Discontinuities in Islamic Perspectives on Cultural Diversity

Sulayman S. Nyang

The purpose of this chapter is threefold:

1. The first objective is to identify the factors and forces responsible for continuity and discontinuity in Muslim opinions on and attitudes toward cultural diversity. This paper works on the assumption that the Muslim World managed to maintain its cultural integrity while assimilating peoples from different cultural and civilizational backgrounds in the Middle East and beyond; it also considers the symbolic and substantive mechanisms that Islam and Muslim peoples created to keep their *Ummah* united and assertive in world affairs in order to demonstrate that the expansion of Europe and the colonization of the Americas contributed to cultural continuities and discontinuities in Muslim societies and cultures.

2. The second objective of this chapter is to show how and why the European conquest and colonization of Muslim lands created the cultural and philosophical transformations that led to the enthronement of nationalist ideas among Muslims.

3. The third objective is to elicit from these findings clear conclusions about the impact of seven developments identified as crucial in the making of the crisis of cultural alienation in Muslim lands.

SEVEN MAJOR DEVELOPMENTS THAT CHANGED THE MUSLIM CULTURAL LANDSCAPE

The first development was what Western historians call the Age of Discovery. It was an age of discovery for the Westerners because they were first coming upon lands long occupied by the Native Americans and because they knew little about lands lying to their east. But the lands bordering the Indian and Pacific oceans were not completely unknown to Muslims. India and China, the two principal civilizations bordering these two major oceans, were known to the Muslims and their traders, who had long established a brisk exchange with them in a wide range of goods and services. Muslim traders, accompanied by their Jewish counterparts, were in these parts of the world long before Columbus sailed for the Americas, and before Bartholomew Diaz and Vasco da Gamma headed for India by way of the Cape of Good Hope.

The industrial revolution—and the attendant rise of European power— was the second development that contributed to the present Muslim efforts at cultural adjustment to the challenge of modernity. The long duel between the two Abrahamic civilizations on the Mediterranean Sea was raised to a new level. Since the late eighteenth century, the industrial revolution has changed the power equation between Europeans and other peoples of the world. With its industrial might, Europe gradually transformed its values, its material bases of living, and its institutions. Factories and powerful banks became a common feature of industrializing Europe and America. The bank, an institution whose most powerful instrument of exchange, the check, was a Muslim invention, was taken to higher levels of utility and performance by the Europeans and later the Americans.

The third development that has also affected the nature of the Muslim world and the modern Euro-American world was the European colonization of the Muslim lands in the nineteenth century. The industrial success of the European nations enabled them to extend their dominion beyond their immediate geographic neighborhood. Fueled by intra-European rivalry to lay claim to the growing planetary market emerging before their eyes, the major European powers extended their imperial reach into the domain of Islam.

Thus, the Age of Discovery of Vasco da Gamma was the prelude to the European colonization of the world. The European invasion and peopling of the Americas preceded the colonization and settlement of lands east of the Americas. European hegemony led eventually not only to the colonization of Muslim lands, but also to a changed demography of many of those lands through the transplantation of peoples from one region to the other. Such transplantation occurred elsewhere as well: witness the Chinese of the Southeast Asian states of Thailand, Malaysia, Indonesia, and the Philippines; the Indians in the East African coastal states; the Frenchmen and women in North Africa; Europeans in Southern Africa; Indians and Chinese in the Caribbean territories; the white settlers of Australia and New Zealand.

Here we have stressed the impact of Western European colonization. The Russian conquest and colonization of Central Asia are usually overlooked by anticolonial and anti-imperial nationalists of the Third World. Recent developments in Central Asia have brought this home to us after the collapse of the former Soviet Union.

The fourth development that has also affected the Muslim understanding of cultural diversity is the transplantation of nationalist ideas and their acceptance by Muslim intellectuals and their political leaders. This intellectual current has changed the self-understanding of many Muslims. Not only have Muslims given greater prominence to territorial and geo-historical particularities, but they have also come to embrace a new political mythology that goes against their religious universalism. These psychological and psycho-political transformations are the intended or unintended consequences of the Islamic flirtation with borrowed European theories of nationalism.

The fifth development was the rise of communism and the establishment of collectivist regimes in Russia and Eastern Europe after World War II. To many Islamic intellectuals Marxism seemed another alien demon to be repelled from the hearts and minds of the Muslim peoples. The legacies of communism in the Arab world and in central Asia certainly remind us that the problem of cultural continuities and discontinuities will remain a challenge to Muslim leaders and led for sometime in the future.

The sixth key development was the eruption of the Iranian revolution under Imam Khomeini and its reverberations throughout the Muslim World and beyond. This revolution, which has produced many images and stereotypes of the Muslim peoples of the world, has contributed positively and negatively to the problem of continuities and discontinuities in Muslim lands.

The seventh and last is the collapse of the former Soviet Union and the resulting growth of Euro-American global hegemony in both the military and cultural life of modern human beings. The globalization of the Western way of life has created new opportunities and new challenges to

Muslims, especially the younger generation, to assimilate Western ideas, values, and material goods. Here the Islamic world faces the challenge of Western materialism and consumerism, what some have called the "MacDonaldization" of the world. An American cultural commentator described the post– Cold War era a contest between "Jihad and MacWorld."

THE AGE OF DISCOVERY AND THE CULTURAL CHALLENGES TO MUSLIM SOCIETIES

Any student of world cultures of the past five hundred years must reckon with the impact of the West on the rest of the world. In writing about cultural continuities and discontinuities in Muslim lands, one must raise the question: What has been the legacy of the Muslim encounter with the West? Many books and essays have been written by Muslims and non-Muslims on this encounter. Here we are not reinventing the wheel; rather, we are trying to identify factors and forces responsible for the changing perspectives in Muslim self-definition resulting from the encounter with the West.

Three issues of importance to Westerners and Muslims resulted from their encounter following the Age of Discovery. The first concerns the definition of the human being and the divergent attitudes between the Muslim slave owners and the Spaniards in the Americas. When the European encountered the native peoples of the Americas, their conceptual screens did not register the humanity of these peoples. This is the legacy of the Spanish conquistadores.

The Muslim attitude toward such matters must be inferred from a spotty historical record; not much was written about Muslim opinions on and attitudes toward the American slave trade, although there is some literature on Muslim slaves in the Americas. One can try to form judgments from the limited sample of opinions in Muslim slave narratives and the practical diplomacy of Muslim rulers such as the Sultan of Morocco, who intervened in the liberation of Abdurrahman ibn Sori, an African prince from the Fula kingdom of Futa Jallon who spent about forty years in slavery in Natchez, Mississippi. Such documentation encourages the conclusion that that Muslims did not conflate race, color, and creed into one metaphysical criterion by which some are elected and others are damned.

But if the Muslim contemporaries did not know much about the exploits of the Spaniards in the Americas, they saw the negative consequences of the fall of Grenada. Not only were Muslims booted out of the Iberian Peninsula in large numbers, but Jews and wavering Christians were also ejected forcefully and mercilessly by the victorious crusaders and the leaders of the Inquisition.

As argued above, though the Muslims in the East did not know fully what was happening in the Americas, there is overwhelming material evidence pointing to Muslim reactions to the persecution of Muslims and Jews by the triumphant Spaniards under Ferdinand and Isabella. This differing view of diversity that was best represented by the different treatment the Turks gave to the Jews at this critical moment in their history. During this horrible period of persecution the Church fathers and their agents took the lives of follow human beings simply because they did not toe the theological line of the day. It is true that slavery existed in Muslim lands during the same period, but there is no historical record to suggest an ideology of discrimination on racial and religious grounds.

The second issue that grows out of the Age of Discovery was the commodification of human beings and of human relations. In a world in which humans were racially and theologically defined, those who did not fit this metaphysical Procrustean bed became the objects of derision and exploitation. If the individual victim was not put to the sword, his life was reduced to that of the hewer of wood and the drawer of water. This racialization, sectarianization, and commodification of life led to the creation of a caste system that paralleled the Aryan-imposed order in India, where the *Sudrahs* (untouchables) willingly or reluctantly accepted their position in light of Hindu metaphysics. The Spanish conquest of the New World set the stage for the emergence of a similar system in the Americas as well.

Muslim societies which were increasingly affected by their contacts with the defenders of this new dispensation, gradually and sometimes unconsciously found their peoples abandoning the old worldview of their geographers and their men of learning. Let us illustrate this point by referring to the Muslim sources. We know that during the height of Muslim power and glory, especially in the Ummayyad and Abbassid periods, Muslim geographers such as al-Masudi divided the world so that the Arab Muslim was at the center of creation. This un-Islamic ethnocentricism, wrapped in the riddle of secular anthropocentrism, was further complicated by the Ptolemaic astronomy of geocentricism. Such a conception of human diversity and cultural ranking of humans was akin to the Greek aversion to the barbarian and the Hebrew contempt of the *goyim*. Yet these various philosophies speak of human dignity and equality at the highest levels of abstraction in their metaphysics.

The Age of Discovery not only led Spaniards and other Europeans to see themselves as different from the "natives" of the world, but it also inspired them to create the world in their own image, to smash the mirrors of the other cultures so that from now on they would not and could no longer see themselves in their own terms. This cultural conquest, which took its greatest toll in the Americas, later manifested itself in Africa, Asia, and the Middle East. As a result many peoples from various parts of the world were scattered into areas far from their original homelands. The Age of Discovery played an important part in this global transformation. The term America can be a metaphor for many things, one of them the massive relocation of human beings from their old uniform cultures into a bewildering new world of pluralism.

What the Islamic historical records suggest is that military and political defeat of one's foes should not entail the denial of humanity to the vanquished, even if the subjugated refuses to embrace the religion of the conquerors. Even though Muslims were affected by the Age of Discovery, their societies did not pattern themselves after the racial and religious antagonism that increasingly characterized a triumphant Europe extending its might beyond the seas.

The third issue that developed out of the Age of Discovery was the gradual secularization of the world, fueled in large measure by the pursuit of gold that attended the European expansion of the fifteenth and sixteenth centuries. The competitive mercantile culture that ensued from the race for gold among these European powers gradually led to the widening of the gaps between the classes of Europe. This class separation and the culture of indifference that fed on it planted the seeds of the political revolutions of the eighteenth century.

How did these developments in Europe and the Americas affect the Muslims in their understanding of economic inequalities in human societies? Though serious economic disparities existed in certain parts of the Muslim World during this time, there is a body of literature that teaches Muslims not to use wealth as a marker separating one human being from the other. In this sense, although Muslim states and societies were gradually losing ground to the emerging Euro-American hegemony, their peoples were not rigidly divided by class culture on the European model. The political economy of the Muslim World did not support an urban society where structural and functional differentiations were fundamentally altering human relationships. Furthermore, the intellectuals and thinkers of this period did not come up with a Muslim equivalent to the Calvinist doctrine that portrays economic success in this world as evidence of divine grace.

THE INDUSTRIAL REVOLUTION AND ITS IMPACT ON MUSLIM UNDERSTANDING OF CULTURAL DIVERSITY

The industrial revolution wrought changes in the way we view our world, in the way we relate to our world and in the way we manage and organize time in the workplace and elsewhere in our social universe. Its major impacts registered first in Europe and later throughout the world, making the factory, already known to Muslims and to others along the Mediterranean, to the predominant form of mass production. Not only did this revolution redefine the relationship between human and human, but it also helped redefine the relationship between humans and machines. Homo Faber was no longer a single entity in the universe of creation; rather, he was now a part of a system of management and production whose processes seemed as much in control of people as vice versa. In the agrarian world, all men could till the soil and grow food for their sustenance and, if necessary, barter or sell the balance of production for profit, but the industrial revolution changed all that. From now on, those who controlled capital and owned factories decided who was employable and for how much. This factory culture, which was developing within an urban milieu first in England and later elsewhere in Europe and beyond, altered the nature of the old relationship between man and man. It also created a new relationship between Man and his tools. The potential sense of alienation of the worker from his working environment has been captured in the literature on the luddites and their destructive attitudes towards the inanimate objects directly and indirectly competing with them for managerial attention and accountability.

How did this emerging industrial culture affect the Muslim peoples? And in what manner did it affect Muslim understanding of diversity? Four points deserve our attention here. The first relates to the nature of culture in Muslim societies and Muslim leaders reacted to the growing industrial challenges of the Western European peoples. If we define culture as a human enterprise that is best characterized by three important components—the material base, the value base and the institutional base—then in Muslim societies the industrial revolution affected all three.

The first notable reaction of Muslim societies to the industrial revolution was in the field of military science. Taking note of the immediate impact of the industrial revolution on the power balance between nations and peoples, and determined to maintain themselves at all cost, the most powerful Muslim empires, Ottoman and others, tried to emulate the magical martial powers of the Europeans. This quest for military power through the genie of industrial transformation registered powerfully in the Ottoman drive to modernize and Westernize simultaneously. The leaders of the Ottoman Empire belatedly realized that Europe was breaking away from the human pack on the path to material development and that Muslims and other non-European peoples could only catch up by catching up with the scientific and technological knowledge of Europe. To transform themselves to meet the demands of the new dispensation, the leaders of the Muslim World, especially the Ottoman, began to get the knowledge, buy the technology or purchase the services of European technicians. This attempt to get science technology from Europe created a new cultural presence for Europeans. Not only were these Europeans received as traders and travelers, but increasingly they were brought in as technical experts. Their presence and the prestige accorded them by the Muslim rulers would gradually create a psychocultural phenomenon of xenophilia that spread to all Muslim lands. This association of technical competence with Europe led some Muslim thinkers of the nineteenth century to identify science and technology with Western Christianity.

EUROPEAN COLONIZATION OF THE GLOBE AND THE CHALLENGES TO MUSLIM PERSPECTIVES ON CULTURAL DIVERSITY

The European colonization of Muslim lands is the result of the industrialization of Western Europe and the decline of Muslim power. Historians have examined the manner in which European states gradually rose above the pack of nations in the world since the fifteenth century. We have discussed, in a previous section, the Age of Discovery and the manner in which the establishment of new trading powers enhanced the stocks of Europe and opened new doors of opportunities to them. In this section I intend to identify and discuss three issues that have affected Muslims in their understanding of themselves and in their relationship with Europe.

The first point relates to the colonial experience and its impact on the psyche of the colonized Muslim. Frantz Fanon and Albert Memmi both addressed the colonial question and the manner in which it affected North Africans. Fanon was a black man from Martinique whose links to France later led to his employment in a hospital in embattled Algeria under colonial rule. Memmi grew up in North Africa as a colonial Jew. Both authors wrote about the colonial experience and how it affected the peoples of that part of the continent of Africa. What makes Fanon particularly significant is his impact on Muslim thought, although he himself was more secular than religious. His influence is indirect and comes by way of the writings of Ali Shariati, one intellectual source of inspiration in the Iranian revolution.

Fanon identifies several characteristics of the colonial state. He argues quite forcefully that the colonial powers created a Manichean world between the colonized and the colonizer. To him, the colonial master dominates not only the physical space of the colonized but his mental world as well. The imperial master carries out this policy of political and cultural domination by splitting the colonized society into two camps: the urban population and the rural communities. Through its education system the colonial power creates a socializing agency that gradually weans its subjects away from their cultural heritage.

This socialization of the Muslim child creates a world of ambiguity. A Senegalese novelist, Cheich Harnidou Kane, captures this perilous state of cultural ambivalence in his widely celebrated book *Ambiguous Adventure*. As psychoanalyzed by Fanon and as fictionalized by Kane, the colonial education system produces black Frenchmen in sub-Sahara Africa; Arab Frenchmen in North Africa and the Middle East; and Southeast Asian Frenchmen in Vietnam, Cambodia, and Laos. This replication of the French mind in the colonial territories has led to the cultural alienation of some elites and to what Myron Wiener called the "elite-mass gap." Such pathologies also created personalities such as Ferhat Abbas, the Algerian nationalist leader, and Hastings Kamuzu Banda, the Malawian leader who rose to the presidency of his country. Colonialism robbed these men of their native tongues. Both of them developed such command of the colonial language that they "forgot" the languages of their ancestors. Abbas's case is the Muslim Arab example that applies more closely to our study of cultural diversity in Muslim lands.

The colonial powers also exploited anthropological data about the colonized peoples. In many Muslim lands where religious minorities existed, there were attempts to pit such groups against the majority Muslim population. Even in areas subject to the indirect rule policy of Lord Lugard, such as northern Nigeria, there is still some limited evidence of this divide-and-conquer policy. Nigerian nationalists have always argued that northern Nigerian Muslims were skillfully pitted by British colonial officers against their Christian brethren in the south. The political divisions of postcolonial Nigeria area bitter testimony to the heritage of such policies.

The same technique was applied Southern Sudan. Though the postcolonial leaders of Sudan cannot run away from their responsibility in the current state of affairs in that pan of Africa, the fact remains that British colonial interest shaped and directed the political outcome we now call Sudan. The deliberate policy of effective separation of the peoples of the north and south in this vast country planted the seeds of discord, and the postcolonial agitation of the southern peoples is the belated outburst of political a long-standing political grievance.

THE TRANSPLANTATION OF EUROPEAN NATIONALIST IDEAS AND THEIR IMPACT ON MUSLIM THOUGHTS ON CULTURAL DIVERSITY

Islam has introduced five major transformations in human life and culture. The first was to demolish the idols of the ancestors and to uphold radical monotheism. Although Judaism was the first of the Abrahamic religions to challenge the hegemony of tribal deities among the ancients and to advocate unflaggingly the primacy of one God, *Yaweh,* its claims to a special covenantal dispensation with the creator separates it from both Islam and Christianity. Whereas the Hebrew people, the children of Israel, usually see themselves as the chosen people, the Muslims and Christians made more universal claims that accommodate others not genetically linked to Abraham and his progeny.

The second revolutionary transformation of Islam was the teaching that all humanity derived from one source of creation, Adam. This combination of the demolition of the idols of the tribes and the advocacy of a common parentage in Adam and Eve for all humankind gave Islam a distinct character among world religions.

The three other revolutionary transformations in human thought engendered by Islam are as follows: (a) the teaching that faith in a single Creator (*Allah*) is the highest and most legitimate basis of allegiance for believing Muslims; (b) that the basis of human merit should not be the physical, external characteristics of the person but his or her capacity for pity (*taqwa*); (c) that power should not be monopolized by any royal family but by caliphs given oaths of allegiance by their Muslim peers. This last teaching remained a guiding principle for many centuries until the Muslim societies became increasingly dominated by the emergent

European powers in the nineteenth century.
In the early 1960s, Bernard Lewis wrote,

> Every student of Islamic history knows the stirring story of how Islam fought against idolatry, in the days of the Prophet and his Companions, and triumphed, so that the worship of the one God replaced the many cults of pagan Arabia. Another such struggle is being fought in our own time, not against Al-Lat and al-'Uzza and the rest of old heathen pantheon, but against a new set of idols called states, races and nations; this time it is the idols that seem to be victorious.[1]

Lewis later adds that the modern idea of nationalism did not take root in Muslim lands because descent, language, and habitation were all of secondary importance. He concludes that "it is only during the last century that, under European influence, the idea of the political union has begun to make headway. For Muslims, the basic division, the touchstone by which men are separated from one another, by which one distinguished between brothers and sisters-is that of faith, of membership of a religious community."[2]

Notwithstanding Bernard Lewis's views on the longstanding Islamic idea of Ummatic solidarity in the modern period, the fact remains that believing men and women in the Muslim World still embrace this idea and would like to see it realized in the establishment of a global political order in which Muslim solidarity is undisputed and Muslim cooperation again approaches the highest levels of human possibility.

Yet one cannot deny the penetration of the nationalist idea in the Muslim World. Over the last century and a half, the ideas of European nationalism have crept into the imagination and consciousness of almost all Muslim peoples, thanks largely to the colonization of Muslim lands and the persistence among Muslims of residual tribal and ethnic loyalties that have been cynically exploited by local Muslim politicians. As we will see later in this paper, the expansion of European colonial rule led to the political manipulation and exploitation of ethnic and religious minorities and majorities in areas where Muslim power was dominant for centuries. This is clear in Africa, Asia, and in what was formerly the Soviet Empire.

Since the modernization drive of the Ottoman, the nationalist idea has remained a fascinating proposition to many a Muslim intellectual bent on imitating and hobnobbing with the Westerners. The successes of the Young Turks and the establishment of the Turkish Republic under Kemal Ataturk after the First World War imparted a lasting impetus to the nationalist idea in the Islamic world. The Turkish example has been copied and followed faithfully by the Arab states that came into being after the collapse of the colonial empires in the Middle East and North Africa. The Iranians, who did not suffer the humiliation of colonization, saw the nationalist path to self-definition as a European alternative to the Islamic paradigm. In the aftermath of the World War II, the Pakistanis, the Bangladeshis, the Indonesians, the Malaysians, and the Africans all decided unilaterally to follow the path of nation-building on the European model. With the collapse of the Soviet colonial empire in Central Asia, the newly liberated Muslim lands have taken their seats as independent political entities in the United Nations and in the Organization of Islamic Conference (OIC).

The second point that deserves out attention here is the fact that the penetration of nationalist ideas from Europe has led to the polarization of Muslim lands between the majority group and its minorities. The Turkish insistence that the Kurds of that land accept the Turkish national language and the cultural victimization that accompany such a nationalist policy is the mirror image of the enforced Bulgarization of the Turkish minority in Bulgaria. Similarly, the victimizations of the Kurds by the regime of Saddam Hussein of Iraq and the denial of Kurdish aspirations for a separate nation in the region have again created a state of unrest in both Turkey and Iraq. The situation is not radically different in Iran, where the Kurdish minority has served as political football in the power game between the Iranian government and the leaders of Baghdad.

This prevalence of nationalist loyalties in the Muslim World has created a serious rift between the loyalists to the old Muslim ideology of Pan-Islamism, as Jamal al-Afghani and his followers became known, and the secular nationalists who pedal their political wares under the names of Arab nationalism, Baathism, Panchasila, Pan-Africanism, and many other "isms." Whatever their differing origins and perspectives, all these varieties of Muslim nationalism are united in their recognition and acceptance of the European-imposed colonial boundaries. The coagulation of the colonial boundaries has given new meanings and new realities to old borders; the emergence of social and economic classes with vested interest in the new order has made it possible for the political elites to champion the new nationalism.

The Cold also helped in the cultivation of the seeds of Third World nationalism. By recognizing the legitimacy of these states and by wooing and winning them into their ideological orbits, the Cold War rivals in both camps gave credence to new born polities and leaderships of these emerging Muslim countries.

The adoption of the nationalist ideology of the Europeans by the Muslim states has created opportunities for ethnic leaders to pit one group against another. These opportunistic policies have been reported in almost all Muslim lands where cultural pluralism and ethnic differentiation are either deeply rooted or have been rekindled by the divide-and-rule tactics of the old colonial and imperial masters. Indeed, the ethnic divisiveness is not peculiar to old colonial territories. The fate of Afghanistan since the Soviet invasion shows not only the effectiveness of Islam as a means of mobilizing opposition to communism but also the potential destructiveness of ancient, smoldering ethnic hatreds among Muslims. The rise of the Taliban in Afghanistan and the havoc wrought by this brand of Islamism has made it categorically clear that Islam could be used as "a wallpaper to cover the cracks in the wall of Pashto nationalism." The same problem could derail the developmental efforts of Malaysia and Indonesia and of the predominantly Muslim states of Sub-Saharan Africa.

THE RISE OF COMMUNISM AND ITS IMPACT ON MUSLIM THOUGHT ON CULTURAL DIVERSITY

Except for the central Asian Muslim territories and the Muslims of Bosnia and Albania, no other Muslim lands lived under communist rule until the Soviet invasion of Afghanistan, a failed gamble that eventually contributed to the downfall of the Soviet Union. In this section of the paper we intend to explore the encounter between the communist message and the Muslim peoples. We also wish to study the manner in which this body of ideas affected Muslim thought on cultural diversity.

There are three ways in which communism affected the Muslim lands. The first and most significant was the poisoning of the Middle Eastern political climate. The dissemination of communist ideas in the Middle Fast, especially after World War II, injected the Cold War into an Arab World that was just coming out of the colonial experience. By competing with the Western powers who had a vested interest in capitalism and by recruiting young Muslims from this region of the world and beyond, the communists planted suspicion among the peoples of the region. Whereas in the past non-Muslim could exist side by side with Muslims, the prospects of a communist takeover of the state and society in the postcolonial era made the communist members of society political lepers who were often targeted for long jail sentences or physical elimination. This acrimonious state of affairs was fostered by the Western allies of the

Muslim anticommunist forces.

One version of the course of modern political history in the Middle East pits the radical nationalists—who embraced some form of Arab socialism—against those who flirted with capitalist powers. What some have called the Arab Cold War was the offspring of the rivalry between the Soviet Union and the United States. From the perspective of Muslim cultural history, the two cold wars, one regional and the other global, were detrimental to the self-definition of the Arab states and the pursuit of their individual and collective interest.

The second issue to explore here is the impact of the Cold War on the internal affairs of Muslim lands. In the Middle East, Central Asia, and Southeast Asia the communist parties were dominated by members of the ethnic minorities. In the Arab world, Jews, Greeks, and Armenians have generally been identified with such parties, although many ethnic Arabs also embraced some form of Marxism. This ethnification of Marxism in Arab countries led to a wall of suspicion between the members of these ethnically based communist parties and the majority communities. In such an unhealthy climate of suspicion, the rights and privileges previously accorded to such peoples in Islamic tradition were eroded, not in the name of Islam but in the name of state security. The spirit of the Cold War made this kind of policy and practice acceptable and legitimate. It also gave greater power and respectability to the secular state and its officials.

As far back as the period after World War I, some Muslim leaders who wanted to liberate their societies from the yoke of foreign rule briefly flirted with the idea of working with the communists. One example was Enver Pasha, who had in 1918 launched the "Army of Islam" ostensibly to help liberate the Muslims from the Russian Empire. After the communists came to power, this Turkish Muslim settled in Moscow. In 1921 he presided over a Congress of the Union of Islamic Revolutionary Societies in Berlin and Rome. This attempt at revolutionary Islam failed, however. Pasha, who was sent to Central Asia to help the newly installed communist regime, changed sides and became a part of the Muslim nationalist campaign against Russian rule. He was killed in 1922 fighting the Red Army.

Another example is Sultan Galiev, the Tartar schoolmaster who worked with Stalin at the Commissariat of Nationalities in 1918 and conceived the idea of revolutionary international colonial people independent of the Comintern. He was arrested in 1923 for "nationalist deviations" and disappeared in a later purge.[3]

THE IRANIAN REVOLUTION AND ITS IMPACT ON MUSLIM
THOUGHT ON CULTURAL DIVERSITY

The Iranian revolution of 1979 has had an incalculable impact on the subsequent course of the theory and practice of Islamic nationalism, especially in regard to questions of pluralism and diversity. Its most immediate effect was the explosion of the myth of the cultural and historical inevitability of modernization. The Iranian revolution challenged the dominant notion that Islam and other religious belief systems were archaic survivals destined for extinction. This idea that "traditional society was passing away" received a serious setback when the Shah of Iran was overthrown and his place was taken by a mullah backed by the bazaaris and most of the Iranian masses; the middle classes in this Middle Eastern country somehow abandoned the modernizer in favor of the traditionalist Imam Khomeini.

Of course there were many reasons for this change of heart. We are not focusing on this point. Rather, we are trying to show that the cultural transformations that the modernization process in Iran caused were reinterpreted if not outrightly reversed by the train of Islamic revivalism. Under the White Revolution of the Shah, the big landlords were beginning to feel the growing power of the modernizing state, as was the religious establishment, whose members had enjoyed for centuries certain agrarian privileges. Modernization did not sit well these classes. Whereas the modernization effort of the Shah widened the circle of control of the state while fostering functional and structural differentiation, the Iranian revolution helped redefine the nature of relationships between ethnic groups, gender groups, regional groups, ideological groups, and religious groups because of the doctrine of *wilayat al-fiqih* (Islamic jurisprudence). This reordering of the political and cultural hierarchy of Iranian society has led to the revival of classical Muslim thought, especially those aspects that have helped Shiites to grapple with the challenges of the human condition.

In addition, the Iranian Revolution changed the nature of the relationship between Iranians and other Muslims in the Middle East and beyond. Since the revolution was perceived by most Muslims as a boost to their self-confidence in their relationship with the two dominant ideological camps in the Cold War, it helped to form a bridge of reconciliation between the Sunnis and the Shiites. Even if this was a temporary phenomenon, we now know that these two antagonistic Muslim groupings saw the rise of Khomeini as a Muslim resurgence and a second chance for Islam to redefine itself in the realm of human thought and action. This short-lived honeymoon between these two sects of Islam, however, was truncated by the Iran-Iraq War and the new phenomenon of "re-ethnification of the Arab-Iranian relations," the propagandistic misuse of the Battle of Qadisiyah by President Saddam Hussein and his Baathist collaborators in the Arab World. Sensing the potential of the Iran Revolution as a source of inspiration and subversion in the Muslim World, and determined to join forces with any and every powerful group to contain this threat, the Iraqi and Gulf states found in Sunnism a new weapon to bash the Iranian revolutionaries. This strategy of the Arab supporters of the Iraqis again drove a wedge between Shiites and Sunnis.

Still another innovation of the Iranian Revolution was in the area the treatment of local minorities. Under the Shah the religious minorities fared well. This was particularly true for the Nahais. Many Iranians would now concede that the Shah was very generous to the Baha'is. This act of generosity was sometimes seen negatively by Muslim Iranians who saw the invisible hand of the Baha'is in virtually every major event in their country. This resentment of the Baha'is, which goes back to the rise of this new religion in Iran in the last century, adversely affected the Muslim view of cultural diversity. The Baha'is were treated by the Shah's regime as just one community out of many seeking religious space in Iran. Under the Shah's modernization program the Baha'is and the Muslim majority were supposed to live under one political roof with equality before the law.

The Iranian Revolution changed the whole political and religious equation for the Baha'is. Seen as heretical by the Islamic revolutionaries and branded as collaborators with the external enemy, the Baha'is were dismissed as unfit to receive the kind of treatment given to *ahl al-kitab* (People of the Book). Since their leader was a renegade Muslim who claimed to be the Messiah and the Mahdi simultaneously, the new religious leadership in Iran changed their lot by rearranging the rights and privileges of citizens living under the Islamic Republic. Contrary to the claims by Baha'is in the United States of America, the Baha'is in Iran are not totally disenfranchised. However, one should hasten to add that their lives are not as secured as in the days of the Shah's regime.

Again, when we look at the impact of the Iranian Revolution on Muslim thoughts on cultural diversity, one quickly realizes that the success of the Iranian revolution has created new opportunities for religious entrepreneurs to pit one sect against the other. This polarization process has reached dangerous proportions in the South Asian subcontinent, especially in Pakistan, where newspapers report daily killings among religious sectarians. Sunnis and Shiites now hunt each other as fair game. This terrorism has now threatened not only the future of the Pakistani state but the unity of the Pakistani people. The glue that kept the Pakistanis united for the last fifty years is being eroded by the resurgence of sectarian and ethnic allegiances. A review of Pakistani history shows that the leaders of the Muslim League were drawn from various sects of Islam. Since the Iranian Revolution and the rise of protagonists and antagonists of the revolution, Muslim societies such as Pakistan and Lebanon have seen new forces and new faces in the circle of leadership in their countries. These groups have come up with their own interpretations of the Muslim experience and are now opposed to one another in the name of Islam. This extremist interpretation of Islam and its heritage in the Middle East has become most violent and most deadly in the hands of the former Taliban government in Afghanistan.

CONCLUSIONS

Eight arguments and points arise throughout this text:

1. The original Muslim formulation of the nature of human identity has undergone transformations not only because of the lapses in Muslim judgment and behavior but also because of the Muslim attempts at emulating external other cultural forms and patterns.
2. The Age of Discovery created the psychological and political climate that led to the violation of the rights of the native peoples of the world.
3. The industrial revolution has presented humanity with novel challenges that have either crippled the defenders of religion or have rearranged their ways of life to such a degree that the idols of the market have now replaced the old idols of the gods.
4. The colonization of the world by peoples of European descent has changed radically the human view of physical space and the philosophy of ownership. The Lockean notion of ownership by simply mixing one's labor with the soil has replaced if not displaced the old communal views of property ownership.
5. The expansion of Europe into the Americas and beyond has led to the conflation of color, creed, and culture into one metaphysical category. The genocidal liquidation of the native peoples of the Americas and Australia have affected the Muslims and others who were not part of the Judeo-Christian world.
6. The rise of European nationalism has affected Muslim lands and peoples to such an extent that they too are bitten by the bug of territorial nationalism;

the fratricidal wars that have erupted across their borders over the last decades are living testimony to the dangers of demotic or territorial nationalism.

7.   The ideological contest between the communist movement and the capitalist world created conditions and circumstances that militated against any independent Muslim exercise in critical self-definition. The Cold War distorted Muslim sentiments and polarized Muslims as they offered their friendship to one or the other of the two superpowers.

8.   The 1979 Iranian Revolution briefly opened the floodgates of Muslim solidarity, but they were slammed shut soon after by the Iran-Iraq War, solidified the wall of sectarian zeal.

The Muslim world faces new challenges and opportunities in the realm of cultural anthropology and political anthropology. Its ability to do better in the next century will depend greatly on the vision of its leaders and on the reformulation of its philosophy of group relations within the historical framework of Islam.

CHAPTER 4

"True" and "False" Pluralism in the West and Islam

Richard K. Khuri

ON THE LOSS OF IDENTITY AND OTHER POSSIBLE CAUSES OF THE PREVALENCE OF DISCUSSSIONS ABOUT PLURALISM

Today there is a global identity crisis. Europe has not escaped this syndrome; in France, Spain, and Italy, the influx of predominantly North African immigrants has caused serious tension. The French have enjoyed a secure sense of nationhood for a very long time, yet there are stirrings of doubt in some quarters about what it means to be French. One need only look at the ethnic composition of the immensely successful French football team to realize how much things have changed. Only a minority of the players are what one would until recently have called "French."

Across the Rhine, in Germany, the natives eye uneasily the creeping citizenship of millions of Turks originally brought in to do menial work. Meanwhile, first-time visitors to London may be startled to discover the ethnic realities of the new Britain. Many Balkan nations, especially the former Yugoslavia, have yet to come to terms with their minorities: Hungarians in Romania, Turks in Bulgaria, Serbs in Croatia, Croats in Bosnia, Albanians in Serbia and Macedonia, Romany (gypsies) everywhere. Elsewhere, Tatars, Chechens, and others resist Russification, while Russians struggle to preserve their communities in the Baltic republics and in Central Asia.

In the so-called developing world, much of which is quite well developed by now, there is an even deeper source of anxiety: the fate of local culture and tradition. Independence from European colonial powers has forced many in those emergent states to ask themselves who they are. Once the question was asked, a plurality of apparently (and sometimes genuinely) irreconcilable answers was unfortunately forthcoming in all too many cases. The diverse and clashing answers to this question have led to violent upheavals: the break-up of India; the Nigerian, Lebanese, and Algerian civil wars; Kurdish rebellions in Iraq and Turkey; and the Iranian revolution.

Globalization has compounded such problems. The United States itself, an immigrant nation par excellence, harbors many who are disoriented by the pace of cultural change and afraid that they might lose whatever identity they have evolved in a comparatively short time. In France there are real fears over how much of French culture will survive the lopsided economics of globalization, much less the ethnic diversity of contemporary French society. Under a global regime of extreme free-market capitalism, the French have good reason to ask whether there will be enough books, songs, and films in their own language; already the proliferation of electronic media has taken a toll on the vibrancy of Parisian café life.

Well known in discussions about political or cultural change, insecurity over ethnic and cultural identity has two very different sources: rapid demographic change and movement; and anxieties bred by rapid cultural change. A culture can embrace pluralism with less difficulty than is usually imagined, but to what extent can a culture become pluralistic in its heart and soul without ceasing to be a culture? We may speak coherently of a plurality of cultures, in the same place and at the same time, but what would a truly pluralistic culture look like? One the one hand there is the clash of rival cultures, say Muslim and Hindu on the Indian subcontinent (not to mention the many rivalries within each major group), and on the other the common threat they all face from an emergent global culture or anti-culture. It makes sense to describe India as a pluralistic society (Pakistan rather less so), but what does it mean to speak of a "pluralism" that joins India with contemporary fashions? Local culture will be transformed, no doubt, but will it persist as a distinctive culture or it will not. There is no pluralism to speak of there. If no forceful resistance is forthcoming, then every conceivable film will be mainstream Hollywood glitz.

Where talk about pluralism is loudest, the overt intention is to persuade recalcitrant to include other groups in their political and cultural life. But in such cases the dominant local group, its culture already weakened by internal decay and the successive assaults of colonialism, neocolonialism, and the brute material power of global anti-culture, is often pushed towards cultural dissolution, along with most of the groups it is urged to include in the name of pluralism. The result is nominal pluralism, a gathering of diverse cultural relics, lorded over by the highly mobile, geographically decentralized, virtual instruments of global anti-culture. Calls for pluralism, often with the best of intentions -- witness the dedication and conscientiousness of organizations such as Amnesty International -- may well result in a dreary cultural monism.

There is no conspiracy here, just an extraordinary convergence of diverse development whose consequences have not been subjected to adequate reflection. How else could so much liberation end with so much consumerism? Such dangers inspire a looming anxiety in some quarters over the imminent demise of local culture, which, they believe, can be saved only by exerting total control over their own society and then mobilizing it for the "great war" of local culture against global anti-culture. Hence, the specter of global monism breeds a plethora of local monisms. Either way, pluralism dies out, trampled by the moral-religious police or submerged in the kaleidoscopic diversity that subserves as a politically expedient veneer for the diffuse interests that drive and sustain global anti-culture.

In contrast, where cultural experience allows a more transparent view of the means by which global anti-culture might gain dominance, genuine pluralism can be both tolerated and maintained. There, the "only" problem is that passions be alive and commitments strong enough for people to choose resistance in the first place and to be effective in their action. In this global context, "pluralism" has taken on diverse connotations, among them the following: (a) Pluralism can refer to the nature of the political system and social order required to accommodate multiple ethnicities. Such a pluralism can be part of a nation's birthright—as in Malaysia, Syria, Turkey, South Africa, Belgium, Spain, the United States, and Guatemala—or it may be a recent graft, as in France, Sweden, and the newly independent Baltic and Central Asian republics. (b) Pluralism can be knowingly used as a rallying cry by those who understand that a shallow diversity erodes cultural resistance to the spread of global anti-culture. It may also be used less hypocritically by those simply caught up in the contemporary spirit of the times. In both guises, it is a worldwide phenomenon and it has indeed facilitated the sweep of globalization's icons. (c) Pluralism can underline acceptance of significant differences in opinion, irrespective of one's ethnic identity or socioeconomic standing. This meaning of *pluralism* faces extinction from various quarters. For instance, many seem to find it difficult to imagine that individuals have a personality and identity beyond that of their social group. A similar conceptual block afflicts many vehemently anti-Marxist economists and scientists.

Pluralism is closely linked to notions of identity, another concept with a multitude of possible meanings. With greater eloquence and violence, such pluralism, as we have just seen, also loses out to the monism of global anti-culture and the lesser monisms of those who resist it zealously. Once we have come to grips with the different ways that "pluralism" is used, we can determine how closely related increased talk about it is to a growing sense of insecurity over identity. Identity can apply to groups or individuals, both of which seem caught up in a global pandemic of insecurity about maintaining their own sense of identity in the face of incursion from other groups or from the faceless imperatives of globalization. Both Nietzsche and Kierkegaard believed that an anguished and conflicted intensity, the sort that may breed intolerance, is preferable to the pluralism of mass somnambulance in which the other is not so much tolerated as given just enough room to contribute his mite of apathy to a mass of socially engineered herd animals.

What sort of pluralism are we talking about, then? To what end is it prescribed? What is the present condition of the Muslims, both as societies and individuals, at the receiving end of friendly pleas or pontifications? How have they regarded the other when they controlled their own destiny? Do we care that they regain a strong sense of who they are, and not necessarily in the manner of the extremists who caricature Islam? Or is the task merely to haul Islam onto the bandwagon of globalized anti-culture, to render it just another color in the global kaleidoscope of diversity?

Pluralism is nothing new. There were several instances of it in ancient times. The Phoenicians, for example, were well aware of cultural diversity through trade and travel. It left them quite unperturbed. Exposure to a variety of cultures and worldviews did not lead to any upheavals within their own dominions. They assimilated some of what they had learned with ease and ignored the rest, all the while remaining distinct from other

Semitic peoples in the region. A similar kind of exposure, far from forcing retrenchment, impelled many ancient Greeks toward the development of a cultural framework that in Hellenized form spread throughout the Mediterranean basin and eastward to Mesopotamia, Persia, and India. That framework gathered extensive Eastern and Egyptian sources into itself.

It should therefore come as no surprise that the Muslims, who ruled the very same lands from the middle of the seventh century, openly embraced Hellenism. It helped that the Muslims were then at the height of their confidence. The case of Xenophanes (c. 570-480 B.C.) is of special interest. This ancient Greek philosopher and poet was able to break through to a monotheistic vision precisely because he knew about the diverse portrayals of divinities in different cultures. He observed that images of the divine resembled the anatomy of whoever crafted them. He then realized that what is truly divine could bear no such resemblance and therefore had to transcend all human specificity. His great contemporary Pythagoras, who is believed to have had contact with the Babylonians, Egyptians, and possibly the Indians, also became aware of a universal, cosmic presence beyond any of its particular manifestations. Thus began a line of mystically inspired theological philosophy that, reinforced by Heraklitus, Parmenides, Empedocles, Plato, Aristotle, and Plotinus, has never died.

This central theme of spiritual awareness had its origins in a rich civilizational pluralism. The grandeur and openness of the oneness of which enlightened ancients became aware does not give license to petty campaigns and vendettas. A study of its history shows that its origins differ radically from the zealous caricatures purveyed by later epigoni. Unusual tolerance for pluralism distinguished the Roman Empire from the time of Julius Caesar onward. The Romans knew very well who they were. They had a clear sense of purpose and a definition of Roman citizenry based on values that disregarded tribal and regional boundaries. They were able to impose their civilizational vision-mostly reflected in Roman law, the use of Latin in administrative and higher cultural circles (except for those who still used Greek), and a brilliantly engineered infrastructure-throughout a vast stretch of the ancient world for many centuries. And so they did not feel threatened by ethnic diversity so long as everyone conformed with that vision. This allowed for the coexistence of an exceptional variety of worldviews in the latter five hundred years or so of the empire's life.

Two outstanding symbols of Roman pluralism have survived. Plotinus, (A.D. 210-275) the greatest Roman philosopher, was a dark-skinned man from Upper Egypt who wrote in Greek and was familiar with hieroglyphs. And the emperor who oversaw the celebration of Rome's millenium in A.D. 248 was known as "Philip the Arab," since he was born among nomads who wandered along the edge of the Arabian desert. His Latinized name became Marcus Julius Philippus, and he may have been the first Christian who ruled the empire.

Even today, the United States is unable to match some of Rome's achievements in pluralism. For can this nation's leading philosopher be anyone not originally from Europe? As for the president, it is rare enough for him to be a Catholic, let alone someone whose origins are as distant from northwestern Europe as Philip's were from Rome. The constitution of the United States affirms universal values, but it also incorporates an underlying sense of Anglo-Saxon Protestant ascendancy (although this has been expanded to include Catholics and Jews of European ancestry since the end of the Second World War). The United States does not have the same kind of confidence in its identity as ancient Rome, and so pluralism here has its limits (Apart from the persecution of Christians, Rome enjoyed much religious pluralism as well. That the Christians would later suppress all other religions, except for limited tolerance of the Jews, makes one stop and think). Pluralism thrived not only in the ancient world, but also later on in the Islamic world (above all in Iberia, the Levant, Mesopotamia, and India), and still later on within the areas of Europe ruled by the Habsburgs.

Before the middle of the nineteenth century, it was probably far easier to live as though there were no other worldviews. There were many more pockets of homogeneity all over the world, many more people who could lead their daily lives in the bliss of stable creeds, without dozens of intrusions that politely or rudely exposed them to other ways. One can imagine a time not so very long ago when the whole world was a mosaic of such homogeneous cultural pockets, while only an elite of traders, clerics, intellectuals, diplomatic, and military officials even knew about other cultures. Our contemporary world, by contrast, is in a crisis of chronic and intense juxtaposition: too many people, too many worldviews crowding in on one another, physically and mentally, propelled towards the absurd theoretical limit where every person is potentially exposed to every possible worldview at all times. Thus one has a better view of how the ground is cleared for global anti-culture: In addition to what has been mentioned already, there is the corrosive effect of being unable to rest sufficiently in a given world view for it to begin to enhance one's ability to live more substantially, with an increased awareness of one's own being and that of one's layered surroundings, from surface phenomena to the innermost drive that (is operative and) becomes partly manifest through our universe. A restless world makes for impatience toward the difficult, the subtle, the profound. The time and space required for deep reflection is swallowed up by the haste and clamor of global electronic anti-culture, with its surfeit of competing images, ideologies, and lifestyles. Continuous simultaneous exposure to diverse worldviews undermines allegiance to any. Those who feel their sacred cultural patrimony threatened might resort to violence.

To the degree that depth of outlook and belief play a big part in how fit one becomes for life, spiritually, psychologically, emotionally, and also in some respects intellectually, the intensity with which worldviews are juxtaposed has become a threat to life. Most who become aware of the threat posed to life by what we may term "pluralistic intensity" are naturally inclined to do away with pluralism altogether, and many among them are liable to resort to violence. The tragedy is that those who withdraw into a localized monism, even suppressing pluralism by brute force, such as the Taliban, are unlikely to realize their goals. In fact, they can become part of the tragicomic spectacle of originally well-intentioned spiritual movements that strangely come to resemble their adversaries in the global anti-culture. Such has been the fate of televangelism and much that passes for "New Age" spirituality, of which the Falun Gong is the Chinese example.

The corrosiveness of pluralistic intensity has another nasty side, evident in the leveling of the value of various worldviews after too many of them have been broadcast at too many people for too long. Too much exposure leads to worldview fatigue—and indifference—amid the white noise of multicultural profusion.

Moreover, the habit of treating worldviews impartially combines with their apparent secondary importance to detach individuals further and further from all worldviews and begin to pass judgment over them as though one were some divinity. Before long, all worldviews are relativized. There is an ineluctable process by which pluralism, if it is intense enough, collapses into relativism. Henceforth, democracy and freedom, wherever they are promoted, subtly impose conditions that favor the absolutization of the system of relativized pluralism. After the initial flush of infatuation with newly won freedom inebriation with freedom, the newly liberated often face some sobering "morning-after" realities:

voting for interchangeable political parties, acquiring more and more useless or superfluous consumer goods, and narcissistically limiting one's company to those who fit the same label or category.

The attainment of real freedom is always hard work, and is often contingent on retaining a sense of the difference between relativism and pluralism. Relativists deny that there is any reality that transcends personal whims, tastes, and preferences. If some people believe that no harm should come to children, others might not. The first belief may be better than the second but lack any axiomatic, universal grounding. (A close examination of relativist methodology will show that the problem is set up in a manner so as to preclude the very possibility of transcendence, in part by confusing it with objectivity, as though moral beliefs with universal import could only gain their status through a process more suitable for highly litigious societies) Pluralism entails neither the denial nor the affirmation of transcendence (which is the philosophical term used to refer to whatever exists beyond the material world and, generally, beyond what can be established by ordinary use of the senses and reason or by scientific experiment). A pluralist might indeed hold transcendent reality dear; what sets him or her apart from the monist is that the former concedes that it is extremely difficult to embody transcendent reality in a definitive interpretation. It is this admission that is the deepest legitimization of pluralism: although transcendent is infinite, human beings can express it only in finite terms. This incongruity forces us to live with the incompleteness of our interpretations and hence to abide with interpretive multiplicity. Language, of course, expresses the infinite and comes most alive when it does so; at least it is the best outward vehicle for striving for transcendence. But to the degree that language has this remarkable capacity, it denies us the ease and comfort of a single and definite interpretation. One may therefore readily acknowledge the legitimacy and spiritual force of several world religions. It is naive for either Christians or Muslims to continue to suppose that the whole of humanity will one day follow their teachings in unison (in this regard, South Asian and East Asian followers of other religions have been wiser). But one need not conclude from such multiplicity that truth is itself multiple-just that it defies invariant linguistic formulation.

It is hard to imagine moral strictures for which there are no exceptions. For instance, is capital punishment always wrong, even if the guilty person is a serial killer of children? Is honoring abusive parents right? Should Muslims fast by daylight north of the Arctic Circle when Ramadan occurs in the summer (or winter for that matter)? Is one bound to a promise the keeping of which might endanger one's life?

We are finally in a position to distinguish between true and false pluralism. False pluralism prevails when there are several choices to be made within a supreme framework that predefines and delimits the range of values and choices. This is not pluralism at all, but a kind of monolithism. No one dares criticize democracy or capitalism in the United States, whereas the most vulgar blasphemies are permitted. Thus democracy and capitalism, neither of which is a worldview or even pretends to be, are now valued far more than the most resonant, far-reaching worldviews. Nothing illustrates the preponderance of false pluralism more poignantly.

True pluralism, in contrast, involves the coexistence of profoundly different but equally valued worldviews. Its topography is varied as opposed to the flat terrain of false pluralism. Transcendence is given its due. Authentic pluralism recognizes the inherent difficulty of reducing transcendence to a single embodiment, however sacred, inspired and ingenious; it fosters earnest personal choice, for one cannot change one's mind daily about, say, how to attain the greatest possible capacity for life or awareness of being, since belief and personality cannot be consumed and discarded as casually as clothing styles or toothpaste. True pluralism encourages more considered political engagement because the contending parties will have more significantly differing visions.

The distinction between true and false pluralism allows me to explain why I prefer "pluralism" to "diversity." Diversity is more noncommittal. It applies indifferently to a variety of types within each category and to a variety of categories as well. We can speak in the same tone of a diversity of religions, languages, lifestyles, ethnicities, consumer products, or species. Repeated use of "diversity" blurs the nature and extent of true differences. It lends itself to relativism and therefore a false pluralism. Pluralism, in contrast, is a more complex and dynamic concept that can encompass the need for coexistence between several fundamentally different philosophical, moral, political, religious, and other points of view. It need not imply a subtle rejection of the possibility that some viewpoints may be more substantial, profound, or otherwise deserving of our allegiance. If pluralism can be false, it can also be true to what is best for human beings. And if what is best for human beings is not always and everywhere the same, this does not justify the listlessness and potential destructiveness of relativism.

It seems, then, that the prospects are slender for arriving at a grounded and authentic way of life in today's global bazaar of competing ideologies, religions, cultures, and marketing strategies, all of which thrive in a relativist atmosphere of coequality. It looks like there is not enough time to become properly rooted in the type of outlook that affords one the greatest capacity for life, nor is one able to select the appropriate path when told repeatedly in one way or another that they are all equally good, nor does one even have the assurance of a definition of human nature that urges one towards a certain level of being. And yet, pluralistic intensity and the requirements for its management are here to stay. So is the paradox that arises from the need to impose a system of management for the peaceful sustenance of pluralistic intensity that before long becomes the sole absolute and relativizes everything else. This collapses pluralism into a more and more tepid relativism. The system necessary for the management of pluralism slowly undermines it and leaves individuals to wander a cultural, emotional, and spiritual desert.

Meanwhile, the human longing for a more meaningful life persists, however susceptible to the comfortingly easy nostrums of cults and political extremists. There is an urgent need for individuals and communities to know who they are. The "who" here refers only superficially to identity. Its ultimate reference is philosophical and metaphysical. On it depends our conception of what it is to be human. What is really human? What are humans meant to be, if anything at all? The less firm and clear one is about where one stands, the more prone one will be to become a plaything in the hands of globalizing marketeers who seek to regiment rather than nourish our common humanity. The unmasking false pluralism reveals the mechanisms through which meaninglessness begins to pervade contemporary life. In countering this pall of anomie, there is still a great deal of wisdom to be mined from the ancient veins of world religions such as Islam. If contemporary Muslim societies do not offer much inspiration, then perhaps the past is instructive so long as one abstains from fantasies about some Golden Age.

THE UNITED STATES AND THE PROBLEM OF FALSE PLURALISM

There is no misprint in the title of this section. Almost everyone today regards the United States as a model of pluralism, ready and willing to bestow the same gift on a refractory and fractious Arab Muslim world. It is automatically assumed that the purpose of any bona fide intervention is to bring about those changes that will ensure for that unhappy region the sort of pluralism enjoyed by North Americans. When a mode of thinking becomes automatic, it ceases to be thought. If for no other reason than to maintain our ability to think, as a thought experiment, let us turn the tables and examine the extent to which the United States is truly pluralistic and whether, therefore, an uncritical adoption of its model is really the cure for the world's ills.

True pluralism no longer thrives in those domains in the United States that are most visible abroad, such as politics, the mass media, and Hollywood. It has become clear that major elections no longer present voters with meaningful choices. The system gamed to practically exclude third parties, and the nontrivial divide between the two persistently dominant parties grows ever narrower. One need only consider how Republican and Democratic presidential candidates are selected or how many senatorial and congressional candidates run for their seats unopposed. The result is voter apathy.

This decline in American democracy has been attended by a triumphalism that has swept the United States in the wake of the collapse of Soviet communism; even as its internal democracy is compromised, the self-image of the United States is that of the world's most desirable political system. Any suggestion that something is amiss with the political and economic culture that rule the United States is met with disdain, amazement, or, at best, polite condescension. This political uniformity is both a cause and effect of a similar groupthink in the mass media, once the principal guardian of meaningful democratic practice but now, increasingly, the echo of the prevailing political line. No conspiracy or overt totalitarianism would succeed in attaining the same level of uniformity as that which spontaneously bedevils the media in the United States, which are now concentrated in a handful of giant corporate proprietors.

How did society founded to maximize opportunities for individual expression and religious freedom become hostage to commercial forces? Part of the answer lies in the ascendancy of the framework for the management of pluralistic intensity at the expense of the competing, juxtaposed worldviews. When the framework matters before all else, there is less and less room for the articulation and dissemination of beliefs that transcend the commercial nexus. The framework that stands apart from specific world views is inherently favorable towards materialism. The preoccupation with an advanced and complex infrastructure that facilitates the flow of capital and goods is otherwise neutral. The framework is the sole possible object of a clear consensus. If it is most important that people agree, then it concerns hardly anyone should what they agree on be of little importance. Money and consumer products flow more and more easily, with the help of ingenious and ever fancier technologies. Everyone's business increasingly becomes business.

The new god, brought into being by an obsession with civic peace (which translates effectively into the need for a greater and greater consensus) is a kind of infrastructuralism from which flows the comic spectacle of applying technological criteria to all of humanity's problems. If the roads are smoothly surfaced and trains and planes arrive and depart on time, then all is well. The universities would ordinarily be islands of true pluralism in the bleak intellectual and spiritual surroundings created by North American infrastructuralism. But they have not been spared. Students in the natural and applied sciences, as well as at business schools, are taught from the first day to exclude themselves from their work, let alone express their opinions about anything, to a degree that would have exceeded the expectations of Marx and Lenin. The use of the first person pronoun is strictly forbidden. The social sciences, ill-conceived as sciences in the first place owing to conditions specific to the dominant culture of late nineteenth century Europe, try as hard as possible to imitate the natural or at least applied sciences (and are captive of the antiquated models of the late nineteenth century). To the extent that they fail, they join the humanities in their predicament: Students and professors (particularly junior members) are required either to follow the prevalent pseudoscientific orthodoxy or join a faction of the official "rebel" coalition (some fashionable "ism" or other), in either case to the serious detriment of the pursuit of knowledge and truth for their own sake.

The universities have also become victims of the commercial invasion: More and more brand name products are now advertised and sold openly on campus, particularly those of the purveyors of fast foods, whereas none were to be seen a mere generation ago, when the university was respected as a sanctuary, immune to commercial predation. Students could eat at a cafeteria that was run as a university concern, without outside affiliations, or buy products at the campus store that were exclusively linked to the university. No more. Even the gates of public schools have been opened to the insatiable hunt for "consumers" (a degrading term with which to describe human beings, as Wendell Berry and others have pointed out). Increasingly the choices facing citizens, students, thinkers are the trivial alternatives of the marketplace rather than the meaningful ones of untrammeled thought and culture. The apparent brand diversity of the market conceals a regimentation and narrowing of nearly every area of life.

Such false pluralism is spreading to other countries as well, most painfully to those that have recently thrown off their communist yoke and others about to rid themselves of despots and other villains. False pluralism is spreading because global change is led by the United States, its homeland. The Third World should approach such pluralism with wariness -- not to shun it altogether but to gain a clearer understanding of the choices being offered them.

For all the corruption, surely there are ways that true pluralism thrives in the United States. Where do we find it? However relentless the drumbeat of conformism, it is not so easy to stifle human individuality and creativity. Let us begin at the university. One always finds the odd professor here and there, more often than not from the older generation, who is an inspiration. At a time when the University of California at Berkeley was, in the words of its own chancellor, turning itself into an education factory, Czeslaw Milosz and Paul Feyerabend became professors there. Milosz is an exceptional poet recognized by the Nobel committee in 1980. He has a unique approach to the idiosyncratic, the particular, and the sacred. He taught courses on Dostoyevsky that were vivid, profound, and unique. Feyerabend raised radical and serious questions about the validity of the claim that science has a superior cultural standing (and challenged every basis for that claim). He personally encouraged his students to think for themselves and engaged them wholeheartedly, whatever their interests, on the condition that they not be narrowly ideological. In general, so long as large numbers of students are required to read Plato, Aristotle, Shakespeare, and other great authors, there will be enough young students whose natural intelligence and astuteness will unmask as rubbish much that passes for culture today, including much that has infiltrated many of the courses they must enroll in. Students of that caliber can also benefit from off-campus activities that sometimes offer better opportunities for cultivation than the universities themselves.

Other informal signs of true pluralism: Visitors who travel across the United States may be startled to find how closely different places resemble one another. The name "Anywhere, U.S.A." has been coined for such generic places. The preponderance of such "Anywhere, U.S.A." towns is a sobering symptom of uniformity. However, more patient visitors will find a healthy contrast in neighborhoods (usually ethnically based), small towns, and among various community organizations, where different attitudes and rhythms of life prevail. All over the country there are, as there have always been, small reading groups that quietly sustain the ability of individual members to think for themselves. Significant numbers of people have removed their television sets from their homes. Movements have formed such as the Promise Keepers, who are not fundamentalists. They simply reject the dominant culture as projected by the mass media and wish to uphold time-honored moral values. In a similar vein, hundreds of thousands of mothers gathered in Washington, DC, to protest gun violence. Other movements, such as the Black Muslims, are taking matters into their own hands in certain urban areas in order to rid them from crime and drugs and provide social services. This is not to say that the Black Muslims themselves are pluralists but that their very existence is confirmation that true pluralism continues to thrive in the United States. One finds similarly strong sentiments and calls for action among certain North American Jewish and Protestant revivalist groups.

It is surprising and disappointing that the United States, conceived as a champion of pluralism, should now harbor it mainly informally. In so many circles, ranging from the government to the media to the corporate workplace to opposition movements to several university departments (especially in the social "sciences" and humanities), whoever thinks differently must resort to guiles reminiscent of those contrived by artists and intellectuals in Kadar's Hungary or Nasser's Egypt. Even so, one must not forget that pluralism in the United States is constitutionally guaranteed. True pluralism lies at the heart of the self-image with which generations of North Americans have grown up. It is deeply resonant. It would take a tremendous exercise of sustained usurpation to bring citizens to the point where they are unable to distinguish between the true and the false. There are enduring legal and moral grounds for rebellion against such usurpation. What is at present informal may become formal in the not too distant future. We just happen to live at a time when the formal expression of pluralism in the United States has become largely bankrupt while the country's military and economic power is at its peak.

THE ARAB MUSLIM WORLD AND SOME SIGNPOSTS ON THE WAY TO TRUE PLURALISM

The usual approach to pluralism in the Arab Muslim world is to consider the state of the political systems in the relevant countries and see how these might be modified appropriately. Unfortunately, such an approach does not penetrate the societies in question deeply enough in order to begin to appreciate what is decisive for the fate of pluralism. One ought to at least give some thought to Islam, which many have been doing belatedly since the Iranian revolution in 1979. However, even though Islam has a more explicit political dimension than any other world religion, the study of Islam in relation to pluralism must go beyond politics.

If political Islam is more visible than other aspects of Islamic life, this does not mean that Islam is mainly political. Precisely those who are most likely to ponder the issue of Islam and pluralism, especially from beyond the borders of the Arab Muslim world, are those least likely to be aware of the inner workings of religion. This is simply the result of generations of academic conditioning, which has presupposed that religion is a stage humanity goes through, just like adolescence. Fortunately, this puerile view of religion has been sharply criticized in the West in recent years, but its influence has yet to wane.

Rather than view religious life as a whole, let us for now limit ourselves to morality. The different ways in which Muslims have regarded morality have been crucial for how well (or badly) pluralism has fared under Islam. Morality continues to inform public life more openly in the Arab Muslim world than it does in the secularized West. No doubt the ruling elites consistently depart from that morality. But this only deepens the resentment among the ruled, who hold their leaders to a high moral standard. It would therefore help us to contrast outer with inner morality, which relate, respectively, to monolithism and (true) pluralism.

A brief exploration of the origins of "outer morality" will slowly reveal its definition. We shall follow the unorthodox path of exploring those origins within individuals and not in their revealed aspect, although we thereby gain an appreciation for why revelation resonates so strongly. Self-aware and self-critical persons run into many occasions that afford them the opportunity to discover their limitations. The discovery of moral limitations is usually a powerful and often painful experience. A swell of good fortune comes crashing down if allowed to grow into hubris. The broad interior expanses with which one may be graced contract excruciatingly through indolence or some other inability to sustain them. Confidence crests and falls. Devotion to something valuable leads to the neglect of another. Ideals that seem so sound to our minds demand physical and emotional exertions that turn out to be beyond us. Above all, those who are keenly aware of a divine presence know just how limited humanity is. This is no more apparent than when humans try to act as though they were gods and promptly visit a catalogue of horrors upon their brethren. In such familiar experiences, we find the basis for our responsiveness to moral commands, particularly those that express strictures. The "Thou shalt not," even if given as a revelation, would meet with disdainful indifference were it not in harmony with the very fiber of human moral life. There are limits because humanity runs up against limits over and over again, limits that seem to touch on the essence of what it is to be human. (The Arabic word for "limits" is *hudud*, a term with strong reverberations because it also refers to the Qur'anic strictures embodied in the *shari'ah*).

It would be silly to think of this as a problem. It is just the way things are with humanity. The problem begins when it is forgotten that morality has a positive source, that morality is also propelled by values before it doubles up as a warning that we not exceed our limitations, that it is a transcendence of nature even as nature keeps it earthbound. The problem is compounded when those who see morality only as *hudud* want to see to it that all are held to the same *hudud*, for only thus can they be satisfied that morality is respected. And the problem is compounded further when those unable to see beyond morality-as-*hudud* inflate the list of *hudud* to an absurd degree, so that morality, originally a source of freedom, metamorphoses into the worst kind of slavery; for those in need of strictures for everything are incapable of anything. People in need of religiously sanctioned moral guidance on how to use the bathroom need something other than morality and religion, as do those who offer them that guidance with a straight face. Outer morality, then, has to do with our limitations. It has to do with the "negative" source of our moral observances. Moral strictures matter because we are all too aware of our fallibility.

What, then, is inner morality? Inner morality has to do with the mystery of our affinity for transcendent values. We are deeply moved by goodness, generosity, charity, mercy, and justice. These have intrinsic appeal. As difficult as the definition of transcendent values may be, Plato saw quite clearly that we respond to those values, that we walk around as though filled with otherworldly deposits, and that nothing in the material world suggests them. The inner force of the best moral philosophy is that it can count on our ability to discover the direct presence of positive values through illumination, inspiration, or some other kind of gift or revelation given and accepted in a spirit of mercy rather than fear. Whenever and wherever outer morality reigned supreme in the Arab Muslim world, there was not much pluralism to speak of, whereas a keen sensitivity to inner morality frequently led to the acceptance of otherness in a manner that would at least correspond with our contemporary notion of true pluralism. The Arab Muslim world has not yet reached conditions that would give rise to false pluralism (as opposed to no pluralism at all), although it is likely to sweep in with changes that so many anticipate.

An overemphasis on outer morality can facilitate a transition to "framework worship." The habit of understanding and applying morality only with regard to its source in our fallibility and limitations easily lends itself to the habit of viewing morality in structural terms. Similarly, a framework designed to ensure the coexistence of different worldviews, when installed with a mechanical notion of impartiality, inculcates the habit of regarding worldviews outwardly and blends seamlessly with the infrastructure that becomes the framework's lifeblood. So, just as millions in the United States have become (Christian) fundamentalists, millions of "fundamentalists" in the Arab Muslim world (many of whom are former Marxists, yet another structure-centered tendency) can turn without difficulty to "framework worship" or infrastructuralism.

Some may object that whatever approximates our notion of true pluralism may result not from a keen sensitivity to inner morality but from pragmatic motives. Even if this is true, a pragmatically installed pluralism does not have a solid foundation. The problem lies with pragmatism itself. It simply does not form a strong enough basis for the acceptance of the other. Pragmatic considerations make one a pluralist today, a monolithist tomorrow. Consider the case of the late Anwar Sadat, often regarded as the paradigm for acceptance of otherness in the Arab world. It is now almost forgotten that the same man unleashed the forces of Muslim extremism for several years in order to consolidate his rule, which required that Egyptians be purged from the aftereffects of the Nasserist epic. Twenty years after his assassination by those same extremists, Egyptians continue to bear the burden of Sadat's pragmatism.

True pluralism is discernible in the origin and essence of Islam. It begins with the consequences of the Prophet's sustained encounter with the infinite, with divine presence, which we must acknowledge whether we are Muslims or not. The embodiment of such an encounter, if it be genuine, is always testimony to the impossibility of interpretive permanence. This is just as true of great poems and other works of art that have spiritual import as it is of holy scripture. Their meaning can never be exhausted because their source is ever beyond the human capacity for articulation. The Qur'an is a book endlessly capable of generating new interpretations that differ significantly from the old. It also refers explicitly to other paths toward the infinite, since it acknowledges other monotheistic faiths. One may even find implicit acceptance of every striving for the divine, because there is a primordial Islam that refers to humanity's general and natural religious disposition. Only thus can we explain how Muslims have coexisted successfully for centuries with Hindus, Buddhists, and the Chinese (whose complex and inherently pluralistic religious life is not so easy to characterize). Surely Muslims have noticed the statues that elicit reverence all over India and the Buddhist world; they have seen the Chinese worship their ancestors. One can confidently dismiss the abhorrent recent behavior of the Taliban as an aberration, a pathology fed by spite for others. That Muslims for many centuries have mostly respected religious practices that clearly defy some of the injunctions of their own faith is supported by abundant historical evidence. The Mohammedan experience provides a solid foundation for true pluralism, which grows from an awareness of the inadequacy of the finite before the infinite, the resistance of truth to definitive linguistic expression. Were the whole world to exclaim "God is great!" there would still be no way to fix the meaning of "God" for every place and time, nor even for a single place and time.

The metaphysical implications of the divide between the infinite and the finite, which form the ultimate basis for a real pluralism, are reinforced for Muslims by the call to respect those that follow other traditions so that one never loses sight of humanity's limitations before the divine, its inability to affirm any metaphysical truth with finality. It is therefore no accident that (a) there are several schools of jurisprudence for the drafting of Islamic law, (b) Muslims were able to engage in interpretation of the Qur'an in a wide variety of ways for many centuries, even occasionally departing from the notion that it was never created or that it is literally the word of God, and (c) they have managed to coexist with Christians, Jews, Hindus, Buddhists, Confucians, Taoists, and pagans (especially in Africa)in many times and places.

Above all, many Muslims have awakened to the spiritual reality of the Mohammedan experience and have sought to recapture it in their own lives. Many distinct mystical groups were ordered around that quest. Many Sufis who belonged to these orders, because they have had access to the inner aspect of religion, and hence to morality, have been at peace with others in a manner that has eluded the more pragmatically inclined.

Alas, Islam has been uniquely vulnerable to a paradox that has also compromised Christian life. Just as the role of imperial politics in the establishment of Christendom distorted its relationship with Christianity, so did the prophet Mohammed's political leadership permanently justify the pragmatic bent of Islam. The paradox has a unique intensity in Islam because, unlike Jesus or the Buddha, the prophet of Islam took it upon himself to lead his community and establish its polity. This forced him to act pragmatically on several occasions, and the Qur'an reflects such pragmatism in many places.

If, however, Mohammed was inspired by the divine, this can be rarely said of those who have since overseen pragmatic politics within the domains of Islam; in allowing their pragmatism to be governed by baser ends, they have contributed to the undermining of Islamic pluralism.

There is a key distinction between the pluralism enjoyed by different Muslim groups among themselves (intra-Islamic pluralism), and that which joins Muslims with followers of other traditions. Intra-Islamic pluralism has receded in many ways. It is most visible in the suppression or absorption of Shi'ism throughout North Africa and in Saudi Arabia, Turkey, Pakistan, and Central Asia outside of Tadzhikistan. In Fatimid times (A. D. 969-1171), Isma'ilism (a branch of Shi'ism) extended from the Maghreb to the domain of the Samanids in and around what is now Uzbekistan. Al-Azhar and the city that hosts it were founded by the Fatimids. Today, Isma'ilism is confined to tiny minorities in Syria, Iran, Pakistan, and India, and finds variant expression in the small Druze and 'Alawi sects in Lebanon and Syria. The suppression of Shi'ism often had pragmatic motives. When the Turks were in the ascendant, for instance, they saw fit to promote Sunnism because they believed it offered them the best chance for establishing a stable polity and gaining the allegiance of non-Turkish Muslims (especially the Arabs). Even within Sunni Islam, mostly outside of the Near East, one school of jurisprudence or another predominates in any given society and has done so for a long time. As a result, it has been possible to form habits that have helped some regard the *shari'ah* in its entirety as divinely inspired. For when generations of Muslims grow up with a single method for the derivation of laws, and those laws themselves remain constant, it is not long before constancy is confused with the eternity of Islam's divine origins.

Sufism is also suppressed or regarded with suspicion in many areas of the Arab Muslim world. This anti-Sufism is due to those for whom outer morality and religion have lost touch with the inner dimension -- so much so that it disturbs them to see that others have access to it. It is a timeless human failing: Whether it be in American education or in the practice of a world religion, there will always be those who cannot rest until everyone else is brought down to their level. In a similar vein, some people can see religious practice endure only through the imposition of its outer forms. For them, emphasis on its inner dimensions is the province of charlatans, collaborators, infidels, or weaklings. Such jaundice has done Sufism so much harm that its current revival veers dangerously towards Islamism. It seems that many contemporary Sufis, mindful of the accusations leveled at them, wish to assure skeptics that they too are at the forefront of the militant defense of Islamdom.

The projection of Islam abroad as an adversary does not help the cause of authentic spirituality either. The most delicate issue that is relevant to our discussion of pluralism is the potential controversy surrounding the Qur'an itself. After centuries of exempting the Qur'an as such from any serious discussion, Muslims have brought a crisis upon themselves. It seems to them by now that to discuss the Qur'an seriously is to question its divine status. Against this sacred illusion stands the need to reinterpret the Qur'an, which arises not from changing fashions but from a far more profound transformation that is inevitable in the temporal world. To be eternal does not mean to be exactly the same across time, but to transcend time. In no way is the eternal compromised if its temporal manifestation changes. Indeed, such change cannot be avoided so long as the eternal and the temporal coexist. Muslims who realize this are in a bind. They perceive the need to discuss the Qur'an seriously, yet they are told that to do so is sacrilegious. Somehow, this unhealthy contradiction must be overcome; otherwise allegiance to Islam and discussion of the Qur'an will become mutually exclusive alternatives.

Because so much that is constructive and creative for the future of Islam comes from non-Muslim sources, it is unfortunate that Muslims allow their suspicion to get in the way. It certainly does not help when non-Muslims assign too much importance to the Mu'tazilites, who were willing to consider the Qur'an as a created work. In the present circumstances, Western enthusiasm for the Mu'tazilites will only serve to intensify the scorn heaped upon them by many Muslims. One must also recall that when the Mu'tazilites were officially recognized as the leading school by the 'Abbasid caliph al-Ma'mun, they promptly suppressed all dissent. If the Hanbalis, now influential in the Sudan and Saudi Arabia, have shown themselves to be monolithic, this is in no small measure due to what they had suffered under the supposedly enlightened Mu'tazilites.

The examples of al-Ghazzali (A.D. 1058-1111) and al-Maturidi (A.D. 853-944) are much more promising. Both religious thinkers have been widely revered by Sunnis, especially followers of the Hanafi school of jurisprudence. Both suggested that the Book of God lay permanently in Heaven. The Qur'an happens to be an Arabic translation (or version) of that Book. This is a subtle reference to what happens when the eternal is embodied in a human language. Hanafis today may find it hard to believe that such thoughts were openly expressed and regarded as entirely legitimate. Pondering their distance from al-Ghazzali and al-Maturidi, both unquestionably devout Muslims of the first order, may be the first step in a process of self-criticism.

There is also the practical matter of the circumstances under which the verses of the Qur'an were gathered into a definitive edition. Some Muslims like Muhammad Arkoun point out that those circumstances were controversial. It is said that those who had recited the Qur'an before it was written down walked out of the meetings that would make it lapidary. It is said that other Muslims with great standing in the community were disturbed by the process of selection. If this is true, then it will not be possible to simply wish the controversy away. Muslims may have to face the challenge one day of disengaging the sacredness of the Qur'an from the exact same text that was put together during the caliphate of 'Uthman ibn 'Affan (ruled A.D. 644 to 656) under conditions highly charged with competing political interests.

The situation is complicated by Western attitudes towards Islam. It is highly unlikely that Muslims will even contemplate serious discussion of the Qur'an while they feel under assault. It is quite easy to accuse any Muslim who wishes to resume that discussion, after a hiatus of more than eight hundred years, of undermining Islam at its core in its hour of need. The dynamics of global politics may be such as to favor the emergence of monolithic Islamic governance that will gradually, with confidence somewhat restored, come to the realization that the sacredness of the Qur'an does not depend on every word gathered into the written 'Uthmanic text, and certainly not on standard interpretations of that text.

It took six centuries for the population in the Near East to shift from its Christian majority to one that is Muslim. This shows that Muslims mostly eschewed forced conversion. They had enough confidence in themselves and their faith not to impose it. For long periods of time, and in many places, their treatment of other communities was unprecedented in its openness and generosity. One need only contrast this with what happened to non-Christians, apart from small numbers of Jews, and to dissenting Christians throughout most of Europe after it became Christianized. Prolonged dominance sadly has its own temptations. Eventually, the social, economic, and political pressures created by Muslim rule were such that conditions favoured the conversion of all but the staunchest adherents to other faiths (which may account for why their remnants are often hostile towards Islam). By the middle of the 'Abbasid caliphate, for instance, it was almost impossible for a Christian to reach a decent station in life. Social services, education, professional occupations, and bureaucratic positions became exclusively available to Muslims. When the Seljuq Turks came to power, they consolidated that tendency by effectively establishing the first Islamic state (in the quasi-modern sense) and building institutions designed to promote only Islamic interests. It is under these conditions that the majority of the population in the Near East finally became Muslim.

In the Middle Ages Islamic rule led to the disappearance of Buddhism from Iran and its drastic contraction in Central Asia. In Anatolia Islam swiftly displaced Christianity as the majority faith as. Christianity vanished among the native peoples of the Maghreb. The traces of Hinduism that survive in Indonesia are so vague that anthropologists continuously debate their extent; Indonesian Muslims can deny that there is any syncretism at all. Non-Muslim communities that survived were periodically subjected to humiliating regulations far from the letter and spirit of the Qur'an. For example, non-Muslims were required to walk on a different side of the street than Muslims and walk on foot; when Muslims could use horses, non-Muslims were restricted to donkeys and mules. In the Balkans, Christians were forced to build churches so that the roof would be lower than the line of sight of Muslim passerby. They were also disarmed and left at the mercy of local Muslim militias whose excesses were not reported to the Sultan. Such practices continued until well into the nineteenth century and persisted under the millet system introduced by the Ottomans that Western and many scholars in the Arab Muslim world admire.

The nadir of Muslim relations with other communities under their rule was reached when it became clear that the European colonial expansion could not be stopped. From the middle of the nineteenth and the end of the twentieth century, the horrific conjunction of nationalism and religious fanaticism has led to the massacre, deliberate starvation, and/or mass deportation of non-Muslims in Nigeria, the Sudan, Turkey, Lebanon, Iraq, Pakistan, and East Timor. Except for the Hindus who lost out through the creation of Pakistan in 1947, all the affected communities were Christian. This is no accident, for amid the madness that gives rise to wanton violence, it is impossible to distinguish between the colonial enterprise conceived by secular, only nominally Christian forces in Europe and the very different kinds of Christian communities scattered throughout much of the Arab Muslim world. The mayhem dissolved the latter into a mere extension of the former.

It is customary to ascribe the retreat from pluralism in the Arab Muslim world to the decline of Islamicate civilization and the attendant European—and now American—ascendancy. But many of the unfortunate developments mentioned in the foregoing few paragraphs go back much further. The suppression of Shi'ism and Sufism has long had a dynamic strictly internal to Islam. They were, respectively, the consequence of political expediency, endemic suspicion, or literal-mindedness. As an example of political expediency, before the Ottomans became engaged in a long conflict with Safavid Persia, the Shi'a and several heterodox sects had enjoyed broad tolerance. The exigencies of the Ottoman-Safavid rivalry combined with pressures from provincial religious leaders in the conquered Arab lands to lead to the imposition of a more narrow-minded Sunnism. Occasional Shi'a support for the Persians did not help their cause within the Ottoman Empire either. And so the Ottomans suppressed the Shi'a. All this had nothing to do with Europe. The Ottoman turn against Shi'ism, most violently expressed in the systematic attempt to destroy Shi'a culture in South Lebanon late in the eighteenth century, is but one in a long series of actions taken by pragmatic Sunni rulers, who had no time for the seriousness with which the Shi'a often took the ideal of maintaining a leadership in the image of the purity of the House of the Prophet.

The logic of and motives for the establishment of Islam as a state religion under the Seljuq Turks was independent from the activities of foreign powers. The waves of puritanical movements that sprang forth from the Maghreb were the collective expression of Islamic zeal. Their leaders were far more interested in banishing music, song, and dance from the halls of Andalusia and the brutal imposition of the fast and the veil than in the relentless Castillian-Aragonese southward drive.

Puritanical movements came to life in Arabia and elsewhere later on because some Muslims were concerned with the degree to which Islam had become emaciated. When Western powers intruded upon the Arab Muslim world, the forces that would cause a steady retreat from pluralism had already been set in motion. The fuel for the defense of the realm was simply poured onto the fire of religious reform (and thanks to the example set by pragmatists, religious reformers and revivalists have found ample precedent for the establishment of Islamic states). The FIS (Algeria), the Muslim Brotherhood (Egypt and Syria), Hamas (Palestine), Hizbullah (Iran and Lebanon), the Taliban (Afghanistan), and the Jami'at Islami (Pakistan), different as they are in their programs and methods, must be viewed in that light.

For all that, we have yet to uncover the grounds for the retreat from pluralism adequately. Once more, we must turn to a persistent human failing. Among human beings, the line between monotheism and monolithism is exceedingly thin. Those who appreciate the implications of monotheism, strict or otherwise, realize that oneness is not only the fearsome transcendence and uniqueness of the origin of all that happens, but a power, being, or presence so inexhaustible as to allow the simultaneous flourishing of every conceivable mode of being, however many, however diverse, holding them all together in an active but unfathomable unity. A monotheism that does not ape dogma and spread it fanatically, but is properly lived and thought through, develops an awareness of oneness that entails neither the tyranny of a static hierarchy nor a tedious monotony, but an infinite, creative, and dynamic capacity for generating and holding all things together, with full regard for the integrity of the individuals thereby unified. If this were not so, it would make no sense to exhort people towards one action rather than another. They would have no choice but to do what is right. They would be preprogrammed for perfect rectitude. It makes no sense to speak of "right" or "good" if one is bound always to do the right thing. To be called towards the right and the good is to be free to do or be otherwise. In this way the integrity of individuals is not violated by the primordial and constant presence of oneness.

Indeed, a belief, in the proper sense of something that one holds dear to one's heart and soul, something to which one is devoted and owes allegiance, can not be represented at all. Beliefs relate to a Presence and not to something represented. Too many people are limited by the ridiculous choice between the uniform "representation" of oneness and its denial. Many who deny oneness are also among those who presume that oneness ought to lend itself to some uniform and empirically verifiable representation. Such people are the prisoners of their narrow minds, dormant imaginations, or unreceptive hearts and souls. If they happen to be religious zealots, then they commit the worst offense against themselves, for in holding oneness within their limitations, they blaspheme against it.

Those who are quick to accuse others of blasphemy are often themselves the worst blasphemers. There never seem to be enough human beings who can live with the paradoxes of monotheism. To accept these paradoxes means to forgo the childish "proofs" that so many seem in need of to assure themselves of the soundness of their beliefs. It means that one must attain, through gift or effort or both, awareness of what monotheism really entails, namely, to say it again, the acknowledgment of an (that is ONE) infinite capacity for the generation and gathering of all things, with full and constant regard for their integrity and individuality (among other aspects).

Philosophy also offers us the alternative of opening up our logic to its greatest possible depth and sophistication. Ancient philosophers like Heraklitus and modern ones like Hegel and Heidegger grounded logic in the logos, a capacious term with a metaphysical-theological dimension that can accommodate what seems contradictory in the eyes of a lesser logic. But a logic that issues from a logos intimately linked with oneness can be developed only in the light of an awareness of oneness. The difference is that the philosopher tries to present the fundamental dynamics of the one and the many, which provides a context for logic to reveal itself in its highest mode.

The Arab Muslim retreat from and the West's lapse into relativism express similar human failings. Both betray an aversion to paradox. From an ordinary logical point of view, of course, it is not easy to sustain paradox, particularly when reckoning with the meaning of one's life, the elusiveness of which is all the more vexing and bewildering amid a plethora of competing worldviews. One cannot always bear the burden of the elusiveness of life's ultimate meaning to standard forms of representation or objectivization, nor is one always able to withstand an incessant assault on one's conception of that meaning in a milieu of pluralistic intensity. The temptation is either to deny the center or reduce it to uniformity. Neither pluralistic intensity (in the West) nor a painful sense of decline and defeat (in the Arab Muslim world) is congenial to the patient attainment of levels of awareness that repel intolerance as surely as disbelief.

The odds seem stacked against authentic pluralism in the contemporary world. But while a pragmatic endorsement of pluralism is better than none at all, we should remain mindful of the problem of the finite in relation to the infinite (and the temporal to the eternal). True pluralism arises when those who care about the infinite (and the eternal) simultaneously acknowledge that the finite can never exhaust the infinite (nor the temporal the eternal). All other pluralisms will inevitably decline into relativism or monolithism, which, from a metaphysical point of view, are the same thing. To deny transcendence and oneness—the infinite, the eternal, and so on—is to cultivate diversity for its own sake, as merely another absolute. To affirm transcendence but deny the plurality of ways in which it can viably dwell among human beings is to impose a monolithism that before long will habituate humanity to a fatal confusion between the meaning of life and the standard ways in which one is forced to express it. The song of transcendence monolithically viewed will conjure images of the Chinese masses singing the praises of Mao Zedong's Great Leap Forward. And just as this misbegotten project led many millions to their starvation, so does religiously motivated monolithism leave in its wake a trail of desiccated or contorted souls.

The Arab Muslim and Western worlds share the same problem and the same hope: the restoration of authentic pluralism. What really matters, however, is not pluralism itself, but its transcendent foundation. Pluralism and cultural diversity are not ends in themselves but, at their best, signs of something more profound. This is the deep sense of the eternal, infinite, and sacred, whose embodiment for us finite humans is always provisional, awaiting a more complete and perfect realization. Without such humility about our own perception of the sacred, we would not be free to grow in our faith--we would blindly follow the dictates and formulas that lead us away from it.

SECTION TWO

Islamic Perspectives on Cultural Diversity

CHAPTER 5

The Conceptual Foundation of Cultural Diversity in Pre-Modern Islamic Civilization

Wadad al-Qadi

The Islamic vision of diversity and authority requires an examination of its roots in the first two formative centuries of the Islamic era as such issues have been greatly shaped by the experience of the early Muslims. That survey will yield some general conclusions about the Islamic tradition of cultural diversity that can then be tested against one of the clear expressions of diversity in early Islam, the Shu'ubiyya movement.

DIVERSITY

The Qur'an expresses two views on diversity: one that considers diversity as natural, and hence positive, and another that perceives it as a consequence of disputation, and hence negative. The Qur'an views diversity as part of the natural order of things that God envisaged when creating human beings. People were created in male-female pairs (49:13; 53:45); they vary in skin color, language, (30:23), beliefs (64:2), and social rank (6:165). Men belong to social groupings which are different from each other (49:13) and fall into different communities, or *Ummah* (2: 213; 10:19). In fact, men were at first one community (2: 213; 10:19), and, if God had willed it, they would have remained one community (11:117; 16:93); but He did not, so they dispersed into multiple communities (2: 213; 6:42; 7:38; 10:19; 13:30; 16:63; 29:18: 35:42; 41:42; 64:18) and continued to do so (11:117). This breaking down is highly beneficial because it enriches the knowledge and experience of humanity's component groups, be they nations (*shu'ab*) or tribes (*qaba'il*), which come to "know one another" (*li-ta'arafu,*; 49:13).The socializing factor of human association lies at the foundation of the Qur'an's positive vision of diversity, according to which the foundation for the vision of civilization is the association of diverse and differentiated groups.

But the Qur'an receives a very different evaluation from the standpoint of the functioning of a single group. Although the Qur'an sees differentiation within communities as normal, even one that obtains by God's design (11:118), it is also fraught with strife. Clashing opinions within communities engender splintering into subgroups and leads to harming each other. (2: 213; 6:42; 7:38; 10:19; 13:30; 16:63; 29:18: 35:42; 41:42; 64:18). This centrifugal tug of diversity necessitates the intervention of God into the affairs of feuding communities, particularly in the form of messengers (2:213), in order to prevent them, in His mercy (11:118), from destroying one another (2:251; 22:40). In fact, had it not been for God's repelling some men by means of others, cloisters and churches and oratories and mosques would have been destroyed (22:40).

The Qur'an's portrayal of the schismatic consequences of diversity is almost always associated with groups viewed as enemies of Islam (*ahzab*; 33:20, 22; 40:30) and with the Pharaoh, who is depicted as breaking up his people into factions (*shiya'*; 28:4). In fact, this factionalism is one of the most distinctive features of polytheists (30:32) and the communities to whom messengers were sent in the past (2:213; 3:19, 105; 4:157; 6:159; 45:17).

Given this negative image of diversity within single communities, the Qur'an speaks of the desirability of strongly united communities, in contrast to the dissenting communities of pre-Islamic times; "Lo, those who sunder their religion (*farraqu dinahum*) and become schismatic (*wa kanu, shiya'an*), you have no concern for them" (6:159), and "And be you not like those who separated (*tafarraqu*) and disputed (*ikhtalafu*) after clear proofs had come unto them; for such there is an awful doom" (3:105).

There is no ambiguity in the Qur'an that the new community of Muslims is a single, united community brought together by its worship of the one true God: "This, your community, is one community (*ummatan wahida*) and I am your Lord" (21:92; 23:52). In fact, according to the Qur'an, unification is one of the main graces that the new religion has brought to them, and as such it is an asset that they should always strive to preserve: "And hold fast, all of you together, to God's rope and do not separate, and remember God's favor unto you: how you were enemies and He made friendship between your hearts so that you became brothers by His grace." (3:103) In so hoping, or demanding, the Qur'an does not to seek to exhort defiance of the natural order of things where diversity is the norm. On the contrary, the Qur'an is replete with references to the differences among the adherents to its message: sexual, temperamental, behavioral, intellectual, and social. Indeed, the Qur'an might very well have meant the Muslims, not humanity as a whole, when it talked about the split of people (*al-nas*) into nations and tribes (49:13).[1] The Qur'an warns against the dissension-related kind of diversity that has historically been shown as pernicious and destructive. The Qur'an counsels the subgroups of Islam to ward off this factional diversity by uniting in the communal identity of their faith. Thus the Qur'an presents an idealized image of the believers as a community acting in unison, with all its members behaving in exactly the same manner, in accordance with Qur'anic codes:

The [faithful] servants of the Beneficent are they who walk pon the earth modestly, and when the foolish ones address them answer: Peace; and who spend the night before their Lord, prostrate and standing; and who say: Our Lord, avert from us the doom of hell . . . ; and those who, when they spend, are neither prodigal nor grudging . . . ; and those who call not unto another god along with God, nor take the life which God has forbidden except in justice, nor commit adultery . . . ; and those who will not give false testimony, and when they pass near senseless play, pass by with dignity; and those who, when they are reminded of the revelations of their Lord, fall not deaf nor blind thereat; and who say: Our Lord, vouchsafe us comfort of our wives and of our offspring, and make us examples for those who ward off evil. Those will be awarded the high place forasmuch as they were steadfast, and they will meet therein with welcome and the word of peace, abiding there forever; happy is it an abode and station (25:63-74).[2]

The Qur'an thus offers a new vision of human association based on the admission of the normalcy of human diversity while still seeking, through faith, the original unity from creation. "O mankind, fear God who created you from a single soul (*nafs wahida*) and from it created its mate and from the two of them spread abroad a multitude of men and women"(4:1).

As Ridwan al-Sayyid has pointed out,[3] this context is essential to understanding two of the Prophet Muhammad's actions shortly after his emigration to Medina: his drawing of the document called "the Constitution of Medina" (*al-sahifa*) and his attempt at "fraternization" (*al-mu'akhat*). Both these actions were meant to eradicate the differences between the subgroups of the potential and actual believers: the various Arab clans and the Medinan Jewish tribes in the first, and the Emigrants and the Helpers in the second. Both attempts, however, failed: the Jewish tribes were either expelled from Medina or killed, and the elimination of the blood tie in favor of the bond of faith was put to a severe test and finally rejected by revelation when the question of inheritance surfaced.

But these failures were only the first signs of the difficulty of implementing the Qur'anic vision of the ideal, united community in real life. Almost immediately after the Prophet's death in 11/632, the believers split over the issue of the leadership of the community, and within a few decades their split had become overtly disputational and schismatic: the Muslim community seemed destined to become just as contentious and divided as the earlier communities to whom messengers had been sent.

Contrary to the previous communities, though, this community was not destroyed by division. Rather, it was transformed within a few decades of the Prophet's death from a small local power in Arabia into a world empire whose armies totally obliterated the mighty Sassanian Empire and rid the Byzantine empire of almost all of its eastern provinces; its lands extended from Spain in the West to the borders of China in the East. But we are not concerned here with explaining the bewildering speed of the Islamic conquests. What concerns us is that their stunning success brought into the Muslim polity a multitude of varying ethnic and religious groups: Persians, Greeks, Aramaeans, Armenians, Khazars, Arabs, Copts, Buddhists, Zoroastrians, Jews, Christians, Sabaeans, and others, many of which had ancient, vibrant and sophisticated cultural traditions (e.g. Hellenistic, Manichean, and Hindu). In the face of such deeply rooted cultural alternatives, the fledgling Islamic tradition could easily have been overwhelmed. But it was not. Rather, it forged from these competitors a new Islamic civilization, one of the greatest of the premodern world.

The rapid spread of Islamic civilization vindicated the Qur'an's positive vision of diversity on the human level, where diversity is seen as the opportunity for differentiated groups to "know one another" and generate a cultural hybrid vigor. This enterprise could not have been succeeded, however, without a strongly developed Islamic vision of authority based on the interaction of text—the Qur'an—and experience—early Islamic history.

AUTHORITY

The Qur'an is clear that all authority in the universe belongs to God, the creator of all things (e.g., 5:40; 9:116). As such, people by definition are God's servants/worshipers (*'ibad, 'abid*; e.g., 39:10; 4:46), and He is their Lord (e.g., 1:2). Hence, the Qur'an repeatedly commands men to be obedient to God, an injunction that extends to God's messenger, the Prophet Muhammad (e.g., 3:32, 132; 8:1). In one verse only (4:59), the Qur'an adds a third entity to whom obedience is due: "those who are in charge among you", *ulu l-amr minkum*.

During the formative period of Islamic thought, in the first two centuries of the Islamic era, these three entities gained further definition, guided not only by the Muslims' further examination of the Qur'anic text but also by their historical experiences. Obedience to God was straightforwardly understood as obedience to His scriptures, the final and most perfect of which was the Qur'an, God's speech as revealed to Muhammad. Obedience to the Prophet was also clearly understood as obedience to him personally during his lifetime and to his judgments and utterances, his *sunna*, after his death. Obedience to the ambiguous "those who are in charge among you" proved the most resistant to clear interpretation and thus generated considerable discussion. In the Sunni interpretation, two main identifications of the "people in charge" were offered: the rulers and the (religious) scholars.[4] Since the Sunni tradition never fully resolved the issue of which of the two entities claims authority to the exclusion of the other, it is best to consider the Sunni view as a single but double-pronged interpretation, whereby both the state (the "rulers") and the religious leaders of the community of the believers (the "scholars") are the third repository of authority as stated in the Qur'an. The identification of these two entities was sharpened by the historical experience of the early Muslim community. Furthermore, it was those two groups of people who charted the road that eventually decided the place of diversity in Islamic society and to some extent delineated the course that Islamic civilization was going to take.

A. The State

Islam produced a form of government almost from its infancy, despite its emergence in Arabia in a society averse to kingship. But the historical context in which Islam first blossomed, its rapid transformation into a vast empire, and the experience of the Muslims in the crucial three decades after the demise of the Prophet-these three factors necessitated the quick emergence of a single Islamic state, and defined the extent of its authority and the structures in which this authority was expressed.

The Prophet's role in the Muslim community transcended that of messenger, i.e., recipient of revelation, in the Medinan period, for he became not only the political and military head of a polity but also its foremost legislator through the wisdom gleaned from revelation and his own judgment. The transformation of that polity shortly after the Prophet's death into an ever-growing empire led inexorably to the need for a strong, unitary state: taxes had to be collected, salaries and pensions paid, money minted, public works conducted, treaties concluded and monitored, appointments made, expeditions sent, the lands of the empire defended, law and order kept within those lands, the day-to-day functioning of the people's affairs attended to, and so on. And when civil strife, *fitna*, hit the Muslim community some twenty-five years after the Prophet's death, where the blood of Muslims was spilled at the hands of fellow Muslims, a wide range of issues was on the table for discussion—responsibility for the strife, sin, legitimacy, justice, rights and privileges. But no one questioned the need for a single state, an identifiable authority to administer the affairs of the residents of the land of Islam, Muslim and non-Muslim alike, and to represent them to the outside world.

In fact, it was the devastating consequences of this recurring civil strife that led Muslims to emphasize the importance of obeying even oppressive or unjust rulers,[5] for it was this single governing body that unify and order the polity[6] in a manner rooted in the ideal vision of the Qur'an and the Prophet.[7] The single Islamic state looked, for all practical purposes, to be seen as the preserver of the "*jamaa*," the communally identified *Ummah* of the Muslims.

But what was the extent of the authority of the state in early Islamic society? The Prophet's authority in Medina was, as we know, all-encompassing; but the authority of the rulers who followed him, from the Rashidun caliphs to the Umayyads to the Abbasids, was also quite broad, most obviously in what was often termed as the "secular" or political realm.

The conquests gave the state practically nearly unlimited control of the resources of the empire, allowing it to have supreme financial might to overwhelm insurgent groups. With these resources in hand, the state was the only body in society capable of administering the affairs of the residents on its soil, both Muslim and non-Muslim. This state's military supremacy gave it the practical and powerful means of enforcing law and order within the land of Islam. And since this power grew was dedicated to preventing factional strife among Muslims, it imparted enhanced legitimacy to the state and an implicit identification between the state's authority and society's stability.

But the state's power went beyond the sphere of the political and "secular"—it also encompassed the religious. In fact, the early Muslim rulers never really understood their role as a primarily political/"secular" one but rather viewed their station as a preeminently spiritual one—just like the Prophet in Medina—that placed them "in full charge" of a community bonded by faith. Nowhere is that perception of their authority more pronounced than in the titles they assumed right from the beginning: "khalifat rasul Allah" (Successor to the Messenger of God), an invocation of their inheritance of the religious as well as the secular functions of the Prophet. "*Amir al-Mu'minin*" (Commander of the Faithful), is an assignment to command of a community of believers; and "*khalifat Allah*" (Viceregent of God) attributes the mandate to God. Less overtly but no less obviously religious were some of the state officials' major duties, often performed as part of their regular (and supposedly "secular") administrative duties. Launching military campaigns had its religious foundation in the doctrine of *jihad*, as did leading the annual pilgrimage, *hajj*, the congregational (*jumaa*) and other prayers, distributing the booty, and executing justice, *hudud*.

The religious element was manifest in even other, less overtly religious, undertakings: it was the rulers (and their governors) who appointed, and sometimes paid salaries to, judges (and later grand-judges) and other religious appointees such as Qur'an reciters (*qurra'*), preachers (*qussas*), and market supervisors (*muhtasib*); indeed, the rulers themselves sometimes presided over hearings that had religious overtones (the *mazalim*). There were some state officials also who even went as far as to define matters of theological disputes and in rare cases to pronounce their verdicts binding on all Muslims.

Despite the expectation of the development of an all-powerful state in such circumstances, the Islamic state developed full-fledged institutions almost only in the limited sphere of administration. In the more broadly political sphere, its contribution was limited and under constant challenge; in the religious domain it was not only more limited but also contingent on the cooperation of other forces in society.

The state's institutional accomplishments in the realm of administration were slow, steady, and long-lasting. Its earliest expressions were 'Umar b. al-Khattab's institution of the Islamic calendar and the military and pension register, the well-known *diwan* of 'Umar. Other expressions of it include the institutions of government departments under the Umayyads and the reforms of 'Abd al-Malik, including monetary reforms, Islamization of the protocols on state stationery, Arabization of the *diwans*, and the clarification of Arabic script. Under the Abbasids, these advances were further developed as government departments came to acquire an unparalleled complexity and new institutions, particularly those of the vizirate and the grand-judgeship, were firmly established.[8]

In the political realm, there is no doubt that the fundamental achievement of the state was the forging of the caliphal form as the sole form of government, with its chief descending from the Prophet's tribe of the Quraysh and elected by those whose voices matter (the *ahl al-hall wa l-'aqd*). The principle of the dynastic succession was swiftly established, whether in implicit or explicit implementation, and had a lasting effect not only due to the work of the state but also due to its support from groups outside of the state structure, mainly the religious scholars with their *fitna*-phobia.

More importantly, the caliphal vision of government did not pass unchallenged; it was obliged to coexist with alternatives such as open elections, direct appointment, divine appointment, and rule from the domain of occultation. By the fourth/tenth century, the caliphal form of government was relegated to a secondary position: not only did more than one regional caliphate arise, but also the original caliphate had to accept coexistence with a new and fundamentally different form of government: the sultanate.

But the limits of the state's accomplishments in the broad political sphere was even more conspicuous in its failure to produce a theoretical statement, a document—a kind of binding constitution—that would legislate for all the forces in the political process and that would have sufficient institutional and operative power to survive its founders. Many early Muslim rulers had enough political acumen and intellectual prowess to formulate such a vision and speculate on the nature of government. But the efforts in this direction—e.g., the statement attributed to early pious caliphs such as Abu Bakr and 'Umar or of great governors such as Ziyad or al-'Ajjaj, the more detailed proclamations of Walid II or Marwan II, or even the revolutionary program of Yazid II—leave an impression of preoccupation with the caliph as the focus of government to the exclusion of alternative models. Thus one gets very little if anything about the rights or duties of the people (other than their solemn duty to obey the caliph) or the distribution of power in government. Moreover, the statements seem to stem from immediate concerns and problems and so offer little of value to posterity. As ideological, propagandistic expressions of the mandates and preferences of individual rulers, they aspired to no lasting or universal precepts of governance; they were inherently factional expressions of this or that group (*asabiyya*), ruler, dynasty, or state. Hence they aimed at preserving particularist interests rather than overcoming them. Sometimes such outlooks were expressly meant to exclude the interests of the other groups of the community.

A society where belief in the *jamaa*, the united body of the community, was very deeply rooted—and, in fact, was a major factor in the consolidation of the state in the first place—was disinclined to accord much credibility to the rulers' pronouncements, thus preventing any institutional momentum. The statements that came closest to attaining institutional status—although only in the area of caliphal government—and that gained wide and lasting acceptance in premodern Islam were written not by potentially biased rulers but by disinterested religious scholars such as al-Mawardi (d. 450/1067) particularly in his *al-Ahkam al-Sultaniyya*. Given this limitation, the state did not develop a political canon that could furnish a constitutional foundation for the powers of the state and that could delineate the rights and the duties of the citizens of the Islamic commonwealth of nations.

The state thus reinforced its authority on the practical rather than theoretical plane, enhancing its legitimacy as the guarantor of stability and the bulwark against dissidence and rebellion. The state intervened forcefully, using all the resources at its disposal, whenever its political authority was challenged by activist dissidents who disrupt law and order in society, i.e., whenever overt rebellions against it took place. Otherwise, the state refrained from intervention in people's lives, even tolerating noncombative dissidence and intellectual opposition, a policy that encouraged diversity in the premodern period.

The last sphere where the state had clear authority was that of religion, yet here, too, there was a paucity of institutional undergirding. Despite their active involvement in matters of religious law, only a few rulers made lasting contributions to the legal canon. Even here, as in their political edicts, their rulings were considered personal opinions rather than binding or foundational and were seldom backed by the state's coercive power. In only one case did a ruler and his two successors attempt to enforce a theological doctrine with the power of the state: al-Ma'mun (d. 218/833) insisted on forcefully propagating his vision of the creativity of the Qur'an. The result of that single incident--the *mihna* ("inquisition"), as it was called--was such a huge failure that it stigmatized the whole notion of state-enforced Islamic religious dogma.

The one instance of successful state intervention into the theological realm was the collection of the Qur'an and the production of the 'Uthmanic *mushaf*, which did yield a lasting institutional framework, but perhaps only because the project was accepted by most of the scholars of the community. Thus the collection of the Qur'an succeeded due to the cooperation with the state of the second most important center of authority in the community: the community's scholars and its religious spokes people.

B. The Scholars: The Community

For the Sunnis, the Qur'anic injunction that "those who are in charge" among the Muslims be obeyed, along with God and the Prophet, was interpreted as referring either to the rulers or the (religious) scholars. The interpretation that accords authority to the state, as discussed above, was the result of historical circumstances that accompanied the rise of the Muslim community in the formative period of Islam, although the state's authority was more firmly rooted in practical politics than in theology. What is more important, perhaps, is that the state's successes and failures were, at least in part, decided by the positions taken by the religious scholars toward them. Thus identifying "those who are in charge" among the Muslims as "the (religious) scholars" has a firm basis in early Islamic history.

The development of the scholars' authority, while somewhat similar to that of the state in some respects, was fundamentally different from it in nature, mode, reach, theoretical foundation, and representation. In spite of that, the kind of authority they claimed--and achieved--was, like the state's, conducive to diversity in Islamic society.

There was scant differentiation between the roles of religious scholar and ruler in early Islamic societies; many of the political decisions they made stemmed from their knowledge of religious precepts or interpretations, and only occasionally were those decisions enforced by the coercive powers of the state. Things soon changed, however, and the religious scholars came to have a separate identity and authority that paralleled rather than intersected that of the state.

The authority of the scholars--at least in the Sunni world--derived from their preoccupation with understanding, explaining, and interpreting the two fundamental sources of the new faith: the Qur'an and the *Sunna* of the Prophet. Working with great intensity and earnestness, those scholars brought the result of their learning to large sectors of society through such activities as teaching, preaching, and writing in the fields of Qur'anic exegesis, Hadith, theology, and law, areas in which the paucity of state intervention led to the undisputed sway of the scholars, who thus exercised broad authority over the mind of early Muslim societies. Such was the vast extent of their moral authority that the state often importuned their support for crucial undertakings—overtly, as in the case of the collection of the Qur'an, or tacitly, as in the case of the accession of Mu'awiya to the caliphate.

For their part, the scholars willingly acceded political power to the state right from the start, for the sake of the preservation of the internal unity of the Muslim community and in order that the state, with its political might, represent the Muslim community in the wider world. When the state, however, exceeded its assigned role and trespassed into their domain, the scholars carefully weighed the sometimes clashing imperatives of politics and religion, and never hesitated to voice their views. To that extent, the scholars domain did extend into politics, but only when politics threatened to breach the walls of theology. In general, apart from crises, the scholars worked in earnest oblivion of the state, which in turn left them in peace to carry on with their work.

The scholars' attitude toward diversity was governed by two aspects of their activity: their tendency to function without formal organizational frameworks and their belief that they represented the totality of the Muslim community, not a particular *'asabiyya* or faction of it. In both of these aspects the scholars differed fundamentally from the state.

The individual and independent character of the scholars' work freed them from organizational imperatives and constraints. Some scholars did indeed at times form structured groups, but only temporarily, to buttress them in occasional bouts of opposition to the state (or other groups): when the opposition ceased, the groups dissolved.

The scholars' activities--especially teaching and writing--helped them to forge intimate bonds with their pupils and through them with the larger community. And when these bonds developed into intellectually differentiated bodies of learning, these bodies were called *madhahib* (trends, orientations, views, normally translated as "schools") and *firaq* (divisions, sections, groups, normally translated as "sects"), which often bore the names of the scholars who inspired them. This emphasis on the personal rather than the institutional meant that, at least in Sunnism, the religious scholars never crystallized into a finely delineated institution, a "school" or "church" that subordinates individuals to a clearly defined hierarchy.

The scholars did not seek to create a single authoritative canon that would serve as the definitive interpretation of the Book of God and the *sunna* of His prophet. This phenomenon is best seen in the manner in which those scholars conducted their research and analysis: They posed questions to one another; corresponded with one another; discussed issues; debated matters of common concern; transmitted materials; and collected in their books and treatises a wide array of opinions. Even when they criticized this or that authority, their work seemed always to be the result of accretions upon accretions of earlier scholarship. They even wrote entire books on the differences between scholars and schools in matters pertaining to law, theology, or exegesis. These collective endeavors seemed always to validate, not annihilate, the individual.

How do we explain this phenomenon? It might be tempting to say that no group of scholars possessed sufficient power to overshadow the others. But this cannot be true, not only because of the scholars' general tendency to shun organization--based power but also because of the testimony of history. For example, in the fourth/tenth century, when the legal scholars decided that there were too many schools, they were able to eliminate the formal validity of many schools and retained only a few and when the Hadith scholars a century earlier found great confusion and fabrication in transmitted prophetic traditions, they invalidated the authenticity of thousands of them.

Another explanation of this phenomenon, thus, must be found. It can be best portrayed by the well--known episode of the response of the jurist and Hadith scholar Malik b. Anas (d. 179/795) to the proposal of the caliph al-Mansur that he assist him in unifying religious law by writing a work that would be binding for all Muslims. Malik refused on the grounds that Muslims would consider this a form of disbelief (*kufr*) and thus he would not wish to be instrumental in any undertaking of the kind.[9] Piety--perhaps excessive piety in the eyes of some--was the reason.

This vignette illustrates a key reality of the religious scholars: they perceived themselves as guardians of the entire community of the Muslims, not one faction, or *asabiyya*, of it. For them, this community was made up of individuals and groups with diverse opinions as legitimate as those of the state; they regarded them all as legitimate voices of the community, none of which could claim a monopoly on the truth. Such an understanding betrays an underlying distinction between God's word, whose truth is absolute, and human's words, whose truth is relative. But beyond that there is perhaps a graver theoretical foundation on which the religious scholars seemed to found their position, the scholars saw the community of the believers as the real repository of the authority in Islam, the entity from which all bodies "in charge among you" derive their authority, the state and the scholars included. It is because of its special status that the community was given great prominence in the Qur'an as the "median community" (2:143) and "the best community that has been produced to mankind" (3:110); and it is because of its standing vis-à-vis the revelation as the supreme repository of God's word and will in the world that the Prophet is the witness of its truth for all the communities of the earth (2:143), all of whom are covered in the call to Islam. In the scholars' view, it is the community as a whole that in entrusted with answering the call to the final truth.

It is in this light, as Ridwan al-Sayyid has suggested,[10] that one should understand the scholars' championing of the principle of consensus, *ijma*, for inherent in this principle is the idea that the community in its entirety decides that a certain matter is wrong or right, thus eliminating the possibility of error, as the traditions of the Prophet have indicated (e.g., "My community shall not agree on an error"). It is within this context that we have to understand the reluctance, nay refusal, of the religious scholars to elevate any single opinion as the definitive one. That they ended up without building a unified code of law which was binding to all was, thus, another consequence of a conceptually clear vision of their limited, though conscious, understanding of how far their representative standing in Muslim society could be. The fact that they, nevertheless, persisted in their role as interpreters of the divine and the prophetic texts indicates that they felt they had a responsibility to fulfill, and they did fulfill it.

The Qur'an had accorded the community as a whole the power to "enjoin the good and forbid the evil" (3:110).[11] But elsewhere it had accorded this power to a group, *Ummah*, from within the community, a group that is to "enjoin the good and forbid the evil" and also "to invite to goodness" (3:104). The scholars could have very well believe that they were that specific group, *Ummah*, but they did not arrogate this title to themselves exclusively; in fact, any other group of the community could be so designated, including the state.

As for the question of how exactly this enjoining of good and forbidding of evil is carried out, the scholars offered several options, basing them on a tradition attributed in various forms to the Prophet:

through the use of force (the sword, the hand), words (the tongue), or silent judgments (the heart). The scholars chose mainly the second course, that of the word. This is what their professions prepared them for in the first place. More importantly, their disputation of others' opinions carried an implicit acknowledgment of the rights of their opponent, against whom they deployed the polemical tools of teaching, preaching, transmitting, debate, or writing. Thus have the scholars bequeathed a legacy so rich in polemical as well as expository and interpretive literature. It is not surprising, then, that they fostered an atmosphere of great permissiveness and diversity.

It is clear, then, that the Qur'an's understanding of diversity in the world at large encourages the interactive relations among diverse groups and considers human association an enriching experience that leads to the accumulation and refinement of knowledge and produces closer ties between the interacting groups. Viewed from the perspective of such an understanding, the growth of complex civilizations out of the associative interaction of various cultures becomes a natural consequence. The Qur'anic view of the world, however, is a fundamentally religious one that holds that God's message to mankind is, despite its various expressions, one and the same and that Islam is sent to all men. As in earlier messages God sent to people before Islam, the message of Islam has been revealed to one of the several communities of the earth through a prophet who speaks a language that the community understands. The Muslim community has a special, elevated status that entails a responsibility of making the rest of the world's other communities aware of God's message. This means that it has both the privilege and duty of leadership towards them. When this vision is coupled with the Qur'an's vision of the interactive process, it could be concluded that, at least conceptually, the Qur'an envisages the Muslim community as a locus of civilizational activity.

The Qur'an envisages a community that is a microcosm of the larger world community, with differences among its subgroups. Ideally, these subgroups, brought together by Islam, should remain unified, for, as pre-Islamic history has shown, diversity within communities is normally the consequence of internal dissension. In order to consolidate the unity of this microcosm community, the Qur'an provides it with characteristics that distinguish its members and give it a unique identity.

Historical developments within the Muslim community shortly after the cessation of the revelation and the demise of the Prophet led to episodes of severe strife. Seeking to avoid the danger of disintegration, the leaders of the community increasingly emphasized the ideal of unity while still recognizing the need for diversity. As a result, the community accorded the state the authority to organize its affairs and to represent it to the outside world while designating the scholars as the interpreters of its religious precepts.

In a society with a minimum of institutional restrictions, inquisitional interests, and coercive interference from the state, coupled with encouragement of a plurality of opinions and doctrines, diversity has its day. The basic vision is the Muslim community leads--acts as a catalyst in the interactive associative process--but does not trample the unique cultural contributions of its component subgroups, which therefore enjoy considerable freedom of movement. Only outright sedition is deemed impermissible. A case study of this vision is the Shu'ubiyya movement, the subject of the next section.

TEST CASE: THE SHU'UBIYYA MOVEMENT[12]

The Shu'ubiyya arose in early Islamic society; it was a complex cultural, ethnically-based movement in which non-Arabs—mainly Persian but also Armenian and Coptic groups—asserted the superiority of their groups over the Arabs. Some members of this movement were accused of heresy, *zandaqa*. In the Eastern Islamic lands, the movement lasted for almost two centuries, from about the middle of the second/eighth until the middle fourth/tenth century, when the Abbasids were at the height of their rule. The movement's proponents were mostly intellectuals, poets, and, above all, secretaries, *kuttab*, in the Abbasid administration. It also emerged in Andalusia and the Islamic West between the fifth/eleventh and sixth/twelfth century in the form of a Slavic and Berber campaign against the Arabs, who mounted their own strong backlash.[13] In both the East and the West, a sizable literature emerged from this movement.

Although no work written by a Shu'ubi in the East has survived, it is possible to reconstruct their claims from the works of their opponents.[14] According to these polemics, the Shu'ubis used poetry and prose, treatises and books[15] to attack and mock the Arabs, chiefly by showing that other nations, especially the Persians, were superior to them. They derided the Arabs for their purported lowly descent (from a slave-woman, Hajar), rough language, ineptitude in rhymed prose, their habits in rhetoric and oratory (such as the use of the stick), pointless mannerisms, rough pre-Islamic lifestyle, dearth of production in the arts and sciences, and deficiency in the military arts; in sum, as Ibn Qutayba put it, they were accused of being devoid of all virtues and possessing all vices.[16]

In an attempt to prove the superiority of the non-Arabs, especially the Persians, the Shu'ubis claimed that other nations were better than the Arabs in descent from a free woman (Sarah), in military expertise, in all aspects of civilizational achievement, and in having had a glorious imperial past. Indeed, the proof for the superiority of the Persians, said the Shu'ubi al-Jayhani,[17] was the fact that God gave them such wonderfully fertile land while He gave the Arabs arid and forbidding land.[18] The same al-Jayhani added that the Arabs did not even study medicine, having failed to produce any books like Euclid's *Almagest*, the *Book of Music* and the *Nabataean Agriculture*.[19]

The Shu'ubi's main problem was the fact that the Prophet Muhammad was an Arab. Unfortunately, all we have on this subject is a statement by one of their opponents that they "discredited the Prophet,"[20] which does not tell us much. The fact that hardly anything specific exists in the anti-Shu'ubi literature on this subject might indicate that the Shu'ubis were circumspect on this topic.

On the contrary, they tried to enlist a specifically Islamic legitimacy for their position by basing it on a Qur'anic verse--49:3--which, as we pointed out earlier, views diversity in a positive light. That verse, they said, talks about the Muslims as being composed of nations, *shu'ub*, and tribes, *qaba'il*; the tribes are the Arabs, and the nations are the non-Arabs. Furthermore, they added, the fact that the Qur'an itself placed the word *shu'ub* before the word *qaba'il* in the verse is a proof that the Qur'an accords the non-Arabs a higher status than the Arabs. It was because the Shu'ubis used this verse that they called themselves "Shu'ubiyya."

But the situation is not that simple. The Shu'ubis might have been careful in expressing any view that would be considered clearly anti-Islamic, but they championed a culture which seemed to have roots in soil other than Islam. Despite the lack of consensus among the modern scholars about the aims of the Shu'ubiyya movement and the forces behind it,[21] there is complete agreement that most of its advocates were loyal to the Persian, Sasanian tradition in which they were educated and propagated its values. Al-Jahiz, for example, angrily stated that they boasted about the policies of Ardashir Babakan and the administration of An-shirwan[22] and took as sole sources of their knowledge the book of Mazdak, the booklet known as *Kalila wa Dimna*, the proverbs of Buzurgmihr, the testament of AnuShirwan, the letters of 'Abd al-Hamid, and the treatises of Ibn al-Muqaffa.[23] More importantly, they brazenly disparaged the Arabic Islamic cultural tradition, mocking the traditionalists and the people's rote, unreflective repetition of transmitted information without examining it.[24] They upheld their own literary products as superior to those of the Arabic Islamic tradition.[25] Thus, although the Shu'ubis were not quite a revolutionary group, a schismatic sect, or a conspiratorial gang, they were certainly nonconformist and probably not fully "innocent";[26] in fact, according to another opponent of theirs, Ibn Qutayba, it was only fear for their lives that restrained them from declaring disbelief.[27]

Some of them were accused of heresy, and others advocated libertinist, *mujun*, life-styles. Therefore, the parties allied with established power in Islamic society considered the Shu'ubiyya dangerous enough to be confronted. Al-Jahiz, one of their most outspoken opponents, considered their ideas potentially subversive to Islam. Noting that most of the skeptics about Islam were inspired at first by the ideas of the Shu'ubiyya, he expressed his fear that protracted argument might lead to fighting:[28]

> If a man hates a thing, then he hates him who possesses it, or is associated with it. If he hates [the Arabic] language then he hates the [Arabian] peninsula, and if he hates that peninsula then he loves those who hate it. Thus matters go from bad to worse with him until he forsakes Islam itself, because it is the Arabs who brought it; it is they who provided the venerable forebears and the example worthy of imitation.

Describing this sense of danger in a broader cultural context, H. A. R. Gibb noted,[29]

> The dangers of the *shu'ubi* movement lay not so much in its crude anti-Arab propaganda . . . as in the more refined skepticism which it fostered among the literate classes. The old Perso-Aramaean culture of Iraq, the centre of Manichaeism, still carried the germs of that kind of free thinking which was called *zandaqah*, and which showed itself not only by the survival of dualist ideas in religion, but still more by that frivolity and cynicism in regard to all moral systems which is designated by the term *mujun*.

How, then, did the people in authority react? If the schema I have suggested above is correct, then the scholars of the Muslim community should have considered the Shu'ubis to be Muslims who had the right to express their opinions, however heterodox they seemed. The best antidote to such ideas would be effective refutation, not suppression. Those who do not like their ideas could refute them; they might even name-call them, belittle them as they belittled the Arabs, and curse them--but they would not shut them up. After all, they were part of the Muslim community—they avowed a belief in God's unity and the prophethood of Muhammad and observed the practices and rituals of Islam. Only outright renunciation of the Islamic faith would require state intervention.

The opponents of the Shu'ubiyya's claims reacted accordingly.[30] In their rejoinders they adopted a defensive form of refutation; occasionally they struck a more confrontational tone, but only in writing. Even more: they actually often took a remarkably conciliatory approach in some of their writings, assuring the Shu'ubiyya of their indispensible role in the development of Islamic civilization, which, after all, could grow only with the constructive participation of all its groups, its *shu'ub* and its *qaba'il*.

The opponents of the Shu'ubiyya rose to an eloquent defense of the Arabs, stressing the unique beauty, richness and versatility of the Arabic language[31] and the eloquence of Arabic speech; the refreshingly pure and courageous lifestyle of the pre-Islamic Bedouin Arabs; and the cultural vibrancy of their great markets, which were beehives of literary activity.[32] As for their arid lands, which the likes of al-Jayhani had derided, the outspoken opponent of the Shu'ubiyya, Tawhidi, retorted that fertile or arid land does not produce good or bad cultures;[33] the main thing is what men make out of their circumstances with rational thinking.[34] In fact, this natural habitat, according to Ibn al-Muqaffa', himself a Persian, had a positive effect on Arabs in engendering purity of character and a predisposition to base knowledge on observation of natural phenomena.[35] Ibn Qutayba argued that Arabs were also notable for laudable character traits such as generosity, temperance, modesty, hospitality, and courage.[36] Al-Jayhani's boasting about *Almagest* and medicine was irrelevant since these were achievements of the Greeks, not of the Persians.[37]

The defenders of the Arabs further reminded the Shu'ubis that the Prophet was an Arab[38] and that, although both Arabs and Persians had kingdoms, the Arabs' dominion had superseded that of the Persians.[39] The opponents of the Shu'ubiyya took their cues from a story that Ibn Qutayba cited about the famous Umayyad statesman, Ziyad b. Abihi: When the caliph Mu'awiya claimed Ziyad as his half--brother, people made fun of Ziyad and his sons and cast doubt on the veracity of Mu'awiya's claim. Ziyad was moved to write a book on vices and gave it to his sons, saying, "Whoever discredits you, face him with his own flow!"[40]

According to Ibn Qutayba, the Shu'ubis accentuated the vices of the Arabs and downplayed their virtues,[41] coloring their claims with gross exaggeration;[42] when faced with several interpretations, he argued, they selected the least flattering.[43] Their fanaticism, as Jahi' puts it, was simply fatal.[44] They based their conclusions on texts they misunderstood,[45] language constructions[46] and genealogies[47] of which they were ignorant, they even thought that Zoroaster was a prophet![48] They also willfully took the Arabs' traits out of their proper cultural context[49] and they turned their backs on important realities.[50] As an example of their twists of proper logic,[51] Ibn Qutayba wondered, How can they be proud about being the sons of Sarah, a free woman, while the Arabs are the sons of a slave-woman, Hajar, when Hajar has been purified by God? And haven't Hajar's progeny been great, including the Prophet? And slave women have given birth to some of the greatest of the Muslims.[52] The Shu'ubiyya were an envious lot, he contended, given to all manner of distortion.[53] The opponents of the Shu'ubiyya invoked God to protect them from the Shu'ubis' factionalism, fanaticism, unfairness, and prejudice,[54] and called upon them to be humble and quit their arrogance.[55]

The next level of counterattack against the Shu'ubiyya consisted of highlighting and deriding the Persians' supposed pre-Islamic mores, especially their marrying their mothers and daughters:[56] even animals, they note, do not engage in such heinous violations of the natural order.[57] What is worse is that such repugnant customs were given religious sanction and institutional legitimacy through attribution to Zoroaster.[58] Indeed, it was because of those bad habits, and the Persians' false attribution of them to God, that He ended their dominance and humiliated them.[59]

The opponents of the Shu'ubiyya were not above resorting to personal ridicule. One said that the worst among them were the riffraff (*sifla* and *Hashw*), the rabble of Aramaeans (*awbash al-naba*) and the sons of the little towns of the countryside.[60] Others narrated long stories aimed mainly at mocking them, like the following: a certain al-Hakam b. Qanbar, a client of the tribe of Mazin, had acquired a high position among the tribe of Tamim, but turned Shu'ubi and composed Shu'bi poetry, for which reason he was beaten by the Mazin. When the beating became severe, he cried out for help from—whom else?—the Arab Tamimis, whence a line was composed mocking him.[61] Another opponent could not help but marvel with a mixture of contempt and incredulity at the Shu'ubis' pride about being descended from Chosoroes. He said: "And just what has a simple Iranian got to do with Chosoroes? Is it enough that he and Chosoroes be both Persian to make him so great?! It is like the man who is terribly proud when a horse wins in racing simply because he is the owner of the horse's bridle!!'[62] They even believe they are better than the Arabs through Adam!![63]

The opponents of the Shu'ubis warned them of the consequences of their claims; one of them wrote, *fa-l-wayl al-awil li-ha'ula'i wa l-bu'd wa l-thubur min hadhihi l-'adawa li-awliya' Allah* (long woe, ruin and destruction be upon those people because of their enmity to God's friends),[64] and then more calmly called upon them to quit their ways, for not only were they in the wrong, but they could not win.[65]

But the most interesting and eye-catching attitude of the Shu'ubis' opponents was the conciliatory one, which was expressed in a variety of ways.[66] One was to take a protective position towards some of the Shu'ubis, making them appear as acceptable in some ways, though not in their Shu'ubi tendencies. A good example is Ibn Qutayba's comment on Abu 'Ubayda, the well-known Shu'ubi and author of a book on the vices of the Arabs. Abu 'Ubayda's own descent, he says, was questionable; nevertheless, he would rather not talk about it since Abu Ubayda was an authority on Qur'anic interpretation and Hadith transmission.[67] Others stressed the importance of rational, non-factional dialogue that is free of factionalism and fanaticism and that starts with the understanding that every nation is distinguished in some ways and not distinguished in others.[68]

The Shu'ubis' opponents often took position that all men are equal: they live and die, and have different colors of skin, temperaments, interest, aims, aspirations, and so on.[69] Going a step further, they asserted that every nation had excelled in some ways and not in others,[70] and in every one of them there were the great and the lowly,[71] the superior and the inferior.[72] The Persians were superior in government and statesmanship, the Greeks in science and philosophy, the Chinese in the arts and crafts, and the Indians in legerdemain and magic.[73] When all the nations' points of distinction were taken into consideration, they concluded, the Arabs could not surpass all the others combined.[74] They contended that no one had claimed Arabic superiority to the pre-Islamic Persians.[75] They did, however, advance a broad thesis to explain the Arabs' rise to prominence after the advent of Islam. Historical circumstances, they argued, make one nation superior at one time and another nation at another time. In this respect, the situation of the Arabs is highly instructive regarding how a change in circumstances affects a people's contribution to civilization. Before Islam, the Arabs were desert dwellers with some admirable virtues and a limited degree of cultivation. Islam endowed them with a newly enhanced status and made them masters of diverse lands and nations.[76] It was at this point that all the achievements of those nations were incorporated into their midst. The Arabs welcomed those ancient achievements, matched their level with their own, added to them, and created a new and inspiring synthesis--their very own Islamic civilization.[77]

On this conciliatory note, the scholarly opponents of the Shu'ubiyya, both Persian and Arab, expressed their desire to maintain a unified Muslim community, even incorporating critics of the Arabs. This catholic tendency, which assumes diversity and approves of it, prevailed except in regard to the heretical elements within and without the Shu'ubiyya movement.

As mentioned earlier, some of the Shu'ubis were accused of being heretics, *zanadiqa*. But so few of them actually were that the connection between the Shu'ubiyya and heresy is incidental.[78] Surely both the Shu'ubis and the heretics showed conspicuous zeal about the Sasanian tradition and were interested in reviving its values.[79] But their targets were distinguishable, at least in principle: the Shu'ubis aimed to undermine the Arabs, and hence the thrust of their movement was ethno-cultural, whereas the heretics were dualists (and perhaps also believed in various aspects of the pre-Islamic religions, like light and fire) movement was religious.[80] Here was the outer limit of Islamic society's openness to diversity; the catholic spirit could not go any farther. Thus, the heretics are treated differently from the Shu'ubis: as dualists, they were not monotheists; like all the polytheists, they were enemies of Islam. Legally speaking, since they had been Muslim as some point, they were apostates and thus had no place in Muslim society: barring repentance, they had to face punishment by death. And since the state was the only legitimately coercive force, it was obliged in such cases to intervene in order to protect the social order of the united community—hence their persecution and execution by the caliph al-Mahdi.

CONCLUSION

On the level of the Qur'an, diversity is viewed in two opposite ways: a broadly universal, positive approach vs. a negative, intra-communal one. Once they became a clearly defined community, the Muslims could have quickly fallen into the quagmire of intra-communal strife, indulging only the negative view of diversity. But that did not happen, so another paradox set in: all of their factions demanded a unified state. This state, with its absolutist might, could have again ended the chances of diversity. But, in another paradoxical twist, the unwillingness--or inability--of the state to develop a political code, while it made its intervention unpredictable, allowed for greater diversity within the bounds of civil obedience to it. The authority of the state was further curtailed by the concurrent emergence of the religious scholars as a competing source of authority in society. Hence still another paradox in spite of the great moral power exercised by the religious scholars in early Islamic society, they were unwilling--or unable--to develop a religious code or a structural hierarchy, either or both of which could define the exact boundaries of the permissible and the forbidden. Whereas this unwillingness--or inability--could be seen as a missed opportunity at religious control, it paradoxically led to further growth of cultural diversity. Hence the entire community bore the burden of interpreting the revelatory-prophetic legacy; this communal interpretive practice fostered the polemical tone of much of the literature of early Islamic civilization.

It was because of such permissiveness in Islamic society that a nonconformist, vociferous, and combative movement such as the Shu'ubiyya could continue to speak out for almost two centuries in the Islamic East and for longer than that in the Islamic West without suppressive consequences--except for those few heretics who went beyond the religious pale and hence beyond the political space permitted politically, historically, and conceptually by the state authorities.

This remarkable openness of early Islamic society took shape in the formative period of Islamic thought, when the mentality of a "sectarian milieu" was dominant, when prosperity bred confidence, and when the creative impulse sent its rays in all directions. The first element was irretrievable and the remaining two fluctuated--as they always do, thus accounting for the occasional recession of cultural diversity in Islamic society and civilization in all periods of Islamic history, including the present.

CHAPTER 6

The Islamic Encounter with the Chinese Intellectual Tradition

Sachiko Murata

One of the least explored areas of the Islamic experience of cultural diversity is the Muslim community in China. Historical records tell us that Muslims entered China within thirty year of the Prophet's death, and the evidence suggests that Muslim communities had been established by the fourth century of Islam. Although little is known about the Islamic presence down to modern times, there is no doubt that Muslims did establish themselves and that many became indistinguishable from other Chinese, except in matters of religious belief and practice. Estimates of the number of Muslims living in China today begin at about twenty million.

Scholars have not systematically investigated how the Chinese Muslim perceived themselves within Chinese civilization before modern times.[1] Nor has anyone investigated the nature of Islamic thinking in China or the manner in which it may be similar or different from Islamic thinking in other parts of the Islamic world. In what follows, I summarize the results of my own recent research in this domain.[2]

The secondary literature on Chinese Islam recognizes that a highly significant transformation occurred in the seventeenth century.[3] Up until that time, so far as is known, Chinese Muslims studied and wrote about their religion in their own languages, mainly Persian. In that century, however, Muslim scholars began to write about Islam in Chinese. They did not do this for the sake of non-Muslim Chinese, but rather for the sake of their own co-religionists. It seems that many Muslims did not have sufficient acquaintance with the Islamic languages to master Islamic thinking, especially not when faced with the vast resources of the Chinese intellectual tradition. In short, by the seventeenth century, Islam in China had reached a point where the *'ulama* perceived the danger that Muslims would no longer be able to understand the principles of their own faith and the rationale for their own practices.

A good deal of evidence indicates that these early texts were aimed at Muslims who had been largely assimilated into Chinese civilization. For example, none of the earliest Chinese texts deal in any detail with Shariah or jurisprudence, nor do they address the Qur'an or Hadith in a direct way. Rather, they undertake to explain the nature of Islamic understanding, that is, the domain that is traditionally called "the principles of faith" (*usul al-din*). The texts explain why Muslims look at the world the way they do and how their world-view has implications for the practical realm. The language of these texts is the language of the dominant intellectual school of the day - Neo-Confucianism. These are not apologetic works written for non-Muslims, but rather expository works written for Muslims who themselves had become Chinese intellectuals, so the level of discourse and scholarship is exceedingly high.

It is interesting to note that the Muslims began writing in Chinese a few decades after Matteo Ricci and other Jesuits had begun writing apologetic Christian works in Chinese - works to which a good deal of modern scholarship has been devoted. The well known scholar of Confucianism, Tu Weiming of Harvard, who has spent time with me reading some of the Chinese Islamic books, is of the opinion that the Islamic works are far more sophisticated expositions of the principles of Chinese thought than anything written by the Jesuits and that, in fact, they are significant contributions to Neo-Confucian thinking itself. Tu thinks that the main reason for this is that the Chinese Muslims did not feel themselves in any way alien to the Chinese environment. They write as Chinese, and they offer an alternative interpretation of the basic principles of Chinese thought. This new interpretation clarifies both the necessity for observing the theoretical and practical teachings of the Arabian sage known as Muhammad, and the reasons why these teachings are perfectly in harmony with the Tao of heaven and earth.

THE CHINESE *'ULAMA*

The two most important and influential of the Chinese *'ulama* were Wang Tai-yu and Liu Chih. Wang Tai-yü was born in the late sixteenth century and probably died in 1657 or 1658. He is the author of one major book of 82,000 characters (about three hundred pages) and a handful of short works. He tells us that his ancestor was an astronomer who had come to China from the Islamic world three hundred years before to serve the emperor, and that he himself underwent the training of a Muslim scholar in his own language, though he does not specify which language that was. He had some knowledge of written Chinese as a young man, but he did not begin serious study of the Classics until he was thirty.

Wang's major work is called "The Real Commentary on the True Teaching" (Cheng-chiao chen-ch'uan). It was published during Wang's lifetime in 1642, and has been published repeatedly ever since, the latest edition being that of 1987. It consists of two books with twenty chapters each. The first volume focuses on theological and metaphysical issues, such as the divine attributes, the creation of Adam, predestination, and the nature of human perfection. The second is more concerned with spiritual attitudes, ethics, and certain issues having to do with the Shari'ah. The book has relatively little to say about Islamic practice, and in cases where practice is discussed, the issues are usually those that would look strange in Chinese eyes, such as the prohibition of pork, wine, and gambling.

In the introduction, Wang mentions that a few colleagues had read the book and criticized him for going too deeply into Taoist and Buddhist teachings. He replies that without borrowing his terminology from other traditions, he would have no way to explain Islam to those unfamiliar with the Islamic languages. In the text he almost never mentions Arabic words and makes no attempt to translate Islamic concepts into Chinese in any direct fashion. His whole effort is focused on re-expressing basic Islamic perspectives in the context of the intellectual tradition of the day.

Liu Chih, the second major author of Chinese books, was born a few years after Wang's death, in about 1670, and he wrote his last major book in 1724. He was a good deal more prolific than Wang and has left us with three major books and a number of shorter works. He tells us that his father was a scholar of Islam who lamented the lack of Islamic writing in Chinese. After preliminary training in the Islamic sciences, he began studying the Chinese classics at the age of fifteen. He then devoted six years to Arabic and Islamic literature, three years to Buddhism, and a year to Taoism. He turned his efforts toward making Islamic learning available in Chinese from the age of thirty-three, that is, around the year 1700. Like Wang Tai-yu, he saw no fundamental discrepancy between Islamic teachings on God and the world and the grand philosophical systems of Neoconfucianism, and he wrote that the guiding principle of the Qur'an is similar to that which motivated Confucius and Mencius.

Before addressing the question of how these authors approached the expression of Islamic teachings in Chinese, we need to consider one more important issue: the resources in the Islamic languages from which they were drawing inspiration for their own understanding of Islam. Here the evidence points to the strong influence of the Sufi tradition. For example, so far as I have been able to determine, only five books were translated into Chinese before the twentieth century; three in the seventeenth century, one in the eighteenth, and one in the nineteenth. Although Qur'anic verses were often cited in the Chinese works, the Qur'an itself was not translated in its entirety until the third decade of the twentieth century.

All five of these translated works are Sufi texts, and four of them are well-known enough also to have been translated into English. The most famous and the last to be translated was the *Fusus al-Hikam* by Ibn al-'Arabi (d. 1240), which appeared along with a detailed commentary in 1865. It was dictated and edited by Ma Fu-chu, probably the greatest Muslim scholar of the nineteenth century, a figure who is well-known to historians because of his association with a major rebellion in Yunnan.

The other four texts were all translated from Persian. The earliest of these was also the longest and in many ways the most significant. This was *Mirsad al-'ibad* by the thirteenth century Kubrawi shaykh, Najm al-Din Razi (d. 1256). It was published in the year 1670 by Wu Tzu-hsien, who is said to have been a student of Wang Tai-yü. Within the Persian cultural sphere itself, this is the most famous and the widely read of the four Persian texts. Its English translator remarks that it can be considered "the summation of the historical elaboration of Sufism" down to the thirteenth century, when there was an extraordinary flowering of Sufi literature. It deals in a relatively systematic manner with human beings as the linchpin of cosmic existence and universal equilibrium, while describing the prophets as the guides to the many levels of human perfection. A final section devotes eight chapters to explaining how various sorts of people should follow the path to God - kings, ministers, scholars, the wealthy, farmers, merchants, and craftsmen. Among the qualities that have made *Mirsad al-'ibad* a classic are the clarity, fluency, and beauty of the Persian prose. Although it deals with issues that remain abstruse and obscure when discussed by theologians and philosophers, it avoids technical language and uses the images and analogies of everyday language. The result has been an extraordinarily popular book, read throughout the eastern lands of Islam as a guide to all dimensions of the path to God.

Although understanding *Mirsad al-'ibad* did not demand training in the technical Islamic sciences, it did require a degree of knowledge of Islam that would have made its translation into Chinese no easy task. On the whole Wu Tzu-hsien is as faithful to the original as one could hope. The very nature of the text helps him, because it is rooted more in imagery than in technical discourse. Nonetheless, when the discussion enters areas that would be difficult for Chinese readers to understand without detailed commentary, he is not averse to dropping the passage.

The three remaining Persian books translated into Chinese are shorter and more philosophically oriented. The first of these was *Maqsad-i aqsa* by the thirteenth century Shaykh 'Aziz al-Din Nasafi. It appeared in 1679, only nine years after the translation of *Mirsad al-'ibad*, and was made by She Yun-shan, who also translated *Ashi'at al-lama'at*, by the famous Sufi poet and scholar 'Abd al-Rahman Jami (d. 1492). Jami is one of the most important popularizers of the teachings of Ibn al-'Arabi,and this work is a commentary on the *Lama'at*, a classic of Persian prose by Fakhr al-Din 'Iraqi, who is an important member of Ibn al-'Arabi's school. Since the *Lama'at* is incorporated into Jami's text, we can consider it a fifth Persian work to be translated into Chinese. The last of the Persian works to be translated was *Lawa'ih*, also by Jami, which was completed in 1751 by Liu Chih, whom we have already met. In his translation, Liu Chih presents us with a highly sophisticated interpretation of Islamic thought in Chinese terms. By the very nature of the language that he uses to translate the book, he engages with major intellectual issues of both Neoconfucianism and Buddhism.

THE UNIQUENESS OF CHINESE ISLAMIC LITERATURE

In order to understand the significance of the Chinese Islamic literature, we need to remember that these writings are unprecedented in Islamic history. They present us with the first instance in which Muslims wrote major treatises in the language of one of the great, pre-existing intellectual traditions. Only the Indian, Buddhist, Greek, and Judeo-Christian traditions could compare with China in terms of the richness of philosophical, theological, cosmological, and psychological teachings.

But Muslims never had to express themselves in the languages of any of those traditions. Wherever they went, they took their own languages with them, first Arabic, and then Persian. Although Persia did have a pre-existing intellectual heritage, by the time the Persian Muslims began writing in their own language, it had been totally transformed by Arabic. The other languages that were used to express Islamic learning, like Turkish and Urdu, were also in effect new creations of Islamic civilization itself.

What the Chinese *'ulama* did, then, was to write about Islam in a completely non-Islamic idiom. The only thing like a precedent for the manner in which they assimilated various dimensions of Chinese thought is the way in which Muslims had adopted Greek thought during the first three or four centuries of Islam. The grand difference, however, is that the early Muslims wrote about Greek thought in Arabic, not Greek, and they did not have to worry about responses by the Greek philosophers. In contrast, the Chinese *'ulama* wrote in Chinese, and their books were immediately printed and distributed, so they had to keep the reactions of other Chinese intellectuals in view. It is precisely this point that Tu Weiming finds striking about these works -- they are very much part of an ongoing discussion about the quest for human perfection in the Chinese tradition.

A second point that is worth remembering is that the Chinese *'ulama* were faced with a problem that was not present in any of the other languages used to express Islamic teachings. An author writing in Persian, or Turkish, or English, can always carry over the Arabic terminology into the new language. Indeed, the Islamic languages are largely defined by the massive carryover of Arabic terminology. But in Chinese, this is impossible. The Chinese script simply does not allow for transliteration except in an enormously awkward and even grotesque manner. Thus the name Muhammad, which obviously had to be spelled out in Chinese at least on occasion, ended up being written in a dozen different ways, each of them a cumbersome attempt to present the word phonetically. As a result, the Muslim authors avoided the use of Islamic proper names and Arabic and Persian words. In order to write fluent and readable Chinese, they had to use pre-existing Chinese words to render Islamic ideas, and every one of these words had precedents and connotations in one or more of the three Chinese traditions.

There are numerous important terms known in almost all Islamic languages for which the Chinese authors had to find equivalents. What should be done, for example, with the word Allah? There is no equivalent in Chinese. According to one historian, Muslims referred to God by the term "heaven" in the Tang period and by both "heaven" and "Buddha" in the Sung dynasty. At the end of the Ming dynasty, when books began to be written in Chinese, words like "Lord" (*chu*), "Real Lord" (*chen-chu*), "Real One" (*chen-yi*), and "Real Ruler" (*chen-tsai*) were used. Muhammad was referred to by terms such as "Sage" (*sheng*), "Ultimate Sage" (*chih-sheng*), "Chief Servant" (*shou-p'u*), and "Ambassador" (*ch'in-ch'a*). The Qur'an was called simply the "Classic" (*ching*). Adam was referred to as the "human ancestor" (*jen-tsu*). The angels were the "heavenly immortals" (*t'ien-hsien*). The jinn became "gods and demons" (*shen-kuei*). Satan was called the "chief god" (*shou-shen*) or the "chief devil" (*shou-mo*). Paradise was called "heaven-country" (*t'ien-kuo*) or the "world of ultimate happiness" (*chi-lo*). Hell was named "earth prohibited" (*ti-chin*) or "earth prison" (*ti-yü*). The daily prayer was called "worship" (*li-pai*) and the mosque "the temple of worship" (*li-pai ssu*) or "the temple of the Pure and Real" (*ch'ing-chen ssu*). In all these cases, the Arabic originals are basic to Qur'anic discourse, but the Chinese words are unrecognizable as Islamic terminology except in the context of the Islamic writings.

Besides this religious language, there are also numerous theological and philosophical expressions that were needed for intellectual discussions. For example, the first principle of faith, *tawhid* or asserting God's unity, is often rendered as "returning to One" (*kuei-yi*). In Arabic the theologians discussed God in terms of "essence and attributes" (*dhat wa sifat*), but the Chinese 'ulama talked about "original nature" (*pen-jan*) and "movement/quietude" (*tung-ching*), or "essence" (*t'i*) and "function" (*yung*). They rendered the term *haqiqa* or "reality" by the important Neoconfucian term "principle" (*li*). They discussed the two basic worlds of the cosmos - the "world of the witnessed" (*'alam al-shahada*) and the "world of the absent" (*'alam al-ghayb*)_as "world of color" (*yu-se chiai*) and the "colorless world" (*wu-se chiai*), which are well-known Buddhist expressions.[4]

THE CONTEMPORARY RELEVANCE

In writing about Islam in Chinese, the 'ulama were faced with a problem that is similar to that which modern-day Muslims face when they attempt to write about their religion in English and other European languages. It seems to me, however, that the Chinese Muslims were more successful than contemporary Muslims have been. I see two major reasons for this. One is that they were thoroughly grounded in traditional Islamic learning and, at the same time, they were also masters of traditional Chinese learning. In contrast, modern-day Muslims writing in European languages seldom have much knowledge of their own intellectual traditions, and their thinking is likely to be determined by a rather narrow school of modern thought or politics.

The second and more important reason for the Chinese Muslims' success is that there was no basic conflict between the principles that underlie the Far Eastern religions and Islam. Even if the different schools of Chinese thought were constantly arguing about details, the intellectual environment was essentially congenial with religious teachings. In contrast, the principles that have molded modern thought are largely hostile to religion. I would like to illustrate what I have in mind by showing some of the commonalities of the three Chinese traditions with Islam that were plain to the Chinese *'ulama* and that come out clearly in their discussions of Islamic teachings and their references to Chinese concepts.

As everyone knows, the first principle of Islamic thought is *tawhid* or the "assertion of unity," that is, the assertion of the unity of God, who is the ultimately Real. Throughout Islamic texts, the discussion is carried on in terms of the creation of all things by God and the return of everything to him. As soon as *tawhid* is addressed in the Chinese language, it appears as another version of the assertion of the ultimate reality of the Tao and the manner in which the Tao gives rise to all things. This is a notion that is basic to all Chinese thought, especially Neo-Confucianism. The Buddhists and Taoists were no exception, though they tended to approach the issue of unity in terms of Emptiness or the Buddha nature.

Tawhid is a constant theme in the works of the Chinese *'ulama*, although they rarely employ the Arabic word. Wang Tai-yu's most widely read work may have been his short treatise The Great Learning of the Pure and Real (*Ch'ing-chen ta-hsueh*). "The Pure and Real" designates the Islamic tradition, while the expression "Great Learning" is the title of a Confucian classic that was central to Neoconfucian teaching. Although the significance of the classic was debated among Neoconfucian scholars, they all agreed that its basic point was "that the internal and the external, the fundamental and the secondary, and the first and the last, must be clearly distinguished."[5] This, indeed, is the theme of Wang's Great Learning, and the whole book explains how all such distinctions must be made in terms of the unity of the Real Lord. Wang distinguishes three basic levels of unity that correspond with the well-known Islamic distinction among the divine Essence, the divine attributes, and the divine acts. However, the language and imagery are derived wholly from the Chinese tradition, with numerous terms familiar to Taoists and Buddhists.

A second point on which the Chinese *'ulama* and the three Chinese traditions agree is the sacredness of the natural world, which is the locus in which the Tao displays its characteristics. It is well known that the very concept of Tao has to do with the harmony of heaven and earth and the perfect balance among all the forces that drive the supernatural and natural worlds. However, it is often forgotten that the Qur'an is full of mention of God's signs in the natural world, and that the idea of the balance of heaven and earth is central to its message, as is recognized by much of the Islamic intellectual tradition.[6] The Chinese *'ulama* had no difficulty whatsoever seeing the idea of cosmic equilibrium as a shared feature of the traditions.

It perhaps needs to be stressed that this idea of cosmic harmony is a dimension of Islamic teaching that tends to be forgotten in modern times, when Islamic countries have been rushing to adopt modern technology with all its inherent implications for the destruction of the natural order. This is one reason why so much stress is laid by modern-day Muslims on the social and political discourse that is central to modern Western thought. So long as the cosmological teachings of Islam are ignored, it becomes easy to pretend that Islamic social teaching are the crux of the tradition. Then people can forget that Muslim thinkers have typically seen an intimate relationship between society on the one hand and, on the other hand, "heaven, earth, and everything between the two" as the Qur'an puts it. The latter is the domain that the Chinese tradition names "heaven, earth, and the ten thousand things."

A third major area of agreement between Islam and the Chinese traditions is that the human models of the past are utterly essential for the quest to live in harmony with heaven and earth. In Islamic terms, this is the second principle of faith - that of prophecy. For the Chinese, the teachings of the ancient sages, the Buddhas, and the bodhisattvas are indispensable. In all four traditions, the reasons for the indispensability of guidance is that human beings cannot possibility achieve the goal of life without outside help.

This brings us to a fourth point of commonality, which is that the goal of human life is clearly laid down and agreed upon by all four traditions. It is to achieve perfection. As Tu Weiming puts it in characterizing Neoconfucianism, the fundamental impulse of the tradition is "learning how to be human." This is also a key issue in Taoism and Buddhism, no matter how much the discussion of human nature may differ. In the Chinese Islamic texts, it is completely clear that the *'ulama* saw "learning how to be human" as the fundamental purpose of all the Islamic teachings. When the Prophet said, "Seek knowledge, even unto China," he did not mean knowledge of engineering or politics. He meant knowledge of how to be human, of how to live up to the models established by the perfected human beings of the past. In contrast, if one wants to sum up the general thrust of modern education and even modern civilization, one can hardly do better than to say that it is "forgetting how to be human." The very idea that there could possibly be a human perfection of which the sages and prophets of the past were the models and toward which all human endeavor should be directed has long since been discarded.

A fifth domain of commonality is closely related to that of human perfection. This is the domain of social and political teachings. In the Far East, it is mainly Confucianism that deals with this domain. The Chinese *'ulama*, in fact, found themselves almost completely in agreement with the Confucian teachings, which they rarely criticize, in contrast to certain Buddhist and Taoist concepts. But even Buddhists and Taoists agree that if social reality is to conform to the Tao, it must be built on individuals who live in harmony with the Tao. Thus, in all four traditions, the only way to achieve the equilibrium, balance, and peace of social and political life is for human individuals to achieve perfection. And the only way for human individuals to achieve perfection is for them to follow the models of the great sages of the past, who lived in conformity with the Tao. If each human individual rectifies his or her own internal relationship with the Tao, then alone will the family, the nation, and the world be put back into order. The contrast with the vast majority of modern social and political teachings could hardly be starker.

Let me close my remarks by quoting from Wang Tai-yu's treatise, *The Great Learning of the Pure and Real*, or, as one might also translate the title, "*The Principles of Islam*." Toward the beginning of the introduction, Wang describes the purpose of Islamic teachings. Most of what he says would be unremarkable in any Neoconfucian treatise. Notice, however, the mention of the "Lord" and the "Chief Servant." These, of course, are God and the Prophet. The discrimination that is being discussed is that established by the *Shahadah*, the testimony of faith. At the same time, the text sums up the shared vision of Islam and the Chinese traditions. It lists the essential human duties in their proper order - moving from the individual, to the family, to the social, to the political. The point of his words will not be unfamiliar to anyone who has studied classical Islamic texts, but it is not often mentioned by modern-day interpreters of the tradition.

> If the country is not governed, it is because the family is not regulated. If the family is not regulated, it is because the body is not cultivated. If the body is not cultivated, it is because the words are not one. If the words are not one, it is because the intention is not sincere. If the intention is not sincere, it is because the heart is not true. If the heart is not true, it is because one does not know oneself. If one does not know oneself, it is because one's knowledge is not real. If knowledge is not real, it is because the clear virtue has not become clear. If the clear virtue has not become clear, it is because one does not know the fountainhead of clear virtue. If one does not know the fountainhead of clear virtue, it is because one does not discriminate the Real One from the Numerical One. If one does not discriminate the Real One from the Numerical One, it is because the principle of the utmost greatness of the Lord and the [Chief] Servant has not become clear. When the principle of the utmost greatness of the Lord and the Servant has not become clear, you may do ten thousand good deeds, but they are not worthy of mention. Why? When the taproot of the deed is not pure, its branches and twigs cannot be pure.[7]

CHAPTER 7

Pluralism and Islamic Perspectives on Cultural Diversity

John O. Voll

THE NEW CONTEXT OF PLURALISM

We are entering a major new era in world history in terms of the way humans define other humans who are part of different groups. In the past, diversity, especially cultural and ethnic diversity, was mistrusted, as "others" were seen as threats to a community's identity and means of cohesion. Speaking an unintelligible language was one of the key aspects of the Greek definition of a "barbarian" and, in the story of the Tower of Babel, people identified the diversity of languages as being a product of divine anger. . In many cases, difference was used to define "the other" as somehow being not fully human or possibly even sub-human.

In the modern era, there emerged a sense that diversity and difference should somehow be tolerated in recognition of the fundamental equality of all humans. Toleration became the watchword of many progressive movements, but toleration still rested on an assumption that humans had a right to be wrong rather than that it was good for humans to be different from each other. The spirit was well captured in the often-quoted statement attributed to Voltaire: "I disapprove of what you say, but I will defend to the death your right to say it."[1] Toleration has opened the way for much human freedom of activity, but it remains tied to assumptions about truth in which a person who is "right" accepts the obligation to tolerate the person who is "wrong."

In this context, diversity is seen as a problem to be solved. Ultimately, the world still remains divided into many different groups and each group looks forward to the time when the values or the identity of their group will become universal. This is the kind of tolerant universalist optimism reflected in the name of the liberal protestant Christian magazine, *The Christian Century*. A century ago the magazine adopted that name in recognition of the expectation that the twentieth century would be the "Christian century," during which the world would be "won for Christ." Muslim perceptions of the division of the world into the *Dar-al-Islam* ("the House of Islam") and the *Dar al-Harb* ("the House of Conflict") carried similar long-term expectations.

Increasingly during the twentieth century people began to seek for ways of transcending the patronizing attitude inherent in toleration. There was a search for common elements in faith and worldview that could be the foundations for building bridges across the communal and cultural divides created by diversity. Catholic theologians led by Karl Rahner developed concepts like "anonymous Christianity," which could give recognition to important similarities among the great traditions of religious experience. This line of thinking helped to provide the bases for some of the important statements on interfaith relations issued by the Second Vatican Council of the Catholic Church in the 1960s.

Among Muslims, similar searches for common grounds can be seen in the increasing references by Muslim thinkers to the "Abrahamic tradition" as being shared by Muslims, Jews, and Christians. A good example of this is a presentation by Jamal Badawi. In his perspective, the most significant connection between Jews and Muslims is the Abrahamic connection. Like many scholars I have studied the Qur'an to see what it says about Abraham and Moses and the *commonality* among the basic threads of their teaching. I think equal attention should be given to the study of the Bible in a new light, which may perhaps lead us to discover more and more threads of that *commonality*.[2] The search for commonalities is important in the contemporary efforts for improving interfaith relations. However, while these are very significant and positive perspectives, they remain within the framework of viewing diversity as something to be avoided, circumvented or overcome if it cannot be eliminated.

In recent years, however, a new attitude has begun to emerge that represents a major shift in the evaluation of diversity. Diversity and difference have begun to be viewed by some thinkers as a source of strength rather than a cause of weakness. "Pluralism" becomes a characteristic that provides vitality for a society. Some of the first thinkers to express this type of thinking were discussing the needs of the physical environment in ecological terms. Biologists have long recognized that diversity of species aids in the health of ecosystems and diversity even within a species is seen as essential for survival.[3]

A major social and political catalyst of this pluralist outlook was the beginnings of the change in human terms can be seen in the evolution of the civil rights movement in the United States. The movement, as it gained power in the 1950s and 1960s, affirmed the equality of all humans and sought a society in which the color of a person's skin would be irrelevant. However, by the late 1960s, new movements of affirmation of special identities, like the 'Black is beautiful' movement, began to reshape the hopes and aspirations of peoples. Around the world, recognition of the positive dimensions of cultural diversity has come to play an increasingly important role in defining inter-group and inter-societal relations.

This development contradicted expectations of many of the most important analysts of modernity and its impact on human life. The nature of modern industrial society was seen as creating conditions in which human diversity would be reduced if not eliminated in a standardized world of mass-produced products and human beings. Writers as widely different as George Orwell, Aldous Huxley, and Ayn Rand all saw the future in terms of an increasingly homogenous humanity with diversity of any sort virtually eliminated. When television became an important part of modern society in the 1950s, social prophets predicted that the mass media would create an undiversified mass society.

While social critics decried the world of uniformity enforced by Orwell's vision of the omnipresent "Big Brother," most people welcomed the ideal of the "melting pot," in which racial, religious and other identities which had been the grounds for discrimination in the past would no longer be important for the definition of an individual's place in society. In the 1960s, many people viewed the discovery of "unmeltable" ethnic groups, as described by Nathan Glazer and Daniel Moynihan,[4] as a challenge to the ideals of the civil rights movement rather than as a description of the emerging recognition of the importance and permanence of diversity in American society. Most people also welcomed the world of standardized mass production and the material prosperity that it created. The assembly line "invented" by Henry Ford for the rapid mass production of automobiles became a symbol of the success of modern technology. The assembly line became both symbol and reality in the increasing application of systematic organization to the workplace. Pioneered in the United States, particularly by automobile manufacturer Henry Ford after 1910, the assembly line crystallized earlier efforts to measure and routinize work. The goal was, as Ford's engineers put it, "to make workers as much like machines as possible—to remove any need for thought and reflection."[5] Although later social critics decried the impact of "Fordism" on modern society, for most people in the twentieth century, the modern assembly line's productivity was viewed as a major achievement that many societies around the world worked to duplicate. Assembly line uniformity was simply part of the broader mass uniformity that seemed to be inherent in modernity, and programs of "modernizing" reforms regularly included attempts to create modern assembly line industries.

It was clear, however, by the actual year 1984 that the imaginary world of Orwell's *1984* was not an accurate portrait of the future or the emerging modern historic present. This change is possibly most vividly visible in the development of communications media. The modern 'mass media' of the middle of the twentieth century had been highly centralized and were viewed as the means for the creation of a homogeneous society. However, one of the major sociotechnological developments of recent decades has been the spread of new forms of media whose patterns of control, production, content and consumption differ dramatically from those older forms of mass media. The new media, utilizing personal computers, fax, cassettes, and Internet, constitute a challenge to the one-way, monopolistic, homogenizing tendencies of the "old" media. In effect, the new media render the Orwellian vision of monolithic consciousness control, a possibility of the past rather than the future; 1984, indeed, has come and gone.[6]

One consequence of this is that major social critics in the 1990s reversed the position of earlier critics. Many observers identified the greatest threat to human peace and prosperity as being not a uniformity imposed by some huge governing apparatus or all-powerful mass media, but chaos. By the end of the twentieth century, the proliferation of means of affirming diversity was a major dynamic of world history. The assertion of cultural diversity at all levels from local communities to large national-ethnic groups was viewed, by the creators of those identities, as a liberating development. However, the results of these developments of increasing assertions of diverse identity and affirmations of the constructive reality of "multicultural" created dismay and grave concern among many analysts. Looking at the impact of multiculturalism in the United States, Arthur M. Schlesinger, Jr. spoke of the "disuniting of America" and noted that the "attack on the common American identity is the culmination of the cult of ethnicity."[7] In terms of world affairs, in the view of analysts like Senator Patrick Moynihan, the result of all this diversity was the potential for "pandamonium," and the need is to find "order in an age of chaos."[8] While the old debate was whether or not "Fordism" would lead to Orwell's Big Brother, the new debates relate to the issue of whether or not recognition of the legitimacy of diversity will lead to a destructive chaos or a constructive pluralism. The old advocates of a toleration which might in the long run reduce diversity are faced with the challenge of a real pluralism which a growing number of thinkers are recognizing as a necessity for human survival. A positive acceptance of pluralism as necessary for human survival becomes an important dimension of new emerging perspectives and worldviews.

Much of this new expression of diversity and communal or local identity represents an affirmation of religious traditions and is frequently spoken of as the "resurgence" of religion in the late twentieth century. Increasingly this resurgence has come to be understood not simply as a movement of opposition to globalization but rather, as an inherent part of those processes.[9] One popular characterization of this situation sees it as a competition between affirmations of local identities (or "*jihads*") and the dynamics of a standardizing globalization leading to the creation of "McWorld".[10] These two dynamics are intimately interrelated: "in history's twisting maze, *Jihad* not only revolts against but abets McWorld, while McWorld not only imperils but recreates and reinforces *Jihad*. They produce their contraries and need one another."[11] Affirmations of diversity, in other words, are a direct component in the processes of globalization. This interaction of the forces of globalization and local assertions of identity has led some analysts to argue that the best term to use for these interacting processes is "glocalization".[12] The world of "glocalization" is a world context in which pluralism can have a positive meaning. This is the new context for pluralism and the definition of the role of the other in human life.

RELIGION AND PLURALISM

Within the major monotheistic religious traditions, where diversity tended to be most suspect, there is an emerging re-evaluation of pluralism. This involves both a new analysis of theological foundations and a reexamination of the historical experiences of the great communities of believers. This is more developed within the thinking of Christian theologians but important initiatives are also being put forward by Muslims.

One interesting example of the rethinking can be seen in a redefinition of the Tower of Babel experience. In a recent authoritative interpretation it is stated:

> Ordinarily, we regard unity in the human community as desirable and in tune with God's purposes for the creation. But here [in the story of the Tower of Babel], because the unity desired and promoted stands against the divine will to spread abroad throughout the world--God must resist it. The right kind of unity occurs only when the community encompasses the concerns of the entire world and encourages difference and diversity to that end.[13]

In much of the religious thought of the late twentieth century, there is a growing emphasis on this concept of "the right kind of unity," which involves the *necessity* of diversity. Pluralism is seen as a positive dimension of human life and is to be encouraged, not overcome. In this sense, pluralism is interpreted as the product of divine action and not in opposition to it.

If one views religious traditions and revelations as sources of inspiration for all peoples in all times rather than a fixed body of doctrines and definitions which are unchangeable, one can then ask the question: What are the conceptual resources within a religious tradition for a positive acceptance of pluralism? There is a growing body of scholarship by contemporary Muslim thinkers identifying these resources within Islamic sources and traditions. There is a growing emphasis on the Qur'anic reminders that if God had wished, God could have created all humans alike but instead He chose to create human pluralism and this action has positive implications for human life. In addition, a growing number of Muslim leaders note that the first definition of the community within which Muslims could live effectively as believers, the Constitution of Medina, is a definition of a religiously pluralistic community and that this can provide a model for contemporary humans. In this emerging discourse, people like the South African Muslim intellectual Farid Esack are playing an important role. In his analysis, he argues that "the Qur'an acknowledges the fact of religious diversity as the will of God."[14]

While this viewpoint may appear initially to be "very modern," or, in fact, hermeneutically postmodern, the tolerance for legitimized pluralism is deeply embedded in the Islamic historical and theological experience. It is not that the whole content of the Islamic tradition is "pluralist" but rather, that there are obvious resources for a pluralistic perspective in premodern Islamic history. The "repertoire of cultural and religious ideas" which the early Muslims developed and "bequeathed" to later generations of Muslims[15] included a wide range of concepts and images which made historic and ideational pluralism possible.

PLURALISM IN THE ISLAMIC HERITAGE

When one views major world view traditions as "repertoires of ideas," or as "communities of discourse," or as "discourse-based world-systems,"[16] it is possible to recognize that some "religions" have a broader conceptual basis on which to ground concepts of pluralism and acceptance of diversity than others. The discourse resources of Islam are especially rich in the potential for pluralist perspectives, although it should also be noted that, like all of the Middle Eastern ethical monotheistic traditions, Islam also has rich conceptual resources for articulating closed exclusivist perspectives. One of the great dynamics of the history of the Muslim community is the on-going debate involved in the interactions between peoples and groups articulating Islam in inclusive, pluralist terms and others presenting a more exclusivist perspective.[17]

In the historical development of Islamic institutions and discourses, even in the medieval *ummah* (community), there was an openness to some forms of diversity. Within the Sunni tradition, one important dimension of this diversity can be seen in the development of Islamic conceptualizations and articulations of "Islamic law." In the early centuries of the Islamic community, there was no standardized version of "Islamic law," and there was no clerical institution that had the power to define such a monolithic canon law. When the Sunni definitions of 'the Law' became in some sense standardized, the *Shari'ah* was not limited to legal matters and it emerged with *four* distinct equally legitimate schools of law.

One conceptual resource that was used to recognize this and other diversity was the Qur'anic recognition of the possibility of legitimate difference: *ikhtilaf*. *Ikhtilaf* became an important conceptual tool in the framework of willingness to accept diversity in "traditional" Muslim societies and remains an important part of Muslim discourses.[18]

Among the four Sunni schools of law there were distinctive differences in definition of specific requirements and obligations. In discussions of these differences, a frequently noted observation was that difference of opinion "is a blessing on the *ummah*, and demonstrates flexibility in *al-Shariah*."[19]

Similarly, variety of devotional paths (*tariqahs)* and the acceptance of this diversity of paths is another element of legitimized pluralism. Beyond this, the articulation of Sufi devotional theologies provides a remarkably (and sometimes self-consciously) pluralist worldview that goes beyond simply accepting a diversity within the unity of the broader Islamic community. Sufi teachers often presented an inclusive vision of faith and community that extended beyond the strictly Islamic world. This vision is reflected in the often-quoted verses from the writings of the thirteenth century teacher, Muhyi ad-Din Ibn Arabi:

> My heart has become capable of wearing all forms.
> It is a pasture for gazelles and a convent for monks.
> A temple for idols and the Ka'aba for the pilgrim.
> It is the tables of the Torah, and it is the book of the Qur'an.
> I profess the religion of Love, whatever the destination
> of its caravans may be, and Love is my law and my faith.[20]

Ibn Arabi's foundation for this broadly inclusive perspective is generally based on verse 23 of Surah 17: "And your Lord has decreed that you will worship no one but Him," which he interprets as meaning that "every worshiper, whatever the apparent object of his worship, in fact only worships Allah."[21] This was a controversial interpretation but one which resonated in the spiritual experience of Muslims throughout the centuries, illustrating the long term existence of a more pluralistic theological position.

The continuing appeal of this perspective can be seen in the writings of a major nineteenth-century Muslim leader more often thought of as the leader of the military resistance to the French invasion of Algeria -- the Amir Abd al-Qadir. After he was defeated by the French, he lived in exile in Damascus and frequently meditated at the tomb of Ibn Arabi. This jihad leader presented an acceptance of the diverse ways of worshipping the One:

> Every representation which is made of Him is really Him, and His presence in this representation does not cease if the one who represented Him in this way later represents Him otherwise: He will be equally present in this new representation. He is limited for someone who believes and represents Him to be limited, absolute for someone who believes Him

absolute.[22]

There is not uniform agreement on the legitimacy of any of these pluralistic expressions. There were, in fact, many who charged that people like Ibn Arabi had gone beyond the limits of Islam. However, a very large proportion of the world's Muslims still regularly recite Sufi devotional literature that is fully within the discourse that was initiated by Ibn Arabi utilizing the Islamic repertoire. Sufism is possibly the most firmly established Islamic pluralist perspective. It has profoundly deep roots in the experiences of Islamic societies in every region and has inspired pluralist perspectives among non-Muslims as well.

Beyond the Sufi traditions, there is a basic foundation of discussions of the divine origins of human pluralism as defined in the Qur'an. A number of verses explicitly affirm that had God willed, He could have created a uniform humanity:

> If God had pleased, He could surely have made you one people (professing one faith). But He wished to try and test you by that which He gave you. So try to excel in good deeds. (5:48)

> But if your Lord had pleased, he could have made all human beings into one community of belief. (11:118)

> Among other signs of His is the creation of the heavens and the earth, and the variety of your tongues and complexions. (30:22)

> O humans, We have created you from a single pair, male and female, and We have made you into peoples and tribes that you may come to know one another. Truly, the most noble of spirit among you, in the sight of God, are those who are the most Righteous. (49:12)[23]

Many discussions based on interpretations of these verses go beyond the usual acknowledgment that Islam provides a clear recognition of the earlier prophetic religions of Judaism and Christianity. These special verses do not usually deal with the specific issues of relations between the three traditions of the "heirs of Abraham." Instead, they point more broadly to the condition of *human* diversity, and state that condition is the result of the explicit will of God. The diversity is identified as having specific purposes in a divine plan: the diversity is created so that humans can get to know one another or so that they can and should compete in doing good works. These verses provide an important pluralist dimension for the repertoire of Islamic concepts of faith. It is possible to argue that they provide the foundation for an

Islamic pluralist theology.[24]

At the same time, it is important to recognize that not all interpreters of these verses have come to the conclusion that they command a pluralist theology. Historic commentators have often viewed the verses in the context of *intra*-Muslim relations, and the verses are also "amenable to interpretation as elements of a more exclusivist principle."[25] The discussions of the implications of these verses and others for living in a pluralist, "glocalized" world are of great significance for determining the Islamic resources for a theology of pluralism.

In concrete experiential terms, the historical-societal manifestations of Islamic faith also reflect a relatively open acceptance of pluralism by most Muslims. One of the great dynamics of Muslim history is, in fact, the interaction between the more inclusive and the more exclusionary modes of Islamic expression. This is one of the great themes lying behind the history of movements of *tajdid* (renewal) and *islah* (reform) in the *ummah*. Movements of renewal and reform work to eliminate compromises with non-Islamic practices and perspectives. However, in addition, the pluralist modes of openness have been a major force in the dynamic of the expansion of the *ummah* through an inclusive *da'wah* within the non-Muslim world. Without the effective pluralism of the Muslim tradition, the expansion of Islam in Africa, Southeast Asia, and elsewhere is difficult to conceive in historical terms.

CONCLUSION

Islam, like all of the other major religious traditions, has resources both for supporting pluralist and for exercising exclusivism. These conceptual resources are an important part of the discussion of Islam and cultural diversity. While Islam as a monotheistic faith demands a unitary allegiance to the one God, the basic sources are open to the expression of that allegiance in many forms. This potential pluralism is articulated in the contemporary world but while the specific expressions may be 'new,' they are in important ways only the current expression of the pluralism that is always a possible mode of the articulation of Islamic faith.

SECTION THREE

Crisis in Islamic State
and Society

CHAPTER 8

Islamists as Modernizers?

Robert D. Lee

Modernization theory finds patterns in the development of Western societies and institutions and suggests that these patterns constitute a model for the world. It predicts the eventual emergence of a prosperous, liberal, homogenous world as the wheel of history; the advance propelled not by the Marxist dialectic but by the liberal dedication to progress. At the other extreme, there are theories of difference and particularity emphasizing primordial cleavages climaxing in cultural war and civilizational clash; theories of authenticity, for example, emphasize the uniqueness of historical experience and slice the human species into bits without providing a logic for putting it back together again.

Neither scenario appears plausible. Cultural differences have persisted in the most advanced Western nations; in fact, ethnic, linguistic, and religious difference may play a more significant role in Western politics than it did fifty years ago, largely as a result of the very modernization process that was supposed to dispel it. Immigration has carried diversity into countries where there was little. Groups have found the means and the motives to bring old claims of diversity to bear on modern problems. Nevertheless, Huntington's assertion that world politics, despite the effects of globalization, may turn on enduring civilizational allegiances seems farfetched in an age when individual, group, and national identities appear anything but fixed.

The Iranian Revolution dealt a fierce blow to modernization theory. Rather following the "new middle class" toward democracy,[1] Iran followed a clerical class toward original solutions based in Iranian and Islamic culture. What followed was an outpouring of literature on the Islamic revival, much of it echoing Islamist claims of innovative approaches to economics and politics. Islamists denounced modernization theory as ethnocentric, and Western social science, already rocked by the attacks of dependence theory, backed away from ideas that no longer garnered consensus either at home or abroad. It was the "end of development" because "development" no longer signified a path toward progress that commanded consensual support.[2]

While theorists of modernization retreated, social change proceeded largely as before. Despite the "mea culpas" of theorists for their failure to anticipate an Islamic revival and the vociferous denunciations of social-scientific determinism on the part of Islamists, neither economics nor politics underwent a radical transformation in theory or in practice. Islamic banking did not obstruct economic development. The Islamic state in Iran created new institutions but also legitimated Western-inspired political practice. Everywhere social mobilization continued (sometimes fostered by Islamist movements, as with the Shi'a in Lebanon), and everywhere the demand for political participation increased. Twenty years after the Iranian revolution, the modernization hypothesis, though seriously flawed, appears very much alive. Economists, merchants, planners, and politicians all seem to proceed as if they know where they are headed.

A major flaw in modernization theory is its treatment of religion. The renewed interest in religion around the world and especially among Muslims flies in the face of the secularization hypothesis, which is usually regarded as fundamental to modernization theory. One of the most cogent contemporary exponents of modernization theory, Ronald Inglehart, predicts that the Islamic revival will not outlast oil reserves in the Middle East.[3] Interestingly enough, Turkey is the only Muslim country included in his study of forty-three societies. He pronounces Western excursions into fundamentalism aberrant and insignificant. He proclaims the centrality of religion to culture and the centrality of culture to economic and political development. Yet he finds religious developments of the past thirty years to have no profound meaning for the development of either East or West.

The problem is that while modernization theory explains much of what continues to occur in Muslim societies, it fails to account for the renewed prominence of religion. If the truth value of the theory rides on the secularization hypothesis, then it stands condemned by recent history. Yet even if the secularization hypothesis represents a distortion or at least an oversimplification of the Western experience and a nonessential or even contradictory element of the model then a revised version of the theory might still account for contemporary developments. While even the revised account might not be palatable to either Islamists or diehard secularists, to partisans of either cultural confrontation or cultural relativism, it might, by reopening the possibility of analogy between European and non-European experience, also permit a renewal of dialogue and a reevaluation of claims about cultural divergence.

Inglehart argues, following Weber, that a cultural shift in Western Europe triggered the growth of capitalism. He fails to observe, however, that the shift involved the secularization of religion and the sacralization of economic and social behavior. It was the subsequent deep penetration of political life by religion that fostered the need for toleration and the sacralization of political institutions through which participation could be maintained and religious strife prevented. As others have argued, the French pattern of hostility between church and state was rare. The American example demonstrates the utility of religion in cementing fundamental values, legitimating institutions, and fostering competition.

The principal characteristic of the Islamic revival in the Middle East is the secularization (politicization) of Islam and the sacralization of society in ways that parallel the European experience. The theorists of revival from the time of Hassan al-Banna to that of Ruhollah Khomeini have sought to convince Muslims of their own responsibility for the history of their world. God is in retreat; Muslims have taken charge. While Islamists have protested Western materialism and the determinism of Western social science, they have, in fact, helped to legitimize the general course of modernization and perhaps reinforced its penchant for democracy. The plurality of voices emerging to speak for Muslims creates the need for tolerance. Tolerance does not necessarily emerge when it is needed, but the European example suggests that it comes out of conditions of religious fervor, not from conditions of preexisting secularism.

"SECULARISM" IN THE WEST

No name is more linked with modernization theory and the secularization hypothesis than that of Max Weber, the German sociologist. Weber argued that the modernization of society meant the gradual replacement of religiously defined norms with legal-rational rules devised by human beings. He also contended, however, that the great drive toward capitalist accumulation in the West began with the Protestant reformation, which deflected human beings from monasticism toward worldly asceticism. Luther himself thought that the pursuit of material gain could only result in the impoverishment of others. Weber portrays him as preaching obedience to authority and acceptance of things as they were where "worldly duties were no longer subordinated to ascetic ones."[4]

From Calvin came an even more pronounced emphasis upon the separation of human beings from God. No individual could know God or be certain of election for eternal life. No amount of prayer, ritual, song, or good works could assure salvation. The only way to demonstrate one's faith was in service to the world, whose purpose was the glorification of God. God had provided both the golden rule and the guidelines for social organization. "This makes labor in the service of impersonal social usefulness appear to promote the glory of God and hence to be willed by Him."[5] According to Weber, the Calvinists identified true faith with "a type of Christian conduct which served to increase the glory of God." God helped those who, by helping themselves, also helped God with his plan for human society.

Here was decisive cultural shift in Western Europe toward a sacralization of society and a secularization of religion. Far from a rationalization of society, it was the identification of the irrational with secular behavior and purposes, especially but not exclusively with the accumulation of wealth. Protestant princes also sought to bolster their claims to authority in virtue of their contributions to the social organization God had ordained. By the seventeenth century, England was awash in the claims and counterclaims of religiously inspired groups seeking to reshape the polity. Hobbes invoked absolute authority on the basis of a contract struck in the name of worldly peace to counter such problems. He assumed the sovereign would do his duty to God by keeping order according to the "natural law" of God's making. Locke invoked religion more explicitly to legitimate a state based on natural law and the principle of tolerance. Both presupposed the application of religious norms to society, not a separation between religion and politics.

The spirit of the American Revolution reflected the Lockean vision in this as well as other ways. The colonies were seeded by religious groups seeking to implement God's will on earth. As they came together to proclaim their independence, they did so in the name of "self-evident truths" rooted in natural-rights theory and the Christian tradition. While the founders accepted Locke's dictates about toleration and foreclosed the possible identification of the state with any single creed, they imagined a republic consistent with principles discernible in nature. With God in further retreat from the world, human beings were left to do His bidding. While not all the founders were believers, believers rallied to the republic. The founders—like their heirs in contemporary American politics—were doing their best to identify the state with God's work.

Martin Marty calls the American pattern "controlled (ambiguous) secularism."[6] He contrasts it with the "formal and unrelenting attack on gods and churches" more characteristic of continental Europe in the nineteenth century. He finds the American pattern different even from that of England, where "God and churches were increasingly ignored and men made fewer systematic attempts to replace them." He calls the English pattern "mere secularity" and the Continental model "maximal secularity." In America, by way of contrast, "There was no demise of religion."[7] Religion adapted itself to secular life. Religion, he says, continued to speak more and more of this kingdom rather than the next and to acquiesce in a vision of the state that executed God's purposes and acted on his behalf. (Perhaps this helps explain the correlation Inglehart finds among the forty-three states he studied between patriotism and the strength of belief in God.)[8] Religion in America, though operating within constraints established by the political system, underwent continuous change to solidify its place in a changing world. "Denomination, parish, missionary movement, benevolent societies, Sunday School, revivalism, all these are what is meant by the term 'new forms' for the age of industrialism and political democracy, for conquest of the frontier and confrontation of the cities."[9]

John Locke himself, in his "Essay on Toleration," acknowledges that churches and churchgoers have every right to deliberate about public matters and to make their views known. To be sure, any religious group that challenges the civil peace can be pursued by civil authorities. For Locke, the problem is that church figures have sought to use state authority for their own purposes, and state authority has sometimes intervened in religious matters. "Whereas if each of them would contain itself within its own bounds, the one attending to the worldly welfare of the commonwealth, the other to the salvation of souls, it is impossible that any discord should ever have happened between them."[10] But that neat division of labor does not foreclose some real-world overlapping: the state building its legitimacy on widely accepted religious symbols and the mobilization of citizens in the name of religious principles to influence elections or policy.

The ambiguity of American "secularism" appears at several levels. At the level of the Constitution, the place of religious belief in sustaining American institutions is undeniable yet difficult to reconcile with the constitutional separation of Church and state. The Supreme Court continues to wrestle with the problem. U.S. church attendance is higher than in other Western countries, religious groups garner enormous support, and "secular humanism" often seems on the defensive (although Americans also appear less hesitant to express disbelief. The society as a whole continues to endow symbols with mythic authority; modern means of communication, far from destroying the mythic, have enhanced it. New technologies appear to have enhanced the political power of religious groups.

Even the continental path toward secularism is much less uniform than theory might suggest. When liberal, republican forces attacked the Catholic Church in the nineteenth century, the Church moved (in five of six countries studied by Kalyvas[11]) to defend itself by extending its organizational structure. Through women's, youth, and charitable organizations the Church sought to strengthen its hold on the masses, even at the expense of its hierarchical coherence and the intensity of its commitment to members. Then, as the liberal pressure escalated further, the Church decided to engage in politics by encouraging its newly created supporters to favor conservative causes. Finally, as confessional political parties emerged in these five countries, the Church found itself obliged to approve the actions of Catholic parties it could not control. This approval undermined the relationship of the Church and its members, weakened the hierarchical structure of the clergy, and generated a de facto plurality of views and loyalties in the Catholic world.[12] Politicization of religion came at high cost for the Church.[13]

Marty identifies secularization with qualities of religion rather than society. "What is often called 'secularization' is not simple secularization; it is a complex of radical religious changes, in which people act and think religiously in ways which differ from those of the past and from those meanings conveyed by the symbols to which they adhere."[14] That definition fits the changes wrought by Luther and Calvin as well as those pertaining to contemporary American society. The secularization of religion means the progressive revalorization of worldly activities in religious terms. In Europe, the politicization of the Catholic Church in opposing liberal, anticlerical republicanism ultimately brought the Catholic masses into full support of liberal regimes. Confessional parties, like socialist parties created to oppose European liberalism, ended up embracing liberalism in the name of

Catholicism. Faith entered the arena to buttress reason. The secularization of the Church helped produce a sacralization of republican institutions.

Ellul denies that secularization means the de-sacralization of society. The sacred, he says, is not a category of religion. Rather, religion is "one possible rendition of the sacred."[15] Christianity arrived to desacralize the ancient world, but it then became the new standard of the sacred. As a result of the Enlightenment, science, philosophy, and, finally, politics came to dominate the sacred. Now technology is the desacralizing force that in turn becomes sacrosanct. While old symbols are constantly destroyed, new ones emerge, as Ellul writes, to "link this new world to the deepest roots of one's being, and which restore the sacred to its imperial position...."[16]

The dependence of modern societies on myth to shore up economic, legal, social, and political systems casts doubt on the Weberian identification of rationality with modernization. Ellul writes, "All facets of the modern religions bring into prominence the deeply irrational character of modern man. He is not scientific, reasonable, rational, involved in tangible and demythicized matters, devoid of illusions, indeed not!"[17] And perhaps the greatest of the myths to which moderns subscribe is the myth of progress. We have seized upon history to make it serve us better. For Ellul Christianity has debased itself by embracing that myth and arguing that human beings make history for the glory of God. The result is a sacralization of fundamentally secular economic, political, and social activity.

Those Western thinkers who have questioned the myth of progress, with its insistence on Western rationality, have themselves exalted the irrational. For Rousseau, the sentiment of being oneself meant radical rejection of not just the irrationalities of traditional society but the emphatic rejection of the rationally ordered society, both of which alienated the individual. Nietzsche called rationality a trap from which the true human being could escape only by exercise of the will. He upbraided the West for its irrational attachment to logocentrism and at the same time invoked myth as a tool for salvation from the ravages of history. For Heidegger and many other critics of modernity, being takes precedence over becoming, and the understanding of being stretches us to the very limits of rationality and perhaps beyond.

These towering figures of Western thought criticize modernity as well as the rational-legal order upon which it is based. But if they are harbingers of postmodernity, one is inclined to put Iqbal, Shariati, Arkoun, and even Qutb in the same camp (recent champions of the Islamist movement in Turkey share many of these same postulates).

None of these writers would abandon the tools of rationality. None would imagine, on the other hand, that a world without myth would be a tolerable place to live.

If one regards certain nineteenth- and twentieth-century European thinkers as postmodern, it does not make sense to treat Islamist movements in the Middle East as premodern in their stance against modernity. It makes more sense to rethink the secularization hypothesis and to recognize that modernization, as a set of interactions among politics, economics, and culture, is necessarily reflective of existing myth, religious and nonreligious. It is also productive of mythical renewal. The secularization hypothesis, as originally formulated, does not discriminate between the Western experience and that of the Muslim Middle East. It does not offer an adequate account of modernization in either context.

"SACRALIZATION" IN THE EAST

Secularization, defined as a "complex of radical religious changes, in which people act and think religiously in ways which differ from those of the past and from those meanings conveyed by the symbols to which they adhere,"[18] does apply to Muslim countries of the Middle East in the twentieth century. Even in the nineteenth century the *ulama* of Iran began to edge toward a position of political involvement. In the Tobacco Revolution and again in the Constitutional Revolution, some of the Iranian *ulama* entered the political arena in favor of reform. In Algeria the Association of Reformist *Ulama* founded modern schools and began to help Algerians rethink their political identity. The emergence of the Muslim Brotherhood in Egypt, under the lay leadership of Hasan al-Banna, epitomized the new this-worldly emphasis of Islam. The thought of persons such as Muhammad Iqbal and Abu al-A'la Mawdudi supported the trend.

After World War II, a period seemingly dominated by secular ideologies such as nationalism and socialism, thinkers such as Sayyid Qutb, Ali Shariati, and Ruhollah Khomeini laid the groundwork for the further secularization of Islam, a secularization that emerged clearly after the Six-Day War. Islamic leaders, some of them radical, emerged from prison in Egypt to work at politics from within the system or from the outside. In Lebanon, a Shi'i movement led by an *'alim* galvanized the south and demanded the transformation of Lebanese political life. The revolution in Iran and the effort to establish an Islamic state then proceeded.

Everywhere in the region, with varying degrees of intensity and government blessing, Muslims sought change by establishing schools, charities, hospitals, nurseries, political parties, and guerrilla groups.[19] In Algeria, "through an extensive network of mosques, the FIS [Islamic Salvation Front] dispensed religious and socialization programs as well as welfare and social services rarely provided by the government. . . . With more than three million followers, the party involved its members in voluntary activities, including collecting garbage, tutoring high school students, and offering medical care services for needy patients."[20]

This transformation of Islam was inspired by the ideas of thinkers such as Iqbal, Qutb, Shariati, and Khomeini, for whom God recedes into the background and becomes less accessible. ("The Essence Itself is something that lies totally beyond the reach of man, and even the Seal of the Prophets, the most knowledgeable and noble of men, was unable to attain knowledge of the Essence. The sacred Essence is unknown to all but Itself.[21]) Hence, human beings are on their own, equipped only with the Word of God[22] and the example of the Prophet, who was not content with Islam as theory but converted it into a practical reality. ("Our real and basic approach would be to find out what type of practical life [the] Qur'an demands of us. What is that concise concept of the universe and life which [the] Qur'an wants us to establish?"[23]) The world is God's place; it is sacralized. "There is no such thing as a profane world. All this immensity of matter constitutes a scope for the self-realization of spirit. All is holy ground. As the Prophet so beautifully puts it: 'The whole of this earth is a mosque.'"[24]

Like the Prophet, Muslims must do God's work on earth. ("Man is a representative of God in the universe as well as His trustee."[25]) Muslims must strive to implement God's instructions (contained in the Qur'an) to construct an Islamic community on earth. ("It is our duty to create a favorable social environment for the education of believing and virtuous individuals, an environment that is in total contradiction with that produced by the rule of *taghut* and illegitimate power."[26]) These writers call upon Muslims not just to believe Muhammad's words but to emulate his deeds. They must create a modern society according to Islamic principles. ("Once a man has become a true human being, he will be the most active of men. He will till the land, but till it for God's sake. He will also wage war. . . ."[27]). Islam is about making a better world. ("If a Muslim shows no concern for the affairs of his fellow Muslims, he is not a Muslim, the Prophet [upon whom be peace] states this in a tradition, even if he constantly says, '*La ilaha illa Llah.*'"[28]

Each writer claims to echo the most fundamental ideas of the religion: that Islam has always meant concern about the here and now; that Islam is about the pursuit of justice in this world; that it always encouraged the good life; that it never, unlike Christianity, insisted upon other-worldly asceticism; that it puts human beings squarely in charge of their own fate; that it opposes monarchy; that it stands for learning and improvement. They would want their insistence on these points to appear unremarkable, a mere reiteration of standard Qur'anic truths. But the effect of their reiteration has been thoroughly remarkable. Muslims have been energized in the pursuit of worldly goals; all across the Islamic world, these ideas have encouraged Muslims to sacrifice their time, their wealth, and even their lives in the name of a better community on earth.

Both Iqbal and Shariati draw direct analogies between the Protestant reformation and the redirection of Islam they seek to promote. Iqbal writes, "We are today passing through a period similar to that of the Protestant revolution in Europe, and the lesson which the rise and outcome of Luther's movement teaches should not be lost on us. A careful reading of history shows that the Reformation was essentially a political movement. . . . ".[29] Shariati says that an enlightened person "should begin by an Islamic Protestantism similar to that of Christianity in the Middle Ages, destroying all the degenerating factors which, in the name of Islam, have stymied and stupefied the process of thinking and the fate of the society, and giving birth to new thoughts and movements." Such a movement would, in his view, "unleash great energies and enable the enlightened Muslims to" use the resources of existing society to create "energy and movement"; to generate a sense of social responsibility; to bridge the gap between elites and masses; to take the religious weapon away from those who use it to enhance personal power; to launch a religious renaissance that will pave the way to cultural independence, "returning to and relying on the authentic culture of the society"; and to "eliminate the spirit of imitation and obedience" and replace it with a "critical revolutionary, aggressive spirit of independent reasoning (*ijtihad*)."[30]

A broad set of worldly behaviors has acquired fresh and enhanced legitimacy. Some resemble "traditional" behaviors. For example, many younger women whose mothers dress in European style have begun to wear various versions of modest, Muslim dress. Yet such dress, far from forcing women back into traditional roles, appears rather to legitimize their presence and participation in education, the modern economy, and even public life. The separation of women and men in the workplace in Saudi Arabia, invoked in the name of tradition, serves the purposes (perhaps inefficiently) of a modern society. "Islamic banking" honors the traditional ban on usury without seriously disrupting modern finance. Religious programming dedicated to the preservation of tradition constitutes the price for *ulama* acceptance of television in Saudi Arabia. The result is legitimation of the electronic medium.

In Iran, the creation of an Islamic Republic occasioned a rethinking of the secularization hypothesis in the West. Some interpreted government of the *faqih* as a throwback to tradition rather than as an original creation of Ruhollah Khomeini from bits and pieces of the Shi'a tradition. Critics tended to focus on institutions such as the Council of Guardians and on the role of the *faqih*, somehow neglecting the blessing necessarily conveyed by the Islamic Republic on an elected presidency and an elected *majlis*. The constitution identified Islam with elections, and the clerical class further legitimated the institutions by dominating elections and debate. While not all of the clerical class accepted Khomeini's new, secular tack, the politicking and debate on public view in the *majlis* has identified Islam with a plurality of answers and positions that undermines the unity of the clerical class just as the creation of confessional parties in Europe undermined the coherence of the Catholic Church.

What is most striking about Iran is not the originality of the regime or its economic and social policies but rather the degree to which Islam has been used to authenticate a constitution, a war, an elected presidency, and an assembly created in the European-inspired Constitutional Revolution. Some policies inherited from the shah and then rejected by the Islamic Republic, such as birth control, have since been reinstated. Life, in at least some villages that remained relatively impervious to the modernization policies of the shah, appears affected in only superficial ways by the new regime.[31] Regime representatives have sought to convince villagers that they cannot be "true Muslims" as long as they practice magic. It will be interesting to see whether the Islamic Republic succeeds at modernization in areas where the imperial regime failed. Leonard Binder writes, "It is difficult to resist the temptation to argue that, after two decades, the naive optimism of those observers who placed the Iranian revolution within the framework of Crane Brinton's revolutionary stages, and those who predicted that the revolution would be structured by the long-term processes of modernization, have been justified by these recent events."[32] (He is referring to the elections that brought President Khatami to power.)

The secularization of Islam in the Middle East has produced a sacralization of political, social, and economic activities. To attack the leaders of the state has become a religious duty for some; hence, to defend itself, the state has associated itself more thoroughly with religion. In Egypt, the *ulama* of Al-Azhar, once intimidated by Nasser's power, have reemerged as an autonomous political force, drawn into the political battle by the state's need for legitimacy.[33] Twenty years ago economic planners had nothing to say about Islam, and Al-Azhar seemed to have nothing to say about planning.[34] Suddenly no decision can be taken without regard for the views of the Brotherhood and other Islamic activists, whose support for the government is a key to keeping the radicals at bay. The conservative Islamist groups look to Al-Azhar for leadership; the government needs the support of Al-Azhar for legitimacy.[35] As a result, al-Azhar, which only a few years ago appeared a mere appendage of the government, suddenly enjoys leverage once again. Al-Azhar wields secular power while government policy has become increasingly sacralized.

Islamist activity has energized society and politics within the nation-state framework. While the Ayatollah Khomeini urged all Muslims to accept his leadership in the immediate aftermath of revolution, neighboring states read his appeal as a fresh act of Iranian imperialism. The result has not been re-creation of the universal *umma* but a legitimation of the Iranian nation-state, a creature of European political conceptions and Reza Shah's armies. None of the previously mentioned scholars (Iqbal, Mawdudi, Shariati, Khomeini, Qutb, Ben Nabi, Ghannoushi), to my knowledge, have explicitly defended the nation-state as a political unit uniquely suited to the needs of an Islamic state.[36] Yet the political movements built from these fonts have, by dedicating themselves to the capture and maintenance of secular power, reinforced the nation-state framework.

Pakistan, Iran, and the Sudan exemplify sacralization of the nation-state while Algeria and Turkey resist the legitimization that Islamist support might provide; the elites in the latter two countries appear attached to a French version of secularism, a complete separation between religious authority and the authority of the state. Arkoun makes a convincing case that Mustafa Kemal embraced a particularly harsh version of French *laïcisme*, one that does not represent the British experience, much less the American.[37] French-speaking, French-educated elites in Algeria have, like the Turks, seen the Islamist movement as pure threat. The dominant forces in Turkey and Algeria would rely entirely on secular myth to bolster the state if they could. Meanwhile, the Islamists continue to solidify their respective nation-states by their opposition to current governments and policies within existing political boundaries. They are "participating" in politics, albeit in ways that may often be destabilizing.[38]

Even before Manfred Halpern raised the specter of neo-Islamic totalitarianism, a key area of debate was whether Islam would dampen political modernization in the Middle East or whether it would eventually help legitimate a liberal, competitive party system. The answer is not yet clear, but recent studies have cast considerable doubt on the thesis of an unchanging political culture, hostile to democratic development.[39] The Islamist movement reflects an objectification of Islam, a modern consciousness of religion as one aspect of life among others, a consciousness of Islam as a distinct set of beliefs and a set of hypotheses about what Islam ought to be.[40] Thanks to modern communications, this objectification has enlisted more and more voices. Critical thought about the nature of Islam and the duties it imposes has spread far beyond the ranks of the *ulama*. It has become much harder to deny that there are multiple interpretations of the great texts and multiple incarnations of historical Islam, as various individuals and groups seek to implement their version of Islamic faith. Professional groups, benevolent associations, student groups, women's prayer circles, and other phenomena have helped to animate civil societies in many Middle Eastern countries.[41] Vigorous public debate in Iran suggests movement toward greater openness and tolerance.[42] The country whose recent history most epitomizes the contemporary Islamist movement now looks more like a democracy than any of the more secular, Muslim states in the area with the exception of Turkey.

MODERNIZATION EAST AND WEST

The modernization paradigm, suitably reconsidered and revamped, looks better than it did twenty years ago. If it can be shorn of its simplistic hypothesis about secularization (which is closely linked to its dichotomous treatment of tradition and modernity), it may account more accurately for general trends in Middle Eastern countries than an alternative emphasizing Middle East exceptionalism. The current period may well be remembered as one in which a significant cultural shift in Muslim countries, occasioned by the emergence of Islamist movements, pushed individual Muslims toward a greater emphasis on this-worldly achievement in social, economic, and political terms. This cultural shift, when accompanied by changes in social organization, including improved education, may well foster economic growth.[43] In addition, increased prosperity and cultural shift may well be generating a propensity for democracy that modernization theory predicts.[44]

Inglehart regards the Islamist movement as a blip on the radar screen that will soon disappear.[45] He continues to hold to the secularization hypothesis embedded in the approach of Weber and so many others. Yet the objectification of religion, the breakdown of the old division between the City of God and the City of Man, the commitment of religious energies to the building of a better world, the characteristics of the Protestant reformation that Inglehart sees as critical engines of modernization in Europe, are also characteristics of the Islamic resurgence of this century. Inglehart finds religion a key to culture and repeatedly argues that culture is eminently mutable in the long run. Yet he neglects the possibility that religious developments in the Islamic world constitute the sort of cultural change he thinks is critical.

One could object that Weber emphasized the Calvinist transformation of religious asceticism into worldly asceticism. Calvinists showed particular enthusiasm for identifying their spiritual welfare with the acquisition of material wealth. Writers from Iqbal to Qutb have argued that the materialism of the West is repugnant to Muslims. They have tended to see modernization arguments, either liberal or Marxist, as anchored in assumptions about the materialistic tendencies of human beings, which they believe must be subordinated to spiritual values. Yet these writers also remind their readers that Muhammad sought a prosperous, harmonious, unified society. I find in their work no opposition to entrepreneurship and acquisition in the name of building an Islamic society.

The Islamist perspective conforms more closely to Luther's idea of "calling" than to Calvinist formulations. Weber wrote that Luther placed heightened value on the

> fulfillment of duty in worldly affairs as the highest form which the moral activity of the individual could assume. This it was which inevitably gave every-day worldly activity a religious significance, and which first created the conception of a calling in this sense. . . . The only way of living acceptably to God was not to surpass worldly morality in monastic asceticism, but solely through the fulfillment of the obligations imposed upon the individual by his position in the world. That was his calling.[46]

Da'wa, a word frequently translated as "call," figures prominently in Islamist movements everywhere. Mawdudi attacked the secularist materialism characteristic of both Marxism and liberalism, but he did not attack the idea of material improvement. Islam makes "man's material life into a 'thoroughly spiritual venture.'"[47] The Islamists, like the Protestants, vehemently oppose a separation between religious and secular matters. They say that religious standards must infuse social life, and it follows that rewards reaped in the pursuit of God's work through the exercise of one's "calling" should be regarded as signs of righteousness. Muhammad provided for the material and spiritual well-being of his community. Khomeini argued for the government of the *faqih* precisely because God would never have left the Shi'a without leadership to superintend the earthly well-being of his community until the hidden Imam reappears, as claimed in the Twelver theory of occultation.

Although he is not a student of Islam or the Middle East, Inglehart dismisses the Islamist movement as a temporary reversion to traditional values. His views, like many of those expressed in the 1970s and 1980s, reflect belief in the secularization hypothesis, despite the fact his own data show wide variation in the degree of societal secularization among the more prosperous countries of the world. He suggests that societies such as the United States, where a majority believes in God and goes to church regularly, will eventually join the more "progressive" states of northern Europe in greater secularism. It may be that the Islamist movement surged in Iran partly because of the rapidity (or unevenness and inequity) of changes wrought by modernization under the shah. The movement surely gathered momentum in Egypt and elsewhere from many of the more educated, modern elements of the population who recoiled from many of the symptoms of secular materialism of the West: its racy and raucous movies and TV shows and its relaxed standards of dress and contact between the sexes. The theorists of modern Islamism, from Iqbal to the present, start not from an analysis of the Qur'an but from a dissection of modern society and the thought on which it depends. They start from modernism in order to defeat it.

Even if that is their intent, it will not necessarily be the outcome.[48] Inglehart argues that a cultural shift toward an emphasis on achievement, structural social changes, a greater emphasis on education, and a growth of voluntary associations will trigger more rapid economic growth. Religion is a key element in culture, and religion in the Muslim Middle East is undergoing a transformation that both alters the value structure and fosters the growth of voluntary associations. It is probably too early to judge whether Islamist influences on education will reduce the modernist component, will reverse the trend toward the inclusion of girls, or will reduce or promote academic freedom. It seems unlikely, however, that a movement urging its followers to hear the call, seize the reins of power, and transform the world will ignore the potential of modern education any more than it has ignored the benefits of modern communication.

Inglehart links democratic stability to levels of trust in the political culture and levels of perceived well-being. He thus affirms, as have many others, that economic improvement increases the chances for democratic political arrangements. Inglehart adds, however, that culture mediates the relationship between economics and politics. The theory of civil society points in roughly the same direction. Economic development and social mobilization foster a growth in associational life, which in turn builds the mutual trust and civic habits that contribute to democratic growth. Plurality in economic life and in associational life leads toward plurality in political life.

The Islamist phenomenon has produced plurality at several levels. If Muslims are to be judged by their deeds rather than their words, then they are clearly promoting differentiation. If this world is in the hands of believers who must try to do God's will as best they can without benefit of privileged access to God, believers will necessarily take divergent paths. While each group may believe it constitutes the "true Muslims" as opposed to all others, the belief in a monopoly of truth becomes more difficult to maintain. While one group can conceivably seize power and impose its views, the opposition will also invoke Islam. Islam has become the language of politics.[49] If the Christian case is an example, then toleration of non-Muslim groups will probably be easier to achieve than toleration of Islamic diversity. In any case, recognition and toleration of plural viewpoints has become a necessity.

The sort of tolerance implied in Arkoun's view of Islam may nonetheless be a long way off.[50] For him Islam is all that it has ever been in thought and practice, together with what it might be. He would make every outcropping of Islam a separate object of study in the hope of providing a general picture all Muslims could embrace as true. That global historical truth would then be the foundation upon which Muslims can build anew. Arkoun has argued, in general, that contemporary Islamist movements oppose such a vision by virtue of their insistence on exclusive truth. Secular forces in Algeria, Tunisia, and elsewhere tend to argue that the Islamists, like fascist and communists, talk the talk of tolerance and democracy only to win power. Once in power they would inflict their exclusivist, authoritarian views on others.[51]

The question, however, is whether contemporary Islamism is moving the Middle East in a direction that denies the patterned interactions among politics, economics, and culture posited by modernization theory or whether it is reinforcing those patterns. I contend that the

Islamist movement, with its commitment to spiritual and material reform, is bringing Islam toward the direct embrace of the myth of progress, a myth that has been foreign and secular in the minds of many Middle Easterners. We may be witnessing the "Islamization of modernity."[52] Culture is changing, and the future is open-ended. The evidence for a rough-hewn parallelism with Europe outweighs the case for difference.

The Muslim Middle East fits Inglehart's model much better than he thinks. Islamists may be modernizers in spite of their ambivalence toward Western culture and their discomfort with the deterministic overtones of social scientific theory. They need feel no uneasiness with that fact. If the Islamist movement fosters an acceleration of trends toward social, economic, and political modernization, it will be because Muslims, confronted with the circumstances of the modern world, have chosen to move in that direction. They will have seized the world to make it serve them better. The apparent inconsistency stems not from their actions but from the persistence of the discredited secularization hypothesis.[53]

In fact, religion has not disappeared anywhere and the use of religious myth and symbol to bolster political legitimacy and to legitimate social behaviors remains characteristic of the West as well as of the East.[54] The question is not whether religion and modernity mix but how and with what consequences. Under what circumstances does a change in religious culture affect the course of social, economic, and political change? Under what conditions do changes in religious culture result from the evolution of social, economic, and political practices? Under what conditions does religion legitimate change? The queries are not new, but developments in the Muslim world have intensified the need for answers. Hence, both East and West need a more sophisticated understanding of the relationship between religion and modernization.

CHAPTER 9

The Transformation of Iranian Political Culture: From Collectivism to Individualism

A. Reza Sheikholeslami

THE RADICAL PAST

The Persian political vernacular before and immediately after the Revolution of 1978-79 was rife with what some viewed as "Marxist" precepts: conflict was too deep-seated to yield to reform; salvation could be attained only collectively; in a world populated by saints and sinners, compromise was a doomed and immoral aspiration; capitalism had no future.

In this variant of Marxism, capitalism would not generate its own antithesis in a scenario of dialectical inevitability—rather, the system would implode under the weight of its cumulative injustices and inequalities. Revolution would not be an impersonal mechanism of history but a chiliastic drama of moral redress—politics as eschatology. The prevailing social order would descend into a Tartarus from which only the pure of soul would emerge to rule a newly virtuous world. The workers, peasants, and the dispossessed would govern because of their moral, not productive, prowess.

This political outlook, steeped in dogmas of faith and the attendant judgmental polarities about the saved and the damned, bore less resemblance to structuralist Marxism than to the unbending theological certitudes of a revealed religion. Orthodox Marxism views morality, politics, and ideology as the superstructure of the productive base of society; in contrast, these Iranian Marxists upended the traditional theoretical structure by placing those superstructual elements at the base.

The most orthodox version of Marxism in Iran was that propagated by the Iranian Communist Party, the Tudeh. The Tudeh publications had little to offer on economics but instead focused on politics, conspiracies, and the castigation of renegades. The discussion of economics was limited to the immorality of the wealthy and the suffering of dispossessed.[1]

Ali Shari'ati, the ideologue of the Islamic Revolution, borrowed heavily from the Tudeh vernacular to unite religion and revolution. It was politics that determined what was of value in religion. To Shari'ati Shi'ism was a revolutionary political party with membership, organization, and social goals, mobilized to liberate the oppressed. The Shi'i expectation of the *Mahdi*, the Messiah, was no longer a remote prophecy but a summons to an imminent, decisive battle between the just and the unjust. The savior could lead only if the masses were ready to march.[2] As presented in contemporary political language, the faith became embroiled in daily secular concerns. This ideational underpinning of the Islamic Revolution merged primeval human anxieties with the language of scientific explanation. The modernity of this discourse placed the pillars of faith in a contemporary context. The popularity of Shari'ati's writings, although symptomatic of an influential current in Iranian political culture, remain a rhetorical gesture lacking in internal consistency.

Shah Mohammad Reza Pahlavi (1941-1979) was a religious popularizer like Shari'ati, and he also saw the appeal of "Marxist" political language, evoking its aura if not its substance in his own public discourse. The shah was habitually called the "leader of the revolution" by his compliant officials and the media. Instead of defending privilege and status in the manner of a standard conservative monarch, he aimed his rhetoric at the peasants, pointedly snubbing the wealthy landowners who had been among his strongest supporters.[3]

REVOLUTIONARY EXUBERANCE

The "Marxists" opposing the shah had little problem with the monarch's religious opponents. They were both essentially romantic. Under the influence of the Third World movements, the left had aped the attitudes and ideas of movements that exalted the primordial "authenticity" of the masses they saw as pitted against the decadence and mendacity of the urban educated middle class. The spectre haunting power the Third World power elites of the 1960s and 1970s was not Marx's disciplined industrial proletariat but Fanon's wretched of the earth, whose religiosity shielded them against colonization of the spirit.[4] The secular left in Iran abdicated its mission and accepted religious leadership—at times even eagerly. The task at hand was the overthrow of the "American gendarme," the shah. Any discussion that questioned the composition and hierarchy of the oppositional forces was counterrevolutionary. The myth that the religious ranks "stole" the revolution is a convoluted admission of errors by the secular left rather than a statement of fact. The various leftist factions cooperated with the clergy in annihilating one another, and they were still cooperating when they were unceremoniously denounced.

If the capitulation of the left to the clerics did not guarantee it a share in the new power structure, its language influenced the clerical articulation of political demands. The haves and the have-nots were transformed, without much imagination or alteration, into the mostakbar (the arrogant) and the mostaza'f (the oppressed). The clerical animosity toward "godless communism" and the Soviet Union was superseded by anti-American rhetoric and culture. Respect for private property, once the keystone of Islamic economics, was overshadowed by enthusiasm for confiscations. Adjudication, once a divine function from which many a respectable clergyman kept a respectful distance, became a tool of revolutionary justice, meted out hourly in kangaroo courts.

Ironically, many of the liberals in the Islamic Republic of Iran today are the very people who heavily borrowed the ideas and methods of the left during the first post-revolutionary decade. The religious revolutionaries sought to prove that their credentials were just as radical as those of the left. Their political discourse, therefore, remained dominated by collectivism. In economics, a more even distribution rather than more efficient production was the ostensible goal, to be guaranteed by a system of coupons.

The clerics won the power struggle but were still not ideologically secure. Three major events helped to buttress their psychological and political over the left: the takeover of the American Embassy in Tehran in 1979; Iraq's invasion of Iran in 1980; and the collapse of the Soviet Union in 1992. The occupation of the embassy by the students following the Line of the Imam established the clergy as the most conspicuous and seemingly militant opposition to the preeminent world power. The marches around the embassy symbolically clinched the victory of the Iranian dispossessed over "imperialism." This passion play was all the more powerful for enlisting the participation of the public. The public and the spectacle became one. The event created a collectivity that was goal-oriented and hopeful, reveling in its freshly acquired power. All other theoretical discussions of capitalism and international order were dwarfed by this very tangible display of triumphant insurgency.

The invasion of Iran by the Iraqi wedged the left into an even more awkward corner. The defense of the motherland was a widely felt moral obligation. The ardor for peace, rooted in the battle cries of the October Revolution, was swept way in the patriotic rush to wage war. What especially paralyzed the left was the spectacle of an apparently "socialist" state, Iraq, waging a war supported by the Soviet Union and the capitalist camp. Thwarted by inadequacy of its cherished ideals and prophecies in the face of these refractory realities, the left was ideologically muted and disarmed during the war years. In fact, its fall was brought about by what it prophesied for its capitalist opposition: inherent contradictions and failure to recognize objective historical conditions. As young men were killed on the battlefields, their bodies were ceremoniously carried to their hometowns for burial. In the final act of return to one's creator, it was, of course, the clergy who took charge. The dead became the charged symbols for the national community, an abstraction that transcended any theoretical or ideological formulation. The courage and the total sacrifice of the dead stood in stark contradiction to the left's pacifist silence, which struck many as a form of collaboration with the enemy. In short, to borrow a Marxist term, the left in Iran became ahistorical

Moreover, the decline and fall of the Soviet Union, the original socialist state, cast doubt on the overall viability of the socialist project. The Tudeh Party in Iran was traditionally loyal to Moscow's line. The decline of Moscow might have liberated the Party. Instead, it simply killed it. With the rising neoliberal tide of globalization, privatization became the rule. The boundary line between the saints and the sinners blurred. The saints of yesteryear were increasingly willing to negotiate with the erstwhile sinners. The left, which thrived on the crisp polarities of its theory, was once again betrayed by the uncooperative messiness of reality.

THE ROUTINIZATION OF THE REVOLUTIONARY SOCIETY

The ceasefire in 1988 not only brought to an end a "revolutionary war," thus obviating the need for constant mobilization; it also marked a retreat from revolutionary ideology. Soon thereafter, the founder of the Islamic Republic died. Free from the challenge by the left, accustomed to the demands and privileges of rule, and situated in a new global environment in which the culture of the haves was growing in appeal, the ruling elite became more elitist and less revolutionary. While the government was to some extent the prisoner of its own rhetoric, the masses were able to manifest their changing taste through their choice of cultural symbols, their new-found interest in Western-style consumption and free expression. Many of the radical activists who had occupied the American Embassy in Tehran now advocated revolutionary justice as opposed to "bourgeois" procedural norms and manned the tribunals for the distribution of private property to the producers; the have-nots became the most prominent defenders of liberalism. The leader of the Students Following the Line of the Imam published the liberal newspaper *Salam*, the forced closure of which sparked massive student protest at the university. In 1988, after the Iran-Iraq war, President Ali Akbar Hashemi-Rafsanjani opened the country economically, and a spoils system emerged. Poverty was no longer a virtue and prosperity no longer a sin.

The Offices for the Strengthening of Unity, set up by true believers to instill the universities with Islamic values, became centers for the pursuit of liberal political activities. Shari'ati, the embodiment of radical Islamic ideals, was replaced by Abd al-Karim Soroush. In contrast to Shari'ati's massive and unattributed although crude borrowings from the Marxist vernacular, Soroush's work emerges from the thought of Karl Popper, the empiricist theorist of the open society. With Soroush's rise to eminence a cautious liberal relativism has supplanted the confident certitudes of Shari'ati's vision of collective destiny.[5]

The upset victory of Mohammad Khatami in the presidential election of 1997 indicated the degree of political change. Khatami stood for forbearance, nationalism, and cultural openness.[6] He was especially forthright in his advocacy of women's rights.[7] His victory indicated that the electorate had decisively spurned the intolerant radicalism of the revolution's early years. Open joy replaced grim resoluteness as the chief public virtue. Khatami's body language, his willingness to smile, was probably a key to his electoral success. The society wanted some cheerfulness after two decades of blood and sacrifice. The willingness of the establishment to permit Khatami's election was also an indication that the power elite had come to accept the inevitability of change and the need for political and cultural space. In fact, Khatami has brought about little change. But he is the culmination of great social and political transformation.

RELIGIOUS AND NATIONAL BASES OF SOCIAL SOLIDARITY

It is often argued that Iran as a community is deeply rooted in religion. Others argue that nationalism, a strong sense of "Iranianness," is what binds the community. Others that nationalism limits and may even annul the universalism of a community based on a belief system. A closer look suggests the inadequacy of both views.

There are few overt manifestations of solidarity based on either faith or nation in contemporary Iran. Surely there is a sense of generalized religiosity, but it is often expressed in the form of aprivate piety devoid of its earlier collective symbolism and political messianism. The affluent have increasingly dabbled in classical Persian mysticism and Asian philosophies. Such belief systems, however, clash with the official doctrinal principles. One also notices the growth of a commercialized, "packaged" religiosity, its status-consciousness most glaringly evident in the ostentation and ritualized festivity of package tours to Mecca; it is a cultural expression more akin to a U.S.-style, upwardly mobile rite of passage than to spiritual devotion. The festivities in this milieu are less a celebration of a belief system than of an elite social standing.

Nationalism presents a mixed picture. The celebrations that followed the Persian victory over Australia in the semifinal World Cup in 1999 were spontaneous expressions of national pride. The emotional outbursts following the World Cup games in 2001, on the other hand, have been compounded as much of anger as of national pride. Other events that might have symbolized national solidarity have been downgraded. The last Wednesday of the year on the Persian calendar, the ancient Persian ritual, is still observed, but with less pomp than in the past. It is no longer a testimony to the continuity and the historical roots of the community; rather, it has become a catharsis of anger. Firecrackers and even grenades have replaced the gentle, warm, and flickering flames of the traditional burning of a small bush. Such anomic behavior bespeaks not respect for the past but frustration with the present.

There are few references to Iran in the papers or in conversations. Iran is mentioned when people talk about leaving it behind for other shores. The celebration of the No-Rooz, the ancient Persian New Year, used to be a rite of togetherness and rebirth through the symbolism of the nationalistic past. During the early postrevolutionary years, many patriots fought for its preservation in spite of the revolutionary elites' opposition. No-Rooz served as an organic expression Iranian identity separate from and even opposed to the official version relentlessly imposed by the authorities. The celebration of the Shab-e Yalda, the night of the winter solstice, was another occasion of collective recollection. Today, however, these created events have withered into formulaic, empty formalities. Those who cannot travel and thus cannot escape the No-Rooz are compelled to celebrate, albeit, in the quickest, most efficient style. Commercialization and imposed obligation—enforced by fear of social sanction—have replaced what was spontaneous participation in an act of social solidarity and patriotic pride.

This decline of the rites of togetherness might seem to portend the development of an anomic, fragmented, narcissistic, society.[8] However, Persia is not unlike other social systems we know. One does not often see flag-waving citizens in the West, with the partial exception of the United States. And when one encounters flag-wavers, one ponders their motives or their politics. The churches in the industrialized world are not crowded. Citizens are not sacrificing for their fellow-citizens. Once-spiritual holidays like Christmas have become a mass homage to Mammon. The wishes of the youth in Persia are not unlike those of "generation slump" in Japan, a country known for both industry and solidarity. The deterioration of the festival of fire in Persia in March 2001 was akin to the chaos of Thailand's celebration of the ancient festival of water. Thailand, after all, is a country that has seemingly successfully synthesized the tradition of the Orient and the innovation of the West. One often hears stinging critiques of a number of tends in the advanced industrial West: the increasing individuation, the rise in anomic behavior, the decline of the churches, the counterposition of ethnic pride to national unity, and the displacement of collective goals by narrow self-seeking. However, serious observers do not take these as symptoms of the demise of the industrial state.

Some observers seem to take a different interpretive tack in dealing with the Third World. Ethnic identities become synonymous with fragmentation. The search for personal fulfillment is identified as disillusionment with the state. The West tends to view the other, namely the rebellious Third World, through the prism of ideology, nationalism, religious fervor, and mass mobilizations. When such indicators are absent, observers tend to think that the state in question is facing disintegration. In fact, we see few of these social indicators in the developed West.

As Persia gradually integrates into the global system, the indicators for collective sentiments are becoming less observable. Iranian youth wants what their contemporaries want elsewhere: autonomy, joy, and entertainment. As confrontation and crisis yield to routine, active political participation subsides proportionately. Politics becomes the domain of the specialist, and the public becomes increasingly alienated. This has been the trend in the advanced societies. The aroused citizenry of yesterday is the complacently apolitical consumer of today. Persian society reflects this global trend toward depolitication, in which charisma, too, falls victim to routine. The charisma-based authority of Ayatollah Khomeini has given way to the instituitionalzed authority of the office of the *Rahbar,* the leader, which is exercised through a bureaucratic structure. Although this overall routinizing, and individualizing of life will generate a degree of disharmony, it can also be potentially salutary in its potential for critical reappraisal and creative renewal. The major problem that this dislocation has brought about in Persia is that expectations for goods and services have raced so far ahead of the supply.

In 1999, at the campus of Amir Kabir University, the Tehran Polytechnic, a simple play was published in a student magazine with limited circulation. The play became a national cause celebre. It was castigated by Ayatollah Ahmad Jannati, the secretary general of the Council of the Guardians, from the powerful pulpit of Tehran Friday sermons. The bazaar of Tehran was ordered to shut down in protest September 27. Yayha Safavi, the Commander of the Revolutionary Forces, publicly demanded that the shame should be washed away with blood alone. The Supreme Leader was outraged. In October, even the seemingly liberal minister of culture, Attaollah Mohajerani, asked for the punishment of the authors if it turned out that they had undermined religious values.[9]

The play centered on the advent of the Mahdi, the Messiah, and the absence of any followers to support the Mahdi's Messianic struggle to establish justice for all. Apparently, the potential supporters were too busy preparing for university entrance examinations and were, therefore, unable to celebrate the Imam's second coming.

This witty commentary accurately drew attention the decline of the sublime and the ascendancy of the mundane; the ascendancy of materialism over spirituality; the triumph of individualism over collective solidarity. It also indicated the degree to which celestial beings and symbols had been reduced to this-worldly and secularized competitors for attention in a more complex society. Indeed, it was a statement of disenchantment with leaders, particularly the charismatic ones who promise radical sweeping changes.

There were other signs of the blurring of the boundary line between saints and sinner. The utopian political culture of uncompromising battle of pure good against pure evil seemed to have morphed into a distinctly nonheroic accommodation to small satisfactions and the amorphous morality of gradual, pedestrian transformation.

In that very month of September, President Khatami, celebrating Ayatollah Khomeini's centennial, talked to an overflow crowd of ten thousand enthusiastic university students. They had voted for him two and half years ago, expecting that he would open up the political space, enhance social freedom, and bring about an open society. President Khatami's speech was instead a denunciation of the "spineless imitators of the West" and a praise of piety. The students had expected him to attack the monopolization of power and defend the virtues of pluralism. Yet, when the speech was over, the crowd burst with excitement. His name was repeatedly chanted and his pictures were waved on banners.

One cannot argue that the students were misinformed. In July of that year, the president had called the students' reaction to the vigilantes' attacks "the eye of the Satan." His statement denouncing the student movement was widely publicized. It seems that if the students could still support a statesman who had so overtly appeased the conservative power structure, then their search for an avatar was over. The politics of limited goals and compromise has begun. The proceduralist optimism that brought about the astounding electoral victory of Khatami in 1997 has lowered its expectations. Perhaps for for the first time in the history of modern Persia, a modus vivendi prevailed. The students had traded their program of total transformation for one of moderate and piecemeal change. They realized that Khatami is subject to constraints. The utopian impetuosity of the parents, who had felled the mighty shah, had given way to the quiet meliorism of their children.

The populace, including the students listening to the president, turned out in large numbers to vote in support of liberal reformism during the local council elections in February 1999, the parliamentary elections of February 2000, and the presidential election of June 2001—four unusually massive turnouts. Each election has been a clear declaration of support for the reformers, a testimony to the belief that electoral politics may be the route to collective salvation. The belief, so far, seems misplaced. Indications of disaffection with procedural politics are becoming clearer.

In the aftermath of electoral victories, there have been major setbacks for the reformist movements. When the newspaper *Salam* was closed down, the students expressed their anger through massive demonstrations. When Iran's mayor, Gholam-Hosain Karbaschi, the primary force behind Khatami's unexpected electoral victory, was put on trial for his irregular conduct, the sympathetic population stayed up until the early morning hours of the morning to watch the tapes of the trial on the television. The tapes were intentionally arranged to overlap with the most exciting World Cup games. Nevertheless, students, state employees, and taxi drivers stayed up late to watch the trial and vociferously defend the mayor next day.

However, when twenty to thirty newspapers (one cannot be certain of the figures anymore) were summarily shut down and a few of the editors were placed under arrest, there was no public outcry. When Abdollah Nouri, a vice-president and the former minister of interior was put on trial for his ideas, not his conduct, there was little public outcry.

The depoliticization process has been rapid. If collective action and massive and repeated turnouts are not enough to bring a measure of change, then cynicism and indifference soon eclipse confidence and hope. In Persia, as elsewhere, despair is the surest path to mass depoliticization.

Power positions have remained in the same old hands, or similar ones, after repeated and conclusive elections. The main centers of power—the Revolutionary Forces, the Judiciary, the National Radio and Television, and the Council of the Guardians—are not elected. The ironically named Expediency Council, which condemns various readings and analyses of religion, is unchanged. The large organizations that control public resources are subjected to no public accountability or electoral verdict. The Foundation for the Dispossessed employs more than thirty thousand people. It controls 28 percent of textile production, 42 percent of cement, 45 percent soft drinks, and 25 percent of sugar. The Endowment of the Eighth Imam, Astan-e Qods, employs more than nineteen thousand people.[10] Abbas Va'ez-Tabasi, the Chairman of the Endowment, answers to no elected body and arguably exercises more authority in the internal affairs of largest province of Persia than possibly the *Rahbar*. The Foundation for the War Disabled is just another example. These foundations, controlling much of the national economy, pay no taxes and are not answerable to the parliament or the executive. They act almost as sovereign empires. The landslide electoral victories of liberal candidates have not affected their *modus operandi.*

As a small group monopolizes the centers of power and capital, almost 800,000 Persians enter the work force annually. Half of the university graduates are unable to find employment. The political participation of the youth has not brought them a share in the economy or in the distribution of power. The immediacy of the problem of just making has contributed to the decline of political activism.

In March 2001 an extensive statement was issued by the office of the Supreme Leader. Having expressed his gratitude to the chairman of the Expediency Council, he bestowed upon him the necessary authority to supervise the national economy. Matters from water to energy resources and economic stabilization were placed in his hands. The chairman is, of course, Hashemi-Rafsanjani, who had run for a seat in parliament in a scandalous and unsuccessful electoral campaign just a year earlier. Now the direction of the economy, one of the few important areas that had been entrusted to the president, was shifted to another powerful unelected official. Surprisingly, even matters relating to oil and water were placed under the control of a man who was resoundingly spurned by the voters. The disregard for the popular will was indeed brazen. What was more significant was that the people who in the past followed the news were uninformed about the edict and, when informed, professed indifference. In a feedback loop of declining democracy, such usurpations of the popular will now thrive on the very depoliticization they first engendered.

Disillusionment in politics, in part fed by the grind of finding and maintaining a livelihood, is the prevailing tenor of public life in Iran. Much of the political debate among the politically active gains no audience on the Persian "street." "They are all the same" is a common, doleful refrain of indifference.

The inward look, the concentration on the individual's struggle to make a living, the disillusionment with politics, and preoccupation with material goods are particularly evident in the successful Persian films made after the elections of 1997. The films nominated in 2001 for the Fajr Film Festival, a major annual event, dealt preponderantly with material privation and the individual's predicament as opposed to earlier appeals to collective issues and ideals.

The films portray the growing importance of women in the workforce and in maintaining families. Activities previously deemed immoral for women now seemed less so in the absence of the traditional male breadwinner. With their role as family guardian undermined by economic exigency, men are judged harshly as the agents of an oppressive patriarchal social order. The social commentary is conveyed in an intimate, understated style that focuses on the plight of the individual. The films show individuals so overwhelmed by the struggle for meager sustenance that the quest for collective salvation seems an idle indulgence. Because they have been sacrificed themselves, they are unable to make sacrifices for any collectivity larger than their own immediate families.

Under the Moonlight goes one step further by questioning the authority of leaders who cannot be providers. A homeless theological student, living under a bridge, is plagued by doubts about his ability to pursue his clerical vocation. By serendipity, his cloth is stolen by a hungry boy. The right of anyone, even a man of religion, to shepherd his people can be seriously questioned.

The popularity of the film is a barometer of the anomie prevailing in Iranian society, the atomism bred by unrestrained individualism. With traditional moral boundaries softening, the public notes the widening gap between official pronouncements as social reality. Much of the political debate bears no resemblance to the concerns of the ordinary man. Even the reformist agenda, so often vindicated at the polls, has failed to sink deep roots in the electorate, which supports it, but more as a gesture of spite to the conservatives than as a vote of confidence in the liberals. The former are therefore emboldened to dismiss the initiatives of the latter without incurring the wrath of the masses.

According to an analyst writing recently in a government-published newspaper,

> There is no doubt that our people have lost their spirit. . . . Our failures in production and services . . . indicate that the proper outlook does not exist. . . . In the last twenty years investment has continuously declined. . . . Investors regret having invested, and wish they had exported their capital or had served as middlemen. . . . Why are we so hopeless? It makes little difference if you have a job or not. You will not be able to rent a room on a salary. . . . If freedoms guaranteed by the Constitution are restored, if nepotism is controlled, if healthy competition should replace opportunism and *"rant-khari"* (concession through influence peddling), then we will have our enthusiasm restored. At present, however, we most clearly observe depression among the youth. As to the middle-age population, they have accepted that as far as they are concerned, it is simply over.[11]

A scholarly journal published by the Ministry of Islamic Guidance and Culture agrees that since 1989 concern with material values has outpaced religious values. Ever since the revolution, one author points out, the number of congratulations and condolences addressed to government officials and printed on the costly cover page of the two main daily newspapers have increased substantially.[12] He further notes,

> The Islamic groups in high schools have failed although all the resources were available to them. . . . The youth is becoming alienated. Islamic norms and organizations [*nahads*] have been defeated. . . . The Quranic classes have been relatively successful. The Baseej [Revolutionary Mobilization] has utterly failed to appeal to the students.[13]

The decline in religiosity is inversely proportional to the rise in popularity Western popular culture. It is estimated that there were 3.5 million video recorders in Persia in 1995. This means that about 13 million people had access to a video recorder. Most video recorders were used for illegal tapes, some 80 percent of which featured American films.[14] The video spearhead of the cultural invasion has been reinforced by a rearguard of posters, CD's, the Internet and computer diskettes.

Oddly, the Islamic Revolution has eased the march of this cultural penetration. While traditional families in the past prevented their children (especially their daughters) from going to the cinema, attending the university, or participating in group activities, the Revolution extensively deployed the resources of cinema, television, and music, promoting mass participation in their creation. The revolution also mobilized women. The post-revolutionary regime unleashed a pervasive politicization through frequent mass mobilizations. The unintended consequences of such group activities included the breakdown of the traditional family structure, alienation, and the individualist quest for personal joy. In sweeping away the shah, the revolution weakened reflexive veneration of all traditional authority. Religiosity declined as drug addiction rose. Sohaila Jello-Dar-Zadeh, a leading member of the parliament recently stated, "In the course of our meetings with the officials in charge of drug control, we discovered that these officials and the organizations they head are exhausted. As the saying goes, they have given up." She identified unemployment, factory closings, general poverty, and the paucity of entertainment as the chief causes of drug addiction.[15] The escape from depression or boredom appears to arise from the decline of traditional values and authority. As one observer has pointed out, "Our youth are attracted to styles and manners which we had not experienced before. The new style is in opposition to what is being propagated from the official tribunals. The official tribunals propagate the unacceptable. Our youth demand new models of behavior.[16]

In the last two decades, Iran has been radically transformed from a society based on collective values, where "sameness" was the ideal, to a society based on individual needs, where differences are the rule. In Durkheim's terms, "mechanical" solidarity has been replaced by an "organic" one. The revolution's galvanizing slogan, *vahdat-e kalameh*—"oneness of word"—has been displaced by the spirit of the current discussion of religious texts, *ghera'at-ha-ye mokhtalef*—"different readings."

SECTION FOUR

Alternative Models of Coexistence

CHAPTER 10

Religio-Cultural Diversity: For What and with Whom? Muslim Reflections from a Postapartheid South Africa in the Throes of Globalization

Farid Esack

But for the fact that God continues to repel some people by means of others, cloisters, and churches and synagogues and mosques (all places of worship), wherein the Name of Allah is mentioned much would surely have been razed to the ground. (Qur'an 22:40)

The humanism, moderation, rationality, flexibility, and openness that characterize much of the Islamic tradition are highly prized by Muslims and leave many of them disinclined to accept arguments that their religion is a static body of doctrine impervious to change and immune to potentially valuable ideas from the West. Thus, outside observers can easily be misled if they assume that the average Muslim considers the more exotic, reactionary Islamic views to be more consonant with his or her own Islamic tradition than those that correspond to the aspirations of contemporary Muslims for enhanced rights and freedoms. (Ann Elizabeth Mayer pp. 145, 146)

1.   THROUGH THE EYES OF THE BEHOLDER

Quite a while ago a Christian student asked me if I considered myself a staunch Muslim; I felt a bit like Alice in Wonderland when she was asked by the caterpillar "And who are you?" She replied, "I . . . I hardly know, Sir. Just at present, at least I know who I was when I got up this morning, but I think that I must have changed several times since then." I told the student: "Well, it depends on what you mean by 'staunch,' what you mean by 'Muslim,' and on the particular moment that you are asking the question or want the answer to apply to."

In this opening paragraph, I have betrayed/disclosed where I am. Just before the protective barriers against the postmodern demons of tentativeness and heurism are raised, let me hasten to add that this ceaseless transformation of self is not without an undying commitment to Islam, *Tawhid*, and the creation of a world wherein it is safe to be human and everyone free to serve Allah. Yet even as I speak about an "undying commitment," I acknowledge that life and living is a process not entirely unrelated to death and dying. In other words, my commitment is always in various stages of growth and death. It is possible to pursue certain commitments while valuing tentativeness and a space for otherness. In other words, pluralism does not have to be an appendage of a putatively value-free postmodernity.

It may sound awfully vain center my remarks on the question "Who am I?" I have chosen to do this because I believe that disclosure is a precondition for conversation since there are inescapable tinsels that color the eyes of every beholder. The alternative to this disclosure, the insistence on "objectivity" or a privileged gnostic access to the truth, may make for interesting sermons but not for engaging conversation.

The undisputed reference points for Muslims are the Qur'an and the Prophet Muhammad's definitive conduct (*Sunnah*). The unavoidable point of departure from which these reference points are approached, however, is oneself and the conditions that locate that self. In ignoring the ambiguities of language and history and their impact on interpretation, there is no effective distinction between normative Islamic morality and what the believer "thinks" it to be. Both traditionalism and fundamentalism deny any personal or historical frame of reference in the first instance. While they will insist that normative Islamic morality is to be judged solely by the Qur'an and the *Sunnah*, they will throughout their discourse simultaneously imply that they are the only ones who have correctly understood it.

So Who Am I?

I am a Muslim male, the youngest of six sons and one daughter (the daughter's "illegitimate" existence discovered more than ten years after the death of my mother [May Allah have mercy upon her soul]), the son of a mother who died in her early fifties as a victim of apartheid, patriarchy, and capitalism and of a father who abandoned his family when I was three weeks old. As a young South African student of Islamic theology in Pakistan with bitter memories of apartheid, I saw the remarkable similarities between the oppression of blacks in South Africa and of women in Muslim society. Later, in my years as a Muslim liberation theologian-cum-activist in the struggle against apartheid, I deepened my awareness of the relationship between the struggle of women for gender justice and that of all oppressed South Africans for national liberation.

I come from a society where "peaceful coexistence" was initially a deep yearning of the vast majority of our population; later, during the years of the liberation struggle, it became a source of much suspicion. Only recently has "peaceful coexistence" been re-embraced, even if tentatively, as a long-term goal among our people. The language of peaceful coexistence in our country's history was invoked by the apartheid ruling minority when they realized that the game of racial domination was up; we, the oppressed majority, saw our sacred task as one of making apartheid South Africa ungovernable. In our society we found an echo in the voice of Paul E. Salem, who, looking at the problem of peace in a more global context, said, "To the dominated members of the 'pseudo-imperial' world system, peace may be something that they might indeed seek to *avoid*, and conflict may be an objective that they might seek to invigorate in order to destabilise the world system and precipitate its crisis or collapse."[1]

In postapartheid South Africa, I am becoming increasingly aware of the limitations of socioeconomic transformation imposed by the market on so-called free societies such as ours and of the need to locate any discourse on cultural diversity within these constraints.

2.   CENTERING MUSLIM MINORITIES

Muslims inhabiting countries where they are in a minority comprise approximately one third (270 million) of the world's Muslim population.[2] Despite their large numbers, they are a relatively marginalized group in Islamic discourse. Muslim "minorities" are, of course, not the only ones who are being ignored in the attempts to find a new relevance of Islam to contemporary challenges. How well known is the name of Seyyed Hossein Nasr in Arabic scholarly circles? How significant are developments in Islam in Indonesia, a country that has the world's largest Muslim population? How many Urdu, Persian, and Turkish scholars are being read in the Arab world? It is only in the recognition of the endeavours of Muslims and Muslim thinkers all over the world and in our comprehensive embrace of our ever-expanding heritage that we are able to seek the best for our societies and for the *ummah* "minorities," which are often privileged to be free from Muslim governments and have a significant contribution to make the discourse of cultural pluralism and diversity. Liberated from the burdens of "Islam in power," our survival and growth has depended on how we have, for better or for worse, negotiated the contours of this discourse. The most important reason, however, why the Muslim minority experience is critical in attempts to address the issue of diversity is that the religious experience of all of humankind today is essentially a minority experience. In our times one can only speak of a dominant or dominating religion in respect of other religions. However, in terms of the economic system and its global structures that really shape the culture and values of humankind today, all of us are in the same minority boat. While many religious adherents still seek to augment the mass of people who share this or that religious label, vast numbers are being lost on a daily basis to the religion of the market, a faith that allows you to hold on to the illusion of your own religious label while stripping it of all meaning.

3. MUSLIMS IN SOUTH AFRICA: A MICROCOSM OF THE UNIVERSAL UMMAH

South African Muslims, little more than 1 percent of the country's population,[3] are not only a significant part of the country's cultural and sociopolitical landscape[4] but also of the world of Muslim minorities. Composed of labourers, political exiles, prisoners, and slaves, they first arrived in South Africa in 1652 from various parts of the East. Together with local converts to Islam they were usually referred to as Malays despite the fact that less than 1 percent of them came from today's Malaysia.[5] Mainly adherents of the Shafi' *madh-hab*, they were concentrated in the Cape and, under apartheid, they were one of the seven subgroups of "coloreds." As if reflecting the essentially eclectic nature of the community's actual origins rather than a mythologized "Malaysia," the dominant `*Ulama* group resorts to any of the four *madh-habs* (schools of Islamic jurisprudence) in resolving juristic issues in a manner most compatible with the requirements of a changing South African society—even while publicly holding on to the notion that they are Shafis.)

A second stream of Muslims arrived in 1860 from India along with some Hindus to work as indentured labourers on Natal's sugar plantations. Mostly hailing from Surat in India, this group is today mostly located in the provinces of Kwazulu-Natal and Gauteng. A large community originating from Kokan in India who follow the Shafi' *madh-hab* is also found in Johannesburg, Pretoria, and Cape Town. In the past twenty years or so, a number of converts from the Black townships, many of them opting for the Maliki *madh-hab*, have increased the ranks of the Muslims. These postapartheid children, who refuse to be second class in anything, are beginning to own Islam. Even more marginalized are the more recent arrivals, economic refugees from various parts of the world ranging from Pakistan to Nigeria.

The two dominant Muslim groups have coexisted in a workable although sometimes tense relationship, and the present generation of Muslims is the arguably the first one where marriage regularly occurs across the cultural divide with minimal familial acrimony. The various provincial clerical bodies have an unwritten agreement to publicly respect each other's spheres of operation, mostly geographical, but often cultural.[6]

Aside from the plurality of ethnicity, culture and *fiqh*, one also finds a diverse approach to religious life, with Sufi groups coexisting and intersecting with those of a more urban and puritan orientation. While the history of Islam's survival in this part of the world is commonly attributed to the work of the Sufi *tariqahs*, the late twentieth-century proliferation of Wahabi and Deobandi Islam has provided Muslims with a sounder base in traditional scholarship. As elsewhere in the world of Islam, Sufi orders (even if informally organized in South Africa) came more and more to represent the true religious feeling of the people, and the lawyer-theologians to whom the *ummah* are indebted for their cohesion have to make their peace with them. Theology has been adapted to accommodate the more moderate version of Sufism, and the majority of the Sufis themselves adopt a positive attitude to communal life; the consensus of the pious and the learned gradually approves ideas and practices that at first appeared difficult to reconcile with ancestral tradition. In short, everything is done to prevent the cleavage between the two concepts of the religious life resulting in full pluralistic separation of their adherents (Von Grunebaum, 1962:44, 45).

The abuse of ethnic identity under apartheid has often led to the embarrassing description of progressive Muslims as "Indians,"

"Malay," and so on. The term "colored" was viewed as pejorative by those described as such; they usually referred to themselves as "so-called colored." Now, freed from the fetters of apartheid and wooed by the governments of India, Malaysia, and Indonesia, many are beginning to describe themselves as "Malay" or "Indian," and the "so-called" has been unceremoniously dropped as a prefix to "colored."

Furthermore, the country's new constitution values cultural diversity and undertakes to protect not only the eleven of the country's languages but also to promote and ensure respect for Arabic, Hebrew, Sanskrit, and other languages used for religious purposes (Chapter 1, article 5.b.ii). Recent legislation affords legal recognition to customary and religious marriages, and the constitution created a permanent commission dealing with language and culture.

South African Muslims lead shared lives of prosperity and poverty, power and marginalization; the country is equally indifferent to most poor refugees, irrespective of national origin or religious preference. With a few exceptions—mostly related to school facilities—Muslims commune with adherents of other religions in a wide array of milieu: on the factory floor, in business, in sports, and in political organizations. "Now we come to the great problem," said a Christian missionary more than sixty years ago about this shared existence. "Christians and Moslems live next door to each other and often rent rooms in the same house. They grow up from childhood together" (Hampson 1934, 273).

In a truly welcoming sense, the doors of diversity are really only now being flung open in the new South Africa. Having rushed through them, Muslims are only now discovering that some other rather unwelcome pedestrians have also walked through. In a society kept in chains for so long, one has little control over the demons--often one's own—that are loosed when the doors of freedom and diversity are opened. The waning of state authority and the attendant growth of personal freedom had led to a mushrooming of the sex industry and a steep rise in crime in general and the drug trade in particular. Many Muslims are in the forefront of a violent and bitterly controversial public struggle against gangsterism and drug abuse initiated by People Against Drugs and Gangsterism (Pagad).[7]

While numerous committed South Africa Muslims are making a significant contribution to the reconstruction of our society, several segments of the community display a haunting fear of the light of democracy and freedom.

The above brief overview raises significant questions of identity, religion, and history. Who are we? Of our Muslimness and South

Africanness we are certain; beyond those, though, there are several more labels: blacks, coloreds, PDI's (previously disadvantaged individuals), NPB's (newly privileged blacks), Malays, Shafi's, Hanafi, Barelvi, and Deobandi. Is it "or" or "and"? Does it depend on when the question is being asked or by whom? At what point does being a Shafi' or Maliki cease to be a religious-legal issue and become a sociocultural one?

Based on my insights into the South African *ummah*, I want to highlight a few of these issues: the unstable nature of identity, the way the *ummah* transcends geography, the way religious tenacity combines with tenuousness, and the notion of an *ummah* beyond religious dogma.

The Unstable Nature of Identity

We are all made up of multiple identities, depending on where we come from, what we believe in, where we are, and who we are interacting with at a particular moment.[8] The insistence on viewing identity as stable, static, or monolithic is usually reflective of our insecurity, our fear of the unknown parts of our selves emerging when the label is peeled off. So we desperately hold on to the label, although the single certainty about its contents is inescapable uncertainty. Our cultures are increasingly uncoupled from their territorial bases and, as never before, we are becoming the carriers of multiple cultures. The truth is that there is no stable self or a stable other. Every encounter of the self with the other contributes to a continual transformation. Intermarriages, linguistic cross-pollination, migration, the Internet, McDonalds, CNN, and the emergence of Christian Jewish, Muslim, Christian, Buddhist, Hindu worshippers of the Market—these are only the more obvious manifestations of the blurring of traditional cultural borders - if indeed, there were ever borders. In the words of Salman Rushdie,

> We have come to understand our own selves as composites, often contradictory, even internally incompatible. We have understood that each of us is many different people. . . The nineteenth-century concept of the integrated self has been replaced by this jostling crowd of "I"'s. And yet, unless we are damaged, or deranged, we usually have a relatively clear sense of *who we are*. I agree with my many selves to call all of them "me." (*Time,* August 11, 1997).

In quoting the author of the *Satanic Verses*, I am reminded of a saying about Satan attributed to the Prophet (Peace be upon him) and cited by Seyyed Hossein Nasr: "Satan hates sharp points and edges." (1988:131). Yet here I am, not blunting the edges but dealing with the notion that in culture there are no sharp edges. Ali Mazrui speaks of Africa being a "cultural bazaar" where "a wide variety of ideas and values drawn from different civilizations compete for the attention of potential African buyers." (1986:97). Taking a broader sweep, Akbar Ahmed reflects on how "mainstream Muslim tradition combined with local culture to produce interesting mutations [that are] most pronounced in mosque architecture."

> In Africa, the Mali-Songhai mosques are marked by buttresses, pinnacles, and soaring minarets, with exposed beams giving a hedgehog effect. In Java and Sumatra mosques are layered and pagoda-like. In China they had gabled tiled roofs which sloped upward, ending in dragon tails. (1988, 109)[9]

Among the Muslims of South Africa there is a microcosm of the universal *ummah* with its competing and ever-changing historicocultural differences among its overlapping subsets. Islam was the cement of religious belief that held different communities in various states of togetherness and sought to eliminate customs that appeared to be incompatible with those beliefs. Even here the boundaries shifted within specific communities: for example, in 1894 Muslims of the Cape were willing to die in their resistance to inoculation against smallpox, believing it a vain human attempt to defy the will of Allah. Nearly a century later inoculation became a prerequisite for anyone traveling on pilgrimage to Mecca, so the will of Allah was now to ensure health for all via inoculation. In 1886 Muslims rioted in the streets of Cape Town when their ancestral burial place, the Tana Baru, was closed down and they were offered a new burial site some distance out of the city. They insisted that following the bier on foot for the entire journey was a religious requirement and that they could not travel in a horse-drawn cart (cf. Davids, 1984). By 1994 Muslims were walking only a hundred meters or so, with the bier completing the rest of the journey in a Japanese-designed station wagon, its parts manufactured in Europe and assembled in South Africa and painted in green, "the Prophet's color."

While postmodernity has deepened our appreciation of the complexity of identity, these reflections are far from mere theoretical musings for Muslim organic intellectuals (a concept coined by Gramsci), those thinkers who grapple with the challenge of cultural diversity while engaging in a struggle for a more just society.

First, when we deal with the *ummah* or with the "other," we are really dealing with persons who are the carriers of multiple and ever-changing selves. We can no longer speak of "Americans," "Algerians," "Kurds," or "Blacks" but must be willing to understand and appreciate the nuances and distinctness of each community.

Second, we observe that communities are not unchanging entities that we can collectively hold hostage for crimes committed against an equally ahistorical and essentialist group called "our people." "The Jews are our enemies," I often hear, to which I respond: "Well, that may be the case, but tell me, which ones? Where do they live? When did they do what? What were their names? What kind of support did they have and from whom? And, besides, who are the "our" in "our enemies"?

Third, while it is true that the way we deal with others is really a reflection of the way we deal with ourselves, the process of learning to live alongside our own many selves-intracommunity diversity-must accompany, not precede, the process of living alongside the other. When learning to live with the self precedes learning to live with the other, then self-discovery runs too great a risk of degenerating into a narrow narcissism, and the *ummah* develops an obsession with controversies like sighting the moon and the correct method of slaughtering a cow.

An Ummah Beyond Geography

Despite the unwillingness of a previous generation of Indian South African Muslims to allow their offspring to marry Malay Muslims or the still-prevalent racial prejudice against "our Zanzibari brothers," the notion of the *ummah* has not only survived but also continues to give Muslims a deep sense of belonging.

Muslim armies would fight each other, communities in different linguistic areas would, in many regards, go their own way; but no political shifts and hardly any local spiritual divergences, no differences in the customs governing the believers' everyday lives, would detract from their intense identification with the *ummah Muhammadiyyah*, the Muslim community, that had gradually come to extend from the southern Philippines to the Atlantic coast of Morocco, from North Central Asia to South Africa, with some offshoots sprouting as far afield as the Americas. The individual groups might hardly know of one another, the rank and file would be practically precluded by geographical and linguistic estrangement, and visitors might be shocked by mores and practices of other units—yet the *ummah* has remained a pluralistic unit in the strictest sense of the word. (Von Grunebaum, 1962)

While Muslims are not averse to behavior that seeks to reducing Allah to a tribal deity or to a particular nation's hockey or cricket fan, there has always been the assumption that we worship a Universal God-*rabb al-alamin*-who elevated our understanding of self from the tribal and ethnic organizational level to the universal community. The *ummah,* at its best, is thus an open-ended community under one universal God and transcends the boundaries, however elusive, of ancestry or ethnicity. This notion of a universal community under God has always been a significant element in Muslim discourse against tribalism and racism.

While numerous South African Muslims continued to hold those of darker skin pigmentation in contempt, they never attempted to produce a theological justification for their prejudices. On the contrary, a number of sacred texts Qur'anic texts became rallying slogans for nonracialism and inclusivity: for example, the Qur'anic "And we have created you in tribes and nations so that you may understand each other" and hadith such as "There is no is distinction between an Arab over a non-Arab, nor of a non-Arab over an Arab; lo all of you are the children of Adam, and Adam was made of dust."

There is a justifiable pride in this unequivocal rejection of tribalism and racism on the one hand, and rejoicing in inclusivism and diversity, on the other. However, much of progressive Muslim discourse today tends to overlook a fundamental exception: *illa bi'ttaqwa*-except in the fear of God. This point raises two issues: (1) the admirable tenacity of the faith of Muslims and the way they identify with the *ummah* alongside the simultaneous erosion of faith as something personal and dynamic, and (2) the notion of an *ummah* beyond dogma.

Between Tenacity and Tenuousness

It is remarkable that a community at the Southern tip of Africa could have survived in relative isolation from the wider world of Islam for more than three hundred years, never ceasing to see itself as a part of that world. This communal consciousness is a manifestation of the universal *ummah* defying all conventional understandings of community. The *ummah* also thereby affirms the notion of a community based on shared participation or aspiration towards a more sacred life. In the words of Von Grunebaum,

There is nothing in its location in the face of the earth that can force a community, however isolated it may be, to consider itself part of a larger if actually remote community, unless it be its free decision, motivated by a realization that by so doing its members will partake of the higher life, a nobler and more truly human existence than by pursuing their own ways without acknowledging themselves parts of an inter-tribal, international, intercultural entity. (1962:41)

How to account for the steadfast adherence to Islam among those who came the Cape of Good Hope in the early seventeenth century as slaves and political prisoners? Many of them remained Muslim, even using their own sense of community to provide a larger home to non-Muslim slaves. Visitors are often impressed with the apparent tenacity of the faith of South African Muslims, the dynamism of their community life, and their vibrant and very visible role in the country's socioeconomic life.

Yet underneath the surface all is far from well. Marches against gangsterism and drugs have often filled Muslims with a sense of pride that we can turn our drug-infested communities around. Yet alert drug dealers watching these marches from the side-lines have pointed out that among the most vociferous chanters of "Death to the drug merchants" are some of their most dedicated clients.

A year or two ago I was asked by the father of a Muslim girl to speak to his future son-in-law, who was about to convert to Islam. In talking to him about the religio-cultural taboos of the Muslims, I mentioned that pork was forbidden in a Muslim home. He casually mentioned that would not be a problem because his Muslim future wife is a closet bacon-eater. (Meanwhile, his father-in-law regularly passed on manuals on performing *salah* to this convert, who was only interested in learning the physical motions in order to blend in during the occasion of the "Id prayer")

These two vignettes underscore the extent of brokenness and addiction underlying the worldwide resurgence of Islam. Our chant of "Death to America" is also a death wish upon an internal enemy which we do not have the insight or the courage to confront as it is a desperate cry from an addict caught up in a web. Like the relationship between drug merchant and customer, this is a web which, while it dehumanises both supplier and consumer, ends up enriching the former and impoverishing the latter.

These recollections highlight the schizophrenia in everyday Muslim existence. We fit into a Muslim culture during the day and slip out under the cover of darkness at night. Those demons that we encounter during the night persist in muted form during the day. This backsliding proceeds without any announcement and thus avoids the judgment of *takfir* (heresy) and *irtidad* (apostasy); in the words of Mohammed Talbi,

> One continues to circumcise children and to recite the *Fatihah* as a blessing on marriage contracts and over the graves of the deceased, but the heart has gone from it all, leaving just the social phenomenon, a civic religion in the manner of those Ancients who continued to pay respects to the gods without believing much in them-it is no longer a case of individual loyalty to a faith but an overall sharing in an ethnic identity. (1984:7)

There is nothing new about this, for personal identification with the *ummah* and the ensuing loyalty to it are also sociological facts rather than a narrowly defined religious commitment. As von Grunebaum observed, "The abyss separating the Islam of Berber mountaineers from that of the *fuqaha'* of Cairo has, sociologically speaking, no weakening effect on the cohesiveness of the Muslim community." (1962:51). This current backsliding, however, does not reflect multiple identities or subsets of a single religio-cultural identity. Both personally and communally, it is not only a departure into the night but also an entry. It is, in fact, part of a descent into a globalized religion—that of the market. This is also the context that should shape our approach to both cultural and religious diversity.

Religious Diversity: An Ummah Beyond Religious Labels

The South African sociopolitical culture with the all-pervasive ideology of apartheid polarized the people to an unprecedented extent. The struggle against apartheid had a similar effect, albeit along entirely different lines. People on both sides of divide of the struggle had Muslim, Hindu, Christian, or Jewish names. The formidable presence of religious figures and organizations and, especially, the unprecedented Muslim-Christian religious solidarity which formed an integral part of this struggle, ensured that questions of identity, affiliation, and community assumed a stark new dimension. Progressive Muslims moved beyond the political necessity of religious diversity to an appreciation of theological legitimacy for interfaith solidarity against racism and an unambiguous embrace of Christians and Jews as "brothers and sisters" and "believers":

Non-Muslims have shed their blood to oppose apartheid's brutality and to
work for a just South Africa. We are then committed to work side by side
with others for the destruction of apartheid society. (*Call of Islam* 1985, 4)

This commitment to work with the non-Muslims went beyond the
functional or utilitarian to the acceptance of the theological legitimacy
of other faiths. Thus, Imam Hassan Solomon, then chairperson of the
Call of Islam and now a Member of Parliament, said,

All the messengers of Allah formed a single brotherhood. Their message is
essentially one and their religion and teachings are one . . . Let us enter the
future as brothers and sisters in the struggle. May Allah . . . strengthen all
the believers in Him until freedom and justice is concrete for all the
oppressed in our country. (1985, 5)

I believe that this position has it basis in the Qur'an and have
discussed these in some length in my book *Qur'an, Liberation and
Pluralism* (Oxford: Oneworld, 1997). First, the People of the Book, as
recipients of divine revelation, were recognized as part of the *ummah*.
Addressing all the Prophets, the Qur'an says, "And surely this, your
community (*ummah*), is a single community." (Q. 23:52)[10] The
establishment of a single *ummah* with diverse religious expressions was
also explicit in the Charter of Medina concluded between the Prophet
and the Jewish and Christian communities. Second, in two of the most
significant social areas, food and marriage, the generosity of the
Qur'anic spirit is evident: the food of "those who were given the Book"
was declared lawful for the Muslims, and the food of the Muslims was
lawful for them (Q. 5:5). Likewise, Muslim males were permitted to
marry "the chaste women of the People of the Book" (Q. 5:5). If
Muslims were to be allowed to coexist with others in a relationship as
intimate as marriage, then enmity is not to be regarded as the norm in
Muslim-other relations. Third, in the area of religious law, the norms
and regulations of the Jews and of the Christians were upheld (Q. 5:47)
and even enforced by the Prophet when he was called upon to settle
disputes among them (Q. 5:42-3). Fourth, the first time that permission
for armed struggle was given was to ensure the preservation of the
sanctity of the religious life of the adherents of other revealed religions.
"But for the fact that God continues to repel some people by means of
others, cloisters, churches, synagogues and mosques, [all places]
wherein the name of God is mentioned, would be razed to the ground"
(Q. 22:40).

The Qur'anic recognition of religious pluralism is evident not only
from the acceptance of the other as legitimate socio-religious

communities but also from an acceptance of the spirituality of the other and salvation through that otherness. The preservation of the sanctity of the places of worship sought not only to preserve the integrity of a multi-religious society. Rather, it was because it was Allah, the God transcends the diverse outward religio-cultural expressions of that service, who was being worshipped therein. That there were people in other faiths who sincerely recognized and served Allah is made even more explicit in the following text:

> Not all of them are alike; among them is a group who stand for the right and keep nights reciting the words of Allah and prostrate themselves in adoration before Him. They have faith in Allah and in the Last Day; they enjoin what is good and forbid what is wrong, and vie one with another in good deeds. And those are among the righteous. (Q. 4:113)

Moral Diversity

South African progressive Muslims who were actively involved in the liberation struggle and who valued their South African-ness are clamoring for a new *urf*, or custom, often cultural and with a basis of jurisprudence, rooted in our South African-ness. Intrinsic to this new *urf* is the *"humanum,"* the truly human, as an ethical criterion. This notion is invoked to justify a liberal democratic ethos that is really un-African in the same way that Islam is being used to justify the universal values of human rights and democracy that have little to do with the socio-cultural hinterland of Islam.

Among the fruits of South Africa's long march out of Egypt are our new constitution and the Bill of Rights, which are perhaps the most progressive in the world. In addition to guaranteeing all the rights enshrined in the United Nations Declaration on Human Rights, the constitution specifically prohibits "discrimination on the grounds of race, gender, sex, ethnic or social origin, color, sexual orientation, age, disability, religion, conscience, belief, culture or language." Christians, Hindus, Jews, Communists, feminists, lesbians, and gays were also an intrinsic part of the struggle. At the altar of maximum unity among the oppressed, their presence was passed over in silent discomfort. If Muslims have arrived then so have these other groups, all protected by the Bill of Rights. Gay rights, freedom of choice for pregnant women, and the abolition of the death penalty are but some of the principles viewed as "unpleasant fellow passengers" who walked in when the doors of diversity were flung open.[11]

Muslims have fought for freedom, declared that the struggle was a Jihad, and invoked one Qura'nic text after the other to spur the believers on to battle for freedom. Rather belatedly, we are beginning to discover that freedom is indivisible and, for some of us, somewhat frightening; freedom also implies the right of others to be, and we do not always like the face of that otherness. When most Muslims rejoice in the new recognition of the legal rights of all four wives in a polygamous marriage-something quite bizarre by Western standards-then the uncelebrated flip side of the coin is the recognition of gay marriages-something equally bizarre by Muslim standards.

Apartheid theology has alerted us to the relationship between exclusivist and conservative political ideology on the one hand and conservative theology on the other (and to the selective invoking of a kind of morality that is rather vocal on woman as evil and on sex and silent on hunger and injustice.). Many of us who transcended the boundaries of a useful but shortsighted antiapartheid Islamic theology have long since known that we would have to confront the full implications of a new inclusivist morality forged in the struggle for human rights.

While Muslims have every right to articulate the Islamic view of personal morality, it is important to understand that this morality is intrinsically related to a comprehensive Islamic moral worldview. In the same way that one does not demand amputating the hands of thieves in a poverty-ridden society, one cannot insist on capital punishment as the norm in a society that is not governed by the laws and values of Islam. The injunctions of *Shariah* and Islamic morality are parts of an ever-developing whole, and, while the fundamental principles of *tawhid* and justice are eternal, their concrete application to social matters has always been subject to human interpretation. To isolate the rules from their context and argue for their artificial transplantation into a non-Islamic society is to reduce an entire worldview to a set of punishments.

4.   THE CHALLENGES OF DIVERSITY

There are two major challenges that confront the advocates for diversity: the theological and the political.

The Theological Challenge: Where Does One Draw the Line?

With *ubuntu*, the notion of the eternal indebtedness to the other ("I am who I am because you are who are") and the *humanum*-holding sacred the humanness of each person—elevated to the level of ethical criteria, what happens to the "will of Allah" as expounded in the Koran and elaborated in the Prophet Precedent (*Sunnah*)? And what happens to the notion of human beings as sacred because of the Spirit of Allah blown into them and not just because they are human beings?

Pluralism is not devoid of ideology. It is part of a discourse founded and nurtured in critical scholarship that is in turn functions as an extension of nonreligious-even antireligious-Western scholarship, which is an extension of a culture that has dominated the so-called underdeveloped world. Has, then, the postmodernist Muslim has really sold out to neocolonialism, particularly of the cultural type? Tolerance and coexistence are fine for the modernist Muslim. Pluralism, however, takes the next step: it talks about valuing difference and being enriched by it. Allow me to quote a passage from my book (*On Being a Muslim*, Oxford: Oneworld, January 1999: 191):

> Spell out for us how *shirk* (associationism/ polytheism) enriches Islam, what we have to learn from ancestor veneration in African Traditional Religion, what Hinduism and its multiple gods have to teach us. How different is your post-modernity with its absence of boundaries, overlapping gods, and a million ideas from *shirk*? Has it occurred to you that perhaps it is you, your likes and the post-modernity which breeds you all that require scrutiny and re-thinking rather than Islam?

> Your project is rethinking Islam. Where do you draw the line? Postmodernity does not believe in such a thing as lines, does it? Tell us about your boundaries. Where do your equality and justice stop? Gay marriages? Women leading the *Jumu'ah salah*? A Hindu priest conducting a *nikah* in a mosque (with a bit of fire to add character)? In fact, why have any kind of marriages? Isn't that too defined a relationship, too confined a union for postmodernity? Why have *salah* at all? It's a tradition with little rational basis, isn't it? What's the point of one *ruku'* and two *sajdahs*. Why don;t you postmodernists just cancel the whole thing? Please tell us what's on agenda.

> You're pretty neat with all your questions and merely outlining frameworks for possible solutions, what Mohammed Arkoun calls "heuristic lines of thinking." I sense that underneath all your "frameworks for possible solutions" lie definite answers, answers for which you don't have the guts to stand up and be counted.

At the heart of all of these questions is the issue of drawing lines. The assumption that one can draw lines and that these will actually have any impact on our theology or law is problematic. We have this notion that sometime ago the door of *ijtihad* (creative juristic thinking) was closed. (When and by whom?) There is no definable moment where any one person, even the most conservative, stops thinking short of the unconsciousness of death. Human beings will always be confronted with new dilemmas and challenges engendered by new knowledge and deeper awareness. Removing one's shoes, today accepted as an intrinsic part of our prayer preparations, was never practiced by the Prophet. How does one fast from dawn to dusk when you end up at a place where the sun does not set for six months? Are you a traveler and therefore entitled to reduce your prayer units or to abstain from fasting, when a Concorde jet whisks you in a nonce to spot thousands of miles away?

The haunting question of drawing lines is rooted in our desperation for safety and security rather than in any sensible appreciation of the inherently dynamic nature of the human condition. One of the great thinkers in the Muslim world today, Dr Ebrahim Moosa, always answers "Allah, Allah is the limit" when I ask him this question. I am not convinced that this is the best answer. Perhaps his sense of certainty about Allah is greater than mine; perhaps he is less afraid of tumbling off from whatever vehicle we "rethinkers" are riding. However, for the moment, I too have this uncertainty with that as a response.

The Political Challenge: Seeking Liberating Diversity

In the post-apartheid South Africa there is much talk from the economically powerful about letting bygones be bygones. Whites hardly attended any of the hearings of the country's Truth and Reconciliation Commission, and are now loud in their clamor to "forget the past so that we can have peace". Our country desperately needs to have its people together and to have peace, but peace at what price? Most whites in South Africa are committed to change because they believe nothing will change. The fundamental economic injustices of the Apartheid era have remained and will ensure that the "peace" in the new South Africa is based on the principle that "the more things change, the more they stay the same". It is not that I do not yearn for these or that I do not work towards them. Nor, I would like to believe, is my own life bereft of these. I am, however, concerned with the naiveté with which these terms are bandied about. Like the unexamined life that is not worth living, the unexamined diversity is not worth experiencing.

We live in a world where individuals are less and less formed by the wealth of their traditions and their own cultures; instead they are shaped by a market so pervasive that freedom is confined to a consumerism that impoverishes the human spirit. While acknowledging the dangers of so glorifying local community and culture that one glosses over their potential for mean-spirited parochialism (e.g., xenophobia and homophobia), we must also recognize that globalization and the celebration of individual liberty-the core of modernity-are not ideologically neutral. The fundamental question in diversity is not how our cultures and traditions can be absorbed into globalization, but what is concealed by the globalist agenda.

In South Africa, these freedoms were already articulated in the Freedom Charter adopted by the ANC some fifty years ago and were intrinsically connected to the broad-based nature of the liberation struggle. It is however, no coincidence that the liberal democratic notions of individual freedom should find themselves most forcefully expressed in South Africa, the most economically developed African country.

As a Muslim theologian, this represents the single most significant ideological difficulty: I can only truly be who I am in my unceasingly transforming self within the context of freedom. Today this freedom is intrinsically connected to all the ideological baggage of the modern industrial state—the relentless Coca-colonization and MacDonaldization of global consciousness. In other words, my freedom has been acquired within the bosom of capitalism along with all of its hegemonic designs over my equally valued cultural and religious traditions. And so I am afraid of this other that is not another but the juggernaut of the market, nestled in my back pocket in the form of my credit cards.

In a critique of the way some Muslim fundamentalists engage in a blanket denunciation of modernity, Bassam Tibi speaks about the "confusion between two different, even if intrinsically interrelated phenomena: the cultural project of modernity and the institutional dimension in the globalisation processes of modernity." He describes cultural modernity as an "emanicipatory project which has resulted in the liberation of mankind from oppressive traditions and from their quasi-natural religious status," while "globalized institutional modernity has been an instrument of power to establish Western dominance over the rest of the world" (1992: 175-6).

I am unconvinced of this neat distinction. Globalization has not always supported the forces of progress and freedom; one need only consider the aggressive petrofundamentalism in some of the Gulf states, with their "primitive messages of obedience (*ta'ah*), intolerance, misogyny and xenophobia-is inconceivable without the liberal democracies' strategic support of conservative Islam." (Mernissi, 1996:39). Far from being one of the most puzzling marriages in the twentieth century, as Mernissi calls it, is this not merely the reverse side of globalization?

This "emancipatory project," when viewed outside the context of globalized institutional modernity, frees people as objects in relentless marketing strategies. (In its crudest form, we see the abuse of women as sex objects). While it may be valid to link "oppressive traditions" to their "quasi-natural religious status," it is also important to point out how religion has also regularly served to destabilize and eliminate oppressive traditions-from infanticide in pre-Islamic Arabia to racism in Apartheid South Africa.[12]

A theoretically postulated dislocated or decontextualized passion for diversity and pluralism often becomes an excuse for not taking sides. This is the perfect ideology for the modern bourgeois mind. Such a pluralism makes a genial confusion in which one tries to enjoy the pleasures of difference without ever committing oneself to any particular vision of resistance, liberation and hope. (Tracy 1987:90).

5.   CONCLUSION: WHOSE BRIDGES? WHERE DO THEY LEAD TO?

The Muslim backsliding I spoke of earlier is not just a byproduct of pluralism; it is also reflective of multiple identities or subsets of a single religio-cultural identity: a departure into the night but also a descent into a globalized religion; that of the market.

I recently came across an unpublished article by David Loy that notes the alarming influence of global forces on South African domestic policy, most notably in a reduction in social expenditures. Diversity and pluralism are worth little if attained at the price of joblessness, homelessness, and hunger.[13]

The market, Loy argues, "is becoming the first truly world religion, binding all corners of the globe into a world-view and set of values" that has "become the most successful religion of all time, winning more converts more quickly than any previous belief system in human history." Because we insist on seeing the values of the market as secular, we have not been able to "offer what is most needed, a meaningful challenge to the aggressive proselytizing of market capitalism." (n.d.: 1)

Until the last few centuries there had been little genuine distinction between church and state, between sacred authority and secular power.

That cozy relationship continues today: far from maintaining an effective regulatory or even neutral position, the U.S. government has become the most powerful proponent of the religion of market capitalism as the only way to live. (n.d.:6)

The market is not just an economic system but a religion, and not a very good one, for it can thrive only by promising a secular salvation that it never quite supplies. Its academic handmaiden, the "social science" of economics, is really a theology masquerading as a science. (n.d.:10)

Underpinned by globalization, the prevailing form of capitalism is every bit ferocious as the most intractable forms of religious fundamentalism. It seeks to convert all other cultures in its image. "The most insidious aspect of it is the fact that it presents itself as the only way, and appears to claim that outside its pale there is no salvation for the world, but only hell-fire of destruction, or the limbo of "primitivism." (Wilfred, 1995)

In the face of threats, real or imagined, the globalization bares its fangs of intolerance, giving the lie to its pretensions to ecumenical pluralism. The enemy is then painted in the vilest forms and in darkest colours.   The threat to the consortium of advanced capitalist countries could be, for example, the illegal immigrants storming the portals of "fortress Europe"; it could be Islam-with haunting memories of Crusades-or it could be the challenges posed by the cultures and traditions of Third World peoples. (ibid)

Given the glaring injustices that pervade the planet, the imperatives of conscience and compassion have a moral calling to disturb the "peace" of the status quo. Interfaith and cross-cultural dialogue is empty without a firm grounding in solidarity with the oppressed and dispossessed. It is only in the struggle for human dignity for all of God's people, for freedom and justice, that the conversation among world cultures and religions finds its most authentic and effective collective voice.

If I May Return to the More Obviously Theological by Way of Conclusion

The Qur'an does not regard everyone and their ideas as equal but proceeds from the premise that the idea of inclusiveness is superior to that of exclusiveness, that justice must prevail over injustice, and that the *mujahidin* (those who engage in struggle) are superior to the *qa'idin* (those who remain idle). Diversity is not the mere tolerance of every idea and practice. Instead it must be geared towards specific objectives such as freeing humankind from injustice and servitude to other human beings so that it may be free to worship God.

The responsibility of calling humankind to the path of God remains paramount. The task of the contemporary Muslims is to discern what this means in every age and every society. Who are to be invited? Who are to be taken as allies in this calling? How does one define the path of God? These are particularly pertinent questions in a society where definitions of the self and the other are determined by justice and injustice, oppression and liberation. The test of one's integrity as a human being dignified by God one's commitment to defend that dignity and to become a subject in history-not a passive victim of the forces of history but an actor whose only masters are God and conscience.

CHAPTER 11

Personal Reflections on Intellectual Diversity and Islam: The Example of Lebanon

Su'ad al-Hakim*

*Translated from Arabic by Meena Sharify-Funk

The television programs and newspaper articles in Lebanon present themselves as critical evidence of the fact that violence has pervaded the usual religious, philosophical, and political attitudes of a number of groups in conflict. This mentality of violence is often nurtured in environments plagued by disunity and irrationality. Many of these incidents reflect an absence of a centralized government that mediates the relations between these conflicting groups. As a result, intercultural relations are rife with misconceptions and biases that impede communication, mediation, and resolution of the conflict that besets Lebanon. The ambivalence of the interests and perceptions of the parties to the conflict only aggravates the volatility of an already bellicose environment. This instability further contributes to the decentralization of governmental control and perpetuates a vicious circle of ignorance and violence; fear and greed, not an awareness of the others' interests and needs, dominate the relations between the two main Lebanese factions. This fractious atmosphere in Lebanon is an example of the larger problem of Islamic cultural diversity, a case study that juxtaposes a cacophony of contending religious, political, and ideological interests.

Lebanon, like the United States and other countries, has been a host for various different cultures and religious traditions. Islam, however, has been Lebanon's chief influence in religion, culture, and politics, and thus offers unique possibilities as a healing force among the country's clashing communities. However, there is a need to develop a broader perspective of Islam, in other words, to discover and analyze its essential precepts in order to understand how Islam can be utilize to resolve the conflict and reconcile differences among different communities of Lebanon.

1. EXPLAINING THE LEBANESE SITUATION

Seven key points to aid in an understanding of the crises facing contemporary Lebanon:

1. Since the beginning of its modern history, the two chief religious groupings in Lebanon have been the Muslims and the Christians. Though living in a single polity, each has maintained and developed distinct cultural, ideological, and political ideals that are embedded in the early evolution of each group in Lebanon. On the one hand, the Lebanese Muslim community has always relied upon the Islamic tradition for spiritual and structural guidance. In particular, they have sought spiritual guidance from Al-Hijaz, the cradle of the Prophet Muhammed's inspiration, in contrast to Istanbul, which provided them with a model for governmental authority. In addition, firm educational standards have been adapted from both Al-Azhar of Egypt and Najaf of Iraq. This dependence upon established precedents led to the creation of an exclusively Muslim Lebanese culture, independent from that of the Christians.

On the other hand, Christians welcomed missionaries into their midst, seeking solace in Westernized thought, culture, and social values and thus forming an equally insular and exclusive community. The result was the mutual alienation of two great religious communities, each steeped distrust, fear, and insecurity toward the other. The quest for security through the years has tended to harden differences and undermine efforts at reconciliation by encouraging self-interest at the expense of the other groups, instead of promoting coexistence and understanding between them.

2. Following the independence of Lebanon, the political leaders arrived at a national covenant that proclaimed a policy of "no East and no West" in an effort to popularize their new social policy. This policy attempted to achieve a common political and social focus for the two communities, yet Lebanon remained "a nation with an Arab face," in

the words of George Naqash of the newspaper *L'Orient.* Lebanon remains unable to bridge these historical, cultural, and religious divides.

3. Despite the efforts of the political leaders, each group is pulled towards its own center, thus diminishing any hope of unifying the Lebanese nation. This divisiveness has been intensified by the consequential attraction and connection received from the international community; within every group there are exclusive affiliations, some directed solely outward, toward the international community, and others inward. This dualism has led to the inevitable fragmentation of the Lebanese nation.

4. A united Lebanese identity, based on coexistence of these two religious groups has failed to develop due to the feelings of insecurity and fear against each other. In their illusive pursuit of self-security, they weaken the bonds of security for the whole country. Therefore, no progress has reulted from previous attempts to bring the parties together. There have been numerous attempts to create symbols of a unified Lebanese identity. However, each of these symbols has only sparked fresh conflicts, which have then inspired additional searches for unifying symbols, which have in turn fostered more conflicts—a spiral of acrimony without end, it seems.

5. Some of these groups have sought in secularism and civil law a path out of the chronic belligerence. The secularists argue that all the Lebanese people must unite under a nonreligious civil umbrella, but their vision strikes some as insufficiently appreciative of the positive role of diversity.

6. Lebanese culture is pluralistic but not diverse—there is difference but not tolerance of difference. Every group within Lebanon has its own closed culture that negates the others. These groups and minorities briefly come out of their own world only to announce their own opinions to the world outside, and then they return promptly to the sealed sanctum of their own community, whether Sunni, Shi'a, Orthodox, Catholic, Druze, nationalist, or liberal.

Each community in Lebanon reinforces its isolation from the others with distinct and exclusive mechanisms of social reproduction: each one has it own theater, newspaper, and television channels in which they purvey only their own religion and culture. This mentality of segregation is transmitted to children through special educational programs, beginning with cartoons for the youngest.

7. Two major debates have emerged out of these decades of heated ethnic and religious conflict in Lebanon, one for the Lebanese and the other for foreigners. Each group has the ability to balance its own self-

interests with that of the Lebanese community. I believe that with a concentrated effort from both sides, a balanced, gradual approach can direct the Lebanese people toward a future of coexistence and harmony. This balance depends on each group's ability to cooperate with and support other groups.

The Lebanese nationality is a confluence of Arabic and Phoenician currents. The result has been the emergence of a distinctive Lebanese-Arabic culture. There is also, however, an imbalance that feeds conflicts that are magnified by the country's strategic geopolitical location at the juncture of three continents. This potential for conflict makes every follower of every group create their inclusive sanctuaries.

II. THE SITUATION AND THE SOLUTION

The Prophet and the Arabs

The Prophet Muhammad emerged as a messenger for the whole of humanity at a time when tribal identity was paramount. His philosophy of God as One contrasted sharply with the polytheistic convictions then prevailing in the Arabian Peninsula. The Prophet believed that Muslims should seek to unify the different tribes and groups as one nation (*Ummah*).

This goal, however, appears to have contributed to the diversity of cultures in the Arab world, in large measure because of the distinct agendas of inner and outer Islam, both of which preoccupied the Prophet. The first command of Allah was the revelation of the Qur'an to the heart of the Prophet. This act symbolized the opening of all the Qur'anic scripture, which has become a font of cultural diversity because it points to a common foundation for the varied beliefs of humanity. For example, we have the inherited images and stories of numerous prophets: Moses, the prophet of the sons of Israel; Jesus, son of Maryam, also known as the word of God; and Muhammad, the end of all Prophets. Each originates from a common source and represents the cultural ideals of his era. Each prophet and his message complete that of the others to the ultimate benefit of the human race.

The second command of Allah was the designation of the Prophet to resolve the differences between various groups. As a result, the *Sunnah*, or the traditions of the Prophet, was further developed in order to meet the needs of the conflicting groups within the Muslim community. Through the analysis of sources of the Islamic sciences, the essential connection with the teachings of the Prophets is revealed. It is from the Prophet's premises that the jurisprudence scholars of the *Ummah* derived their various schools of thought, whether in theory or practice. The Sufis have been characterized as the closest to emulate the moral conduct of the Prophet, their spiritual strivings exemplifying most closely the Prophet's *Sunnah*. Other groups who concentrated on the *Sunnah* focused their energies on understanding the relationship between the Divine and the human.

The Prophet's way of life was itself a study in diversity. He believed there was no one exclusive way to perform any one action; for example, he stated one cannot always do *wadu* exactly the same way because life's conditions—most basically place and time—are constantly changing, so implementation must accord with the individual's capabilities and living conditions. Hence difference and diversity are incorporated into the very fabric of the Prophet's teachings.

III. LEBANESE UNITY AND SULTAN BEN DUROUDIE

The essence of Islam emerges from two sources: (1) the Qur'an (2) the temporal context of the revelations that followed the death of the Prophet. It was only after the death of the Prophet that actual "Muslim" history began; the Muslims of that era were the sole interpretive custodians of the Prophet's teachings.

The emergence of modern ideas and values has gradually transformed the Islamic cultural diversity of the first century Hegirah. The original message of diversity was initially founded on the principle of unity. Conversely, it is now defined and practiced through Islamic cultural pluralism, or "manyness." All subjects in the Islamic sciences have advanced because of the collective gathering of intellectual and cultural resources. This gathering of knowledge has also benefited the public, for it has resulted in the creation of an unique cultural intellectuality. Unfortunately an agreement has yet to be reached between the sciences.

Paralleling this impasse is the metamorphosis of various races, nationalities, and tribes, who had existed in the one *Ummah*. They emerged from diversity but now find themselves mired in pluralism. The work of Seyyed Mohammed Duroudie al-Hassani al-Nasib (also known as al-Sultun) is an important attempt to overcome the conflicts inherent in this Islamic pluralism. He envisioned that the *Shariah*, Islamic law, focused upon the debate on culture within differing social perspectives. He proposed a specialized a gradual, nonviolent transformative process for a group of Muslims. This process would encourage Muslim society to move from a consciousness of manyness to a Muslim society based in diversity-in-unity.

It is essential to begin with an examination of the differences between pluralism and diversity. In following the Prophet's example, the consciousness of diversity implies unity. Diversity so considered would be as aspect of a single, united nationality that would encompass the entire human race. By contrast, pluralism has no essential foundation in unity; it entails a multiplicity of rules and norms with no anchor in a single tradition, culture, or polity.

Diversity incorporates all races in one human race. Consequently, a son of any race is embraced as a member of the human race. He will act accordingly, classifying others in the same category as himself, that of humanity. Pluralism, by contrast, traffics in racial hierarchies, thus undermining the notion of multiracial solidarity and equality.

The discussion of the One in the context of diversity is certainly attributable to the One of existence and the Many of diversity, but unfortunately there is a tendency to equate unity with that of uniformity. The One, based upon existence as a human reality, is transposed upon the Many within every field. It is, however, numerous in its manifestation within the unity of existence. If such a unity of existence were absent, chaos would be inevitable in all realms. The idea of unity can inspire people to unite under different cultural, social, and political auspices. This will facilitate open discussions, debates, and, hopefully, dialogue that will allow all group's to express their own ideas in relation to others.

Islamic culture originates from the essence of the diverse and the many. It is one, as a whole, and it is Many in beliefs, subjects, and ways of knowing. This "diverse unity" recognizes each group as a part of the whole; in order for the whole to be complete, the recognition of the part is essential for the integrity of the individual's culture. The absence of the part creates an emptiness within the whole. To use a particular example, if we disregard specific groups within Islam, such as the Salifiyyahs or Sufis, we will ultimately be impoverishing the whole Islamic community. This is applicable to every group.

If we are able to recognize on a daily basis that humanity is one and many, we will become empowered with the understanding that humanity is one in essence and many with regard to the rituals and activities of everyday life. For example, I am but a single person in essence; yet I am many in form as a mother, wife, friend, daughter, sister, scholar, Muslim, white, Arab, Lebanese, human, and so on.

Every time a human being grows and develops, he or she increases the levels of inclusivity within his or her reality. Therefore, increasing development is equivalent to increasing one's capacity for open-mindedness. There is no end to such adaptation. Because the individual realizes the importance of diversity, he or she is also empowered with the ability to forgive and accept differences. This recognition of the necessity of the other as a contributing factor to one's own identity is essential in avoiding the dualities of consciousness that contribute to social fragmentation.

For example, I am a Lebanese Muslim, and I have been invited to give a lecture in America, assuming that I have been invited because people are interested in my ideas and that they will listen to me. From my perspective, American society seems to provide tangible evidence of the possibility of a diverse society that actually accepts diversity and the idealistic notion that "the other is one of us."

IV. CONCLUSION: LEBANON AND CULTURAL DIVERSITY

Without an essential collective framework for diversity, we risk the possibility of descent into a pluralistic consciousness that invites chaos. For this reason, it is imperative to seek out those foundational ideas from the work of Sultan al-Duroudie that may be practically applied to the Muslim nation as a whole and to Lebanese society in particular.

The following is a summary of four interrelated conditions that will serve to dispel negative pluralistic tendencies and uphold a positive, healthy consciousness of diversity.

First, unity of existence implies that all Lebanese maintain an identity as individuals within an existing Lebanese collective, as opposed to that of a being confined to an existing collective, or private group inside the borders of Lebanon. This undoubtedly creates a Lebanese identity characterized by interrelationships between all people. It is this identity that contains the potential to unite the people of Lebanon and create a diverse, peaceful society.

Second, for every unified society, there are certain factors in place designed to shield the culture from contamination, whether it be on an institutional or individual level. These shields may be uncovered through an analytical approach. Investigation reveals that in Lebanon it is rare to come across individuals who look past their own self-interests to represent the whole of the nation. Where are the protectors of Lebanon who can reconcile the competing claims of the public and private?

Third, unification cannot exist without national leaders and heroes. The successful leader envisions and then formulates the foundations for unity and organizes relations between various interests. This leader must provide the source of guidance in times of social turbulence. The people depend upon the leader to deliver the official national sentiment, which they will accordingly accept and utilize as a personal opinion. The people of a nation also look to their heroes, often those that have physically struggled to defend the integrity of the unified existence; for these are the individuals that represent adherence to moral and universal human values. However, in the absence of a common leader, hero, or symbol of Lebanese unification, we find every group championing its own leaders, heroes, and symbols rather than those of the nation as a whole.

In all of this, where do we find Lebanon? Where is its united leadership, with visionary leaders and abundant heroes who can strengthen the unity of the country? To answer these provocative questions it is necessary for all groups to share in one love. Such a diversity of cultures could establish a coexistence consciousness of Christians and Muslims, both perfecting each other. The person endowed with this consciousness would be aware that all individuals are a part of the whole. It is not enough to be given our natural human and social instincts, we need to increase our efforts daily towards securing our collective well-being for the long-term of our social existence.

It is unfortunate that in Lebanon we find mothers warning and advising their children everyday to not trust others but instead to trust only oneself. It is no wonder that under the influence of these opinions we are ultimately left with a mentality of distrust. Perhaps we can encourage these mothers to ask themselves, "How can we cooperate, or come to know one another, when we have nursed such distrust within ourselves?" Trust is the key to fostering this spirit of cooperation, but it cannot be realize without an accompanying awareness of our common universal ground of being. Both trust and the organization of all individual groups are essential elements for the future as without the awareness of our unity of existence, Lebanon cannot be managed. Perhaps we can then come to know that any establishment can control and organize a group but that no one establishment has the right to control and organize people's minds. For this reason, unity and cooperation cannot appear only on the surface and cannot lack the depth of human awareness. With the development of the four items that were previously mentioned: existence (unity of society), protectors or cultural shields, leaders and heroes, and the individual who has such awareness, we can come to live as one Lebanon.

CHAPTER 12

Muslim Communal Nonviolent Actions: Minority Coexistence in a Non-Muslim Society

Chaiwat Satha-Anand (Qader Muheideen)

INTRODUCTION

One of the most memorable scenes of coexistence between Muslims and non-Muslims I have ever witnessed took place on a Friday afternoon before a *jumaat* prayer near a local mosque in central Bangkok, Thailand. The scene was typical: Muslims from nearby workplaces arrived for the congregation. The mosque, surrounded by both Muslim and non-Muslim communities, was in an alley reachable only on foot. Most come before *Qutbah* because in addition to being a place of worship, a mosque is also a place where friends meet, people talk, messages are shared, and *halal* food is consumed. Finding a place for Muslim food in Bangkok is not easy because Muslims, though the largest minority in Thai society, are only 7 percent of a country of some 60 million people.[1]

On that day, I and several other Muslims were having our lunch in front of a small stall in the open basement of a traditional Thai house. The space was small and so crowded with customers that it was difficult to walk through. Suddenly we heard a loud voice: "Here comes the pork!" And the crowded customers having their fried rice or Indian-style chicken rice parted as if touched by magic. Silently, and as quickly as she could, an elderly Chinese woman carrying a large bowl filled with a pork dish walked through the throngs of Muslims waiting for their Friday prayers. The Chinese woman tried her best to stay clear from the men around her in that narrow pathway while the Muslims tried their utmost to make themselves as small as they could to avoid contact with the prohibited substance. What is remarkable about this scene is the fact that the warning voices echoed from here and there with smiling faces, that the Chinese woman ambled almost apologetically, that the Muslims expressed no anger, and that this scene of everyday coexistence must have been a common one.

As a matter of fact, in India, where Hindu-Muslim conflicts have flared dangerously in recent years, Ashis Nandy maintained that for every riot reported, there are also "instances of bravery shown by persons who protect their neighbors at immense risks to their own lives and that of their families."[2] Even at the time of the bitter partition of the subcontinent, which saw the deaths of hundreds of thousands of people, both Hindu and Muslims, there were stories of someone from the other communities who helped families of the "others."[3] Such coexistence persists, since of the 2,800 Indian communities identified as predominantly Hindu or Muslim in the 1990s, only about 350 were exclusively one or the other. In addition, some 600 such communities also live with multiculturalism within.[4]

MUSLIM MINORITY'S NONVIOLENT ACTION: A BROAD CONCEPTUAL GUIDELINE

In attempting to understand a Muslim minority's engagement with conflict in a largely non-Muslim setting, we will pose and attempt to answer three basic questions: First, what is the primary purpose of engaging in such conflicts? Second, what is the political context of the majority-minority relationship? Third, what kind of action would allow Muslim minorities to engage in such conflicts meaningfully, constructively, and effectively?

If it is the life of a Muslim minority as a collective identity that is being threatened by the "malady of modernity," then the purpose of engaging in conflict is primarily to defend its community as opposed to fighting to unseat a tyranny. Thailand is a "strong democratic society," judging from the people's rights institutionalized in the constitution of 1997, complete with independent monitoring agencies, competitive electoral politics, and a highly visible civil society. Conflict in such a context would naturally be different from conflict in an authoritarian polity. So the range of potential nonviolent protest for aggrieved parties in Thailand is broad. Generally speaking, nonviolent action may involve "acts of omission," whereby people refuse to perform their expected functions, or "acts of commission," whereby engage in unexpected or proscribed activities.[7] Nonviolent protests to defend Muslim minorities' way of life in a democracy seem to take the forms of "nonviolent protest and persuasion," mainly symbolic actions of peaceful opposition.

DEFENDING MUSLIM COMMUNITIES FROM DRUGS, PATHOLOGICAL DEVELOPMENT, AND GREED IN FISHERY

1. Fighting Against Drugs

One of the most pressing problems facing Thai society is drugs, primarily heroin and amphetamines. According to the United Nations, illegal businesses worldwide generate an annual income of around $600 billion, two-thirds of which is from drug trafficking. In Thailand, profits from drug trafficking were estimated at around 21 percent of world total and twice the country's earnings from exports in 1994. The U.S. Bureau of National Narcotic Matter estimated that the production of opium in Southeast Asia accounted for 75 percent of world production in 1993, most of it originated from the Golden Triangle bordering Thailand, Laos, and Burma. Prices of heroin at sources of the time were between $2,400-3,400 per kg (using current exchange rate of US$1=45 Thai Baht. But when sold in the US, prices jump to $57,000-$122,000 per kg. In 1994-1995, it was estimated that there were more than 214,000 heroin addicts while there were 257,965 amphetamine addicts in 1993. The cost of production of amphetamine is roughly seven to eleven cents per pill, but each could fetch around two dollars in the United States market.[5] The drug business survives and, in fact, thrives because it is protected by dark influences in Thai society, most likely involving the collaboration of some high-ranking politicians and police officers.[6] It is a small wonder that drugs have become such a gigantic problem in Thai society.

It is remarkable when small communities decide to fight back. For a long time, residents of a community in the outskirt of Bangkok lived in fear of powerful drug gangs who traded openly. The 5.2-acre town is called "Mitraparb" (friendship) community but is better known among residents as "Apache Village." It has a population of 800, mostly

Muslims who work in factories and small-scale commercial business. Theft and petty crime were rampant as drug addiction spread among community members. Reliance on the compromised local police proved futile. In October 1997 members of the community decided that "enough is enough" and called a town meeting to mobilize a response to the problem. They decided to set up a round-the-clock security service, with villagers taking turns on foot patrol. The aroused locals were able to apprehend seventeen buyers on the very first night. From October 1997 to June 1998, sixty-four users and/or dealers were apprehended. A community leader reported that most of the pushers were people from outside the community. When they were checked by the community security team, their names and ID card numbers were recorded. All were told that they would be handed to the police if they came back. As a result of their action, the crime rate has dropped sharply. Women and children can walk the streets without fear again.[7]

Seeing its success, the Bangkok Metropolitan Administration has chosen this Muslim community to lead a pilot project in a move to declare fifty communities drug-free zones. Members of Mitraparb community were asked to advise others on possible courses of action. This is a case of an ordinary urban village being threatened by a drug problem that robbed the villagers of their sense of safety that, in turn, created a drive alter the situation by empowering themselves. This Muslim community is admired by both the Thai authorities and other non-Muslim communities that also seek to root out the drug peddlers by such means of empowerment.

2. Fighting Against Pathological Development

Bangkok, a city of more than 7 million people, has it share of urban problems, with traffic congestion near the top of the list. The diagnosis of this problem is simple: too many cars on too few roads. According to the present mayor of Bangkok, there are more than 4 million cars in Bangkok, while there are only 2,812 km. of roads of all type.[8] The mainstream solution is to build more roads.[9] The first National Economic Development Plan, formulated some four decades ago, included proposals to modernize the country's infrastructure; most canals in the city, which had once served as transportation channels and a natural drainage system, were filled with earth to build roads. Recently, numerous megaprojects such as the sky train and a subway system have sprung up in Bangkok as if the city could grow indefinitely. The expressway project is one such megaproject the government planned and carried out in order to alleviate traffic problems.

But to build such an extensive highway at a time when the city is bursting at the seams is to risk a number of crucial problems. For example, appropriation of land already owned by Bangkok residents has become a costly endeavor on the part of the expressway builder and the administration. There are landowners who accept compensation, normally below market prices, without any fight. There are those, however, who do not yield so easily and have taken their cases to court. One of the most famous and instructive examples is the fight of the Ban Krua community.

Some might think of Ban Krua as one of Bangkok's 843 slums. With more than 1.1 million inhabitants, this area includes 14.6 percent of Bangkok's population.[10] So when it was suggested that one of the exits of the second stage expressway had to cut through Ban Krua, the choice seems obvious: a slum vs. a gleaming new road to ease congestion for Bangkok's growing and thriving middle class. The people of Ban Krua had other ideas, however. They have argued that they do not want to obstruct the expressway project; they simply do not want to be forced from their homes for a roadway that then contend will aggravate rather than allieviate the city's traffic congestion. The fight of Ban Krua community has been going on for more than thirteen years, with that expressway exit yet to materialize on the backs of that poor community.

Why have they fought so hard for their community? Commenting on a columnist's remark that there are others whose land and houses were dug up more than once under the cruel claws of these megaprojects, a Ban Krua community leader observed, "What I feel for and will not be able to find elsewhere is much more than houses. It is the air of the community that everyone knows everyone. We can greet anyone from one house to the next everyday. If we are driven away from here, this atmosphere will be gone."[11] This strong communal sense is rooted in the long-standing Cambodian Muslim identity of the area, which was founded some two hundred years ago.[12] In a great battle between the Burmese and the Siamese in the reign of King Rama I (1782-1809), known as "the nine-army battle", the Cham (Cambodian Muslims) volunteered to fight on the side of the King. When the Burmese were defeated, in an act of appreciation, King Rama I graciously granted a piece of land to be the home of the community of these brave Cambodian Muslims who fought and died for Siam and the King. Ban Krua residents also claim that as a Muslim community, they have built both a mosque and a cemetery that cannot be touched or removed because they are *waqf*. Even if the expressway exit were to avoid both sacred grounds, a mosque without any community to sustain it with lives, prayers, and spirituality would not mean much.

The Ban Krua community has fought the modern project using all types of nonviolent methods. Sometimes they sent letters asking for help from the authorities; they also worked with the opposition to pressure the then governments. Internally, they organized themselves to protect their community with guards and patrol teams because, as a slum, the community is susceptible to arsons. In fact, there have been attempts to set fire to houses in Ban Krua, but they were put out by the residents themselves. Everyone helps. Even children in the community are trained to identify any suspicious occurrence or person. They have organized cultural tours of their community, famous for its production of refined silk and its indigenous Islamic cuisine. These nonviolent tactics have proved effective politically and have won wide admiration among non-Muslim segments of Bangkok.

But the leaders of the protest have not shied away from street actions, either. In April 1994, the community descended on the government house, demanding to see the prime minister. They have used all kinds of symbolic nonviolent actions to convey the message that they are serious about their fight and that they are willing to sacrifice whatever it takes to fight for their rights and for what is right. For example, they called for a press conference and digging the grave in the community cemetery to show the public that they were willing to lay down their lives in this fight. Prayers were offered before the demonstration. People put on their "Muslim" garb, including turbans, *kapiyah* or *hijab*. Some carried coffins covered with velvet cloth adorned with words from the holy Qur'an Surah II (Al-Bakara), Verse 156: "To Allah we belong, and to Him is our return." Once they arrived in front of the government house, they set up their community there. Compulsory prayers, uttered five times a day, were offered for everyone to see. They also sent protest letters to several Muslim countries around the world.[13]

After three days, the prime minister came out to meet the Muslims of Ban Krua, who greeted him kindly and with delight. Before he left them, they all made supplications (*du'a*) asking Allah Almighty to bless him with wisdom to distinguish right from wrong.[14] All the leading newspaper columnists agreed on exemplary quality of Ban Krua Muslims' protests. They wrote that the nonviolent struggle of Ban Krua Muslims is a "model" for Thai civil society, "a fight of courageous people's warrior worthy of becoming future lesson," "an example for all to contemplate changes in Thai society."[15]

The Ban Krua Muslims have been fighting to defend their community from a kind of modernization that sacrifices the values of tradition, spirit, and community for the sake of dubious material gains. The most salient quality of their nonviolent struggle is their success in using Islamic religious practices and symbols to assert their identity as a Muslim community with a glorious history of serving Thai society valiantly in the past. A researcher who did her thesis on the protest of Ban Krua community concludes that conditions of their success is based on the leadership's faith in religion and belief that communal responsibility of the leaders is "God's obligation." A community leader told the researcher that, "We are limited in every way. Without God's guidance, would we be able to do this? To move forward in fighting is to walk with God."[16]

3. Fighting Against Greed in Fishery

Thailand has a 2,600-km coastline that extends 1,700-km in the south. In 1990, there were 47,000 households headed by fishermen; the livelihood of at least half a million people depends solely on the ocean, and 74 percent of these people are in southern Thailand. There are two kinds of fishermen: The small operators with small boats or no boat at all number approximately 30,000 households in the south, constitute some 85 percent of the population of small fishermen in the country, and cannot fish beyond 3 km offshore because of the big commercial fishing trawlers, which often invade that 3-km zone and thus infringe on the livelihood of the small operators. If small fishermen choose to invest more in their fishing instruments, they often end up with lots of debts. At present, they earn $526-$927 a year while their expenses amount to approximately $927 a year.[17]

In recent years, as seafood has become more and more commercially viable, big trawlers try to catch more fish by moving closer to the shore with no seasonal surcease. To secure their livelihood against big business' code of greed, southern fishermen from four provinces around Phangnga Bay want the government to expand the coastal zone where trawling is not allowed. They want to extend the protected zone from the existing 673 sq. km to 2,010 sq. km to permit the rehabilitation of fish stocks. On June 24, 1998, Muslim fishermen from the area decided to call on the director-general of the Fishery Department. A fisherman said to his friends, "We all suffer the effects of those big trawlers taking away our resources. We should tell as many people as possible to come and listen to what the government has to say. We don't have any physical force, but if we come in large numbers, we can at least muster some power."[18]

In preparing for the confrontation, a question was asked about measures that could be used to pressure "the other." A Muslim elder of the fishing community answered, "No matter what, don't use violence. It's no good for anybody. We should try our best and aim for peaceful talks." Muslim fishermen around the Phangnga Bay area were all enthusiastic about the initiative. They organized themselves by soliciting voluntary contributions to fund the cost of their nonviolent actions. They also prepared their own food to take along with them. Finally, 3,000 small-scale fishermen went to Krabi City Hall. But they did not enter into a trilateral discussion with government officials and the commercial trawler operators because they were dissatisfied with the number of their representatives allowed to attend the negotiation. Having boycotted the negotiation, Muslim fishermen decided to stage a nonviolent sit-in cum blockade.[19] Protesters made a barricade to stop officials and the commercial trawler operators from entering and leaving City Hall so that they would have to listen to their side of argument.

The way in which they organize their nonviolent action is culturally creative. For example, Muslim women were assigned to guard the gate of City. A Muslim woman in her *hijab*[20] told a reporter that women are gentle, "so we should keep vigil at the gate." Another pointed out, "Muslim women don't only have to live behind the veil and pray five times a day. We can and must exercise our rights. That is what our Imam told us." The barricade sparked a war of words as tensions rose. People were attacked with sticks and stones until both group leaders were able to calm their friends down and separate the contending parties. Finally the governor agreed to talk with the fishermen. An agreement was reached that a committee would be formed in the following four months to study the proposed enlarged protected zone. The fishermen (and women) then prayed to Allah to express their gratitude that their efforts were met with moderate success. A fisherman said, "At least the officials listened to us and left the door of opportunity open for further study." When asked what would happen if the fishermen's demands remained unsatisfied in four months, the fisherman answered, "I believe more of us will go there again."[21]

For a group of 3,000 fishermen with little experience in communal nonviolent action, the degree to which they were able to adjust their tactics in accordance with changing circumstances was quite impressive. Another remarkable feature of the Muslim fishermen's struggle was the fact that they decided early on to conduct their protest nonviolently.

A distinguished Thai journalist wrote that the Muslim fishermen tried everything. When told to get organized, they did. When told to consult the law, they found that the 3-km no-entry law against trawlers was on their side. When told to complain to government officials, moving up the bureaucratic ladder from the marine police up to the head of government, they did that, too. Finally, they took to the streets, which she claims is "the last resort for the poor to air their grievances." Again, they were told to start a dialogue, with every side involved. They did that and organized themselves into a united, regional network. Yet the authorities refuse to act because, the journalist argues, there is a lack of legal enforcement.[22]

Nevertheless, the quality of the fishermen's participation in this conflict is quite instructive. Through their communal actions, they become stronger. They also learned that there is power in numbers.[23] To ensure a large number of participants, efficient organization and creative methods were necessary. The Muslim fishermen were able to get themselves organized through tapping their strength as a Muslim community in their creative and highly adaptive nonviolent struggle against greed.

MUSLIM COMMUNAL NONVIOLENT ACTIONS: SOME COMMON FEATURES?

These three cases of Muslim communal nonviolent actions show some interesting similarities and contrasts. First, each case is different as regards the extent of preparation, experience, and time involved. The Ban Krua Muslims were the most experienced, given their longstanding grievances. On the other hand, the fishermen of Phangnga seemed to move into communal nonviolent action without much experience. The "Mitraparb" urban village showed the most patience before coalescing into militant action to fight the drug dealers.

The fishermen's three days of confrontation and four months of waiting for the result was the shortest episode, while the decade-long and as yet unresolved struggle of the Ban Krua community is the longest. The "Mitraparb" village's eight-month struggle falls in between.

Second, the social background of each community is different. Ban Krua and "Mitraparb" Muslims are quite similar because both communities are urban, with a good representation of small businesspeople and factory workers. On the other hand, the fishermen of the Southern Sea are rural people. In terms of educational background, the Ban Krua Muslims are perhaps the best educated.

Third, the relationship between the communities and state agencies in general is different in each case. While the "Mitraparb" community is on very good terms with the authorities, both the Ban Krua Muslims and the fishermen are not. This is because the causes they are fighting against are different.

Fourth, the "Mitraparb" community's fight against the drug pushers dovetailed with official state policy, whereas the struggles against the highway exit and the big fishermen pitted poor people against entrenched interests defended by the government.

Fifth, the degree to which each community is committed to nonviolent action differs. It seems that the fishermen were most vocal about their commitment to nonviolence, while the "Mitraparb" community most inclined to resort to force if necessary. As a matter of fact, one of their banners read: "We will not forgive the damned drug pushers."[24] The Ban Krua community is distinctive in its varied uses of nonviolent techniques. Most of the methods Ban Krua people fell under the category of symbolic nonviolent protest.

On the other hand, there are five basic similarities in the protests that were significant in help in these minority Muslim communities win the admiration of the surrounding non-Muslim majority.

1. Just Cause

Each struggle was widely perceived as a just cause. The "Mitraparb" crusade against drug pushers struck a chord among both Muslims and non-Muslims afflicted by that plague. Their community has been fighting against drug problems. The Ban Krua community has been fighting against the modernization project that ran against the grain of both Islamic suspicion of human arrogance and a more general suspicion among the city's populace that the highway was a boondoggle likely to create more traffic at the expense of the dignity and welfare of one of the city's oldest neighborhoods. This drama of human values vs. the impersonal juggernaut of urban renewal had a wide appeal that extended far beyond the Muslim community with the most to lose. The Southern fishermen were fighting to preserve their livelihood, and in so doing, to preserve a balance in nature and among humans balance ordained by God. The ocean testifies to God's bountiful mercy as "the Lord of bounties unbounded."[25] For these Muslims God's bounties are meant to be shared and not monopolized, a view equally appealing to the surrounding Buddhist community, which views greed as a form of attachment that impedes the quest for enlightenment. In fact, in all three cases the causes advanced by these

Muslim communities were easily embraceable in the ethos of the Buddhist majority.

2. Nonviolent Actions

Most of the three Muslim communities' actions were nonviolent. The "Mitraparb" community was least explicit in their commitment to nonviolence, perhaps because their approach came closest to vigilantism in dealing with potentially violent opponents in the drug trade. But in the cases of both the fishermen and Ban Krua, participants seem to be quite conscious about their peaceful intent, in part because both were mindful of the need to attract support outside their immediate communities. These three communities' nonviolent actions were primarily "tactical" (i.e. geared towards limited changes) and "pragmatic" (i.e. using nonviolent actions not as a sacred principle or a way of life but because they seemed more effective).[26]

3. Organization

All three communities showed a strong and effective organizational strategy. I would argue that being a Muslim community makes getting organized somewhat easier because there are a number of communal functions that need to be performed such as *Yanaza* (prayers for the deceased) or washing *Mayyid* (body of the dead) or burial of the dead within twenty-four hours. The importance of a closely-knitted *Umma*, notwithstanding, is that these rituals do tighten the community bonds which can prove useful in the course of a civic or political protest or struggle.

4. Faces

One unique feature of these three Muslim communities is the fact that though their leadership are very strong and skillful, they manage not to overshadow the significance of the communities. When one looks at the groups, it is not easy to identify who the leaders are. Although in the cases of both "Mitraparb" and Ban Krua, some prominent members are more visible due to their connection with the authority in the former case and long years of fighting in the latter, it could be argued that it is the community itself that is the star of nonviolent fighting and not the leaders. This seems to be in line with development of nonviolent actions at the global level where the faces of singular leaders (e.g. Gandhi or King or Mandela) are being replaced by faces of courageous people, ordinary mortals fighting with nonviolence against injustices everywhere.[27] This would mean that nonviolent actions are not reserved for extraordinary beings but could be used by ordinary people. To view nonviolent actions from this angle is in itself to empower the others and open up possibilities for more use of nonviolent actions.

5. *Voices*

If the effect of injustice is to silence the victims, nonviolent actions are methods of eradicating those silences. It is not a case of "giving" voice to the voiceless. Rather, it is a case of the previously voiceless deciding to end the silence with their own voices. In this sense, nonviolent actions are communicative. But it is not a one way communication in the sense that the previously voiceless speak. It begins when the previously voiceless decide to speak, speak truth to power, and deal with the consequences while the rest of that society benefits from the struggle. If those who fight for just cause with nonviolence win, that society as a whole will be better off. Even if they lose, that society does learn how to use nonviolent actions and at times feel empowered by them. Nonviolent actions, therefore, are communicative in the realm of power relations because they could alter existing power relations and expand political space for possible transformation.[28] These three Muslim communities managed to emerge from voicelessness and expand political space for just causes with their communal nonviolent actions. What remains to be discussed is why Muslim communal nonviolent actions seem to be accepted as exemplars in a non-Muslim society?

CONCLUSION: MUSLIM COMMUNAL NONVIOLENT ACTION AS AN EXEMPLAR OF COEXISTENCE

In *The Handbook of Interethnic Coexistence*, Gene Sharp, a leading theorist of nonviolent action, argues that ethnic groups in conflict can practice nonviolence while still adhering to their long-term objectives, their fundamental convictions, and even their prejudices; such an approach may not "produce a loving society but a less violent one."[29]

It is the less acute conflicts—such as those pertaining to ecological issues or hyper-development in conflict with nature or tradition—that might dominate the political landscape in the next century as humankind grapples with potential shortages of land, natural resources, and water. Such issues are ripe with the potential for desperate, dehumanizing acrimony among nations and ethnic groups. More than ever, nonviolence seems the only path that can guarantee at least the possibility of human survival through such dire contingencies.

Huntington, in his controversial *The Clash of Civilizations and the Remaking of World Order*, recycles the shopworn notion that "Islam has from the start been a religion of the sword" and that "a concept of nonviolence is absent from Muslim doctrine and practice."[30] There are many ways to counter such unwarranted assertions. Some have indicated pointed to the demonization of Islam by the Western media.[31] Other scholars have shown that violence pervades Muslim public life because violence pervades world orders, old or new, that Islam as an ideology is subordinated to nationalism, and that it is European colonial powers that have used religion to divide and control Muslim societies.[32] Such counterpoints—along with examples such as the three discussed in this article—help to advance the idea that, Huntington notwithstanding, nonviolence does indeed have a place in Islamic culture and politics. In fact, these cases indicate empirically that Muslims can apply the tactics of nonviolence so well that they elicit the admiration of their non-Muslim countrymen. Muslims are "naturally" prepared for nonviolent action thanks to the Islamic tradition of fighting for a just with discipline, empathy, patience, and solidarity.[33] All these qualities are crucial for getting organized and voice their claim for justice.

In a non-Muslim society, when a minority group gets organized for a just cause, the majority might not object to it. Sometimes, the voice of a victim is not welcomed because the larger society would prefer to be blind to the pain of the sufferings and deaf to cries of the oppressed. But there does exist those who long for justice, they might welcome the move. However, with the image of close proximity between Muslims and violence, getting organized, challenging existing power could be feared. The use of nonviolence could lessen those fears. If fear is removed, or at least undermined, the act could be appreciated and Muslim communal nonviolent action could be seen as exemplar: an example of coexistence that goes beyond staying together with tolerance or loving one another, but doing the right thing for a better tomorrow that could be shared by all.

ENDNOTES

Chapter 1

1. This viewpoint is supported in Alvin Rabushka and Kenneth A. Shepsle's *Politics in Plural Societies: A Theory of Democratic Instability.* (SUNY: New York) 1972. The authors argue in their introductory chapter that the results of discord within plural societies are "democratic instability, authoritarian government, gerrymandering, legal and illegal manipulations" p. 7.

2. Locke's discourse is intimately linked to democratic pluralism; the logic of his contractual thinking is evident in the emergence of economic cooperation, as in the EU and NAFTA. As advocated by Ismail Berlin and other contemporary theorists, democratic pluralism encourages a message of free markets and free minds. While this form of democracy enjoins tolerance and cultural differences, the basic precepts are highly significant encompassing values of individualism, secularism, and consumerism, among others.

3. Neil J. Smelser and Jeffrey C. Alexander, eds., *Diversity and Its Discontents: Cultural Conflict and Common Ground in Contemporary American Society*, (Princeton University Press: Princeton, NJ), 1999, p. 15.

4. Joseph Prabhu, ed., *The Intercultural Challenge of Raimon Panikkar*, (Orbis Books: Maryknoll, NY), 1996, pp. 250-251.

5. Brad Stetson, *Pluralism and Particularity in Religious Belief*, (Praeger: Westport, CT), 1994, p. 9.

6. Joseph Prabhu, ed., *The Intercultural Challenge of Raimon Panikkar*, p. 253.

7. Ibid. Raimon Panikkar goes on to say, "Peace and conflict resolution demand such a pluralistic attitude." p. 258.

8. Brad Stetson, *Pluralism and Particularity in Religious Belief,* p. 75.

9. Gregory Bateson, *Steps to An Ecology of Mind: A Revolutionary Approach to Man's Understanding of Himself.* (Ballantine Books: New York), 1972, p. 469.

10. Surah 109:6.

11. Karen Armstrong, *Holy War: The Crusades and Their Impact on Today's World* (Doubleday: New York), 1988.

12. One particular story of the Prophet Muhammed is his encounter with Waraqa b. Naufal b. 'Abdu'l-'Uzza, a Christian cousin of Khadijah (the Prophet's first wife), who was the first to confirm Muhammed's revelation as Abrahamic in content (the God of Moses and Abraham).

13. Karen Armstrong, *Holy War: The Crusades and their Impact on Today's World*, p. 46.

14. CL. Cahen, "Dhimmi," *The Encyclopedia of Islam*, Vol. II, C-G, B. Lewis, Ch.Pellat, & J. Schacht, eds., (Leiden, Netherlands: E. J. Brill), 1965, pp. 227-230.

15. R.D. Grillo, *Pluralism and the Politics of Difference: State, Culture, and Ethnicity* in15. R.D. Grillo, *Pluralism and the Politics of Difference: State, Culture, and Ethnicity in Comparative Perspectives* (Oxford University Press, Oxford, United Kingdom), 1998, pp. 93-96. And Marshall G. S. Hodgson, *The Venture of Islam: Conscience and History in a World Civilization*, Vol. 1 "The Classical Age of Islam", (University Press of Chicago: Chicago), 1974, pp. 305-308.

16. Cyril Glasse, *The Concise Encyclopedia of Islam*, (Harper San Francisco: New York), 1989, p. 98.

17. Marshall G.S. Hodgson, *The Venture of Islam*, pp. 215-216. The First Fitnah Wars occurred between A.D. 656-661, the Second Fitnah Wars between A.D. 680-692, and the Third Fitnah Wars between A.D. 744-750.

18. Majid Khadduri, *War and Peace in the Law of Islam*. (Johns Hopkins University Press: Baltimore, MD), 1955, p. 13.

19. Ibid., p. 6.

20. Armstrong, pp. 45-46.

21. Miguel Asin Palacios. *Islam and the Divine Comedy*. Trans. Harold Sutherland. (Frank Cass & Co.: London), 1968.

22. Annemarie Schimmel, *Islam: An Introduction*, (SUNY: Albany, NY), 1992, p. v.

Chapter 3

1. Lewis, Bernard. *The Middle East and the West* 1964, p.70.

2. Ibid, p.71.

3. Lewis, Bernard. (op.cit.), p. 107.

Chapter 4

Bibliographical note by author: Given the degree to which this paper directly expresses the assimilation of years of reading into my own thought, I did not think it necessary to annotate it. With the exception of the reference to Muhammad Arkoun, my text contains no paraphrase or other requirement for footnotes (For that single reference, the reader may consult Arkoun's *Tarikhiyyatul-Fikril-'Arabil-Islami* [The Historicity of Arabo-Islamic Thought], pp. 288-291). However, I shall list some references for those readers who seek inspiration for the further pursuit of themes that have been introduced here. Today's databases are good enough for the names of the authors and the titles of their works to suffice. Among works that relate to the Arab Muslim world, the reader may consult all three volumes of *The Venture of Islam* (Marshall Hodgson), *A History of Islamic Societies* (Ira Lapidus), Albert Hourani's collected papers, *Religion and Social Change in Modern Turkey* (Serif Mardin), and William Chittick's books on Ibn 'Arabi and Rumi. As for works that relate to modern Western thought, *Kant's Critique of Practical Reason* is important. So are *Concluding Unscientific Postscript and the Present Age* (Sooren Kierkegaard), *Beyond Good and Evil* (Nietzsche), *The Sleepwalkers* (Hermann Broch), *The Mystery of Being* (Gabriel Marcel), and *Faith and Belief* (Wilfred Cantwell Smith). The reader will also benefit tremendously by paying some attention to the Presocratic philosophers, especially Anaximander (for instance, as presented in Paul Seligma's excellent and unjustly forgotten book *The Apeiron of Anaximander*), as well as Plato, Aristotle, and, above all, Plotinus, for whose extremely difficult thought Pierre Hadot's splendid *Plotinus or the Simplicity of Vision* offers the best introduction. Since I made a passing reference to the possibility of a higher logic drawn from an awareness of the dynamic of the one and the many, the reader who wishes to become engaged further with such themes will benefit tremendously from the joint work by Martin Heidegger and Eugen Fink entitled *Heraklitus Seminar*.

Chapter 5

1. Verse 49:13 reads: "O mankind, lo We have created you male and female, and have made you nations (*shu'ub*) and tribes (*qaba'il*) that you may know one another. Lo, the noblest of you in the sight of God is the most God-fearing. . . ." There will be further reference to this verse below in the section on the Shu'ubiyya.

2. Another section that describes the identity of the community collectively through the identical behavior of its individual members is 48:29; it reads, "Muhammad is the messenger of God; and those who are with him are hard against the non-believers and merciful among themselves. You see them bowing and prostrating, seeking bounty from God and [His] acceptance. The mark of them is on their foreheads from the traces of prostration. Such is their likeness in the Torah and their likeness in the Gospel-like a sown corn that sends forth its shoot and strengthens it and rises firm upon its stalk, delighting the sower—that He may enrage the non-believers with [the sight of] them".

3. See his *al-umma wa l-jama'a wa l-sulta* (Beirut: Dar Iqra, 1984), pp. 53-55, 154.

4. Cf. M. Kister, "Social and Religious Concepts of Authority in Islam," *Jerusalem Studies in Arabic and Islam* 18 (1994), pp. 98-99. Other groups who were believed by Sunni scholars to be meant by the Qur'anic "people in charge" were the Prophet's (military) commanders (*al-umara'*), the Prophet's Companions (*sahaba*), or, more specifically, Abu Bakr and 'Umar; see Wadad al-Qadi, "Authority," *Encyclopedia of the Qur'an*, Leiden: E. J. Brill, forthcoming.

5. Kister, pp. 99-111.

6. See Kister, p. 108

7. See Kister, *passim.*

8. See A.A. Duri, "Diwan, *EI* 2, II, 323327, E. Tyan, "Kadi," ibid., IV, pp. 373-375.

9. See G. H. A. Juynboll, *Muslim Tradition*, Cambridge: Cambridge University Press, 1983, pp. 62-63.

10. al-Sayyid, pp. 76-80.

11. See Michael Cook's newbook, *Commanding Right and Forbidding Wrong in Islamic Thought* (Cambridge: Cambridge University Press, 2000).

12. The Shu'ubiyya movement has received sufficient attention from modern scholars to make its broad claims well known. Therefore, while presenting these claims below, I shall not cite particular sources, primary or secondary, except in the cases where the claims mentioned have not received the attention they deserve or when they are of special significance for the student of diversity in Islamic culture. Two sources in particular will be consistently cited: the first is Abu Hayyan al-Tawhidi's *al-Imta' wa l-mu'anasa* (ed. Ahmad Amin and Ahmad al-Zayn, Cairo: Lajnat al-Ta'lif wa l-Tarjama wa l-Nashr, 1939-1944, I, pp. 77-81), which has preserved a very important discussion of the Shu'ubi ideas of a certain al-Jayhani (see below, n. 17) and Tawhidi's retorts to those ideas; no scholar has used this source, as far as I know. The same applies to al-Jahiz's treatise on censuring the secretaries

("Dhamm akhlaq alkuttab"), which is preserved in *Rasa'il al-Jahiz* (ed. 'Abd al-Salam Muhammad Harun, Cairo: Maktabat al-Khanji, [1964], II, pp. 193-209). I have also deemed it useful to give the page references to Ibn Qutayba's *Kitab al-'arab* (in *Rasa'il al-bulagha'*, ed. Muhammad Kurd 'Ali, Cairo: Lajnat al-Ta'lif wa l-Tarjama wa l-Nashr, 1946, pp. 344-377) because of its fundamental importance to diversity-related Shu'ubiyya discussions. For the main studies on the Shu'ubiyya, especially in the Eastern part of the Islamic world, see Ignaz Goldziher, "The Shu'ubiyya," in *Muslim Studies*, tr. and ed. S. M. Stern, London: George Allen & Unwin Ltd., 1967, I, pp. 137-163 (*Mohammedanische Studien* [Halle, 1889-1890], I, pp. 147-176); H. A. R. Gibb, in *Studies in the Civilization of Islam*, Boston: Beacon Press, 1962, pp. 62-73; 'Abd al-'Aziz al-Duri, *al-Judhur al-tarikhiyya li-l-shu'ubiyya*, 3rd ed., Beirut: Dar al-Tali'a, 1981 [1st ed., 1962]; Roy P. Mottahedeh, "The Shu'ûbîyah Controversy and the Social History of Early Islamic Iran," *International Journal of Middle East Studies* 7 (1976), pp. 161-182; H. T. Norris, "Shu'ubiyyah in Arabic Literature," in *'Abbasid Belles-Lettres* [Cambridge History of Arabic Literature], ed. Julia Astiyani et al., Cambridge: Cambridge University Press, 1990, pp. 31-47; Enderwitz, "Shu'ubiyya," *EI* 2, IX, pp. 513-515; Enderwitz's study has an extensive bibliography on the Shu'ubiyya.

13. For studies on the Shu'ubiyya in the West and translations of some of their works, see James T. Monroe, *The Shu'ubiyya in al-Andalus*, Berkeley, Los Angeles, London: University of California Press, 1970; 'Abd al-Wahid Dhannun Taha, "al-Dass al-shu'ubi bi-l-andalus wa mawqif al-'arab fi mujabahatihi," *Dirasat Andalusiyya* 4 (1410/1990), pp. 6-24; Jum'a Shaykha, "Min mazahir al-shu'ubiyya fi l-andalus," *Dirasat Andalusiyya* (1410/1990), pp. 25-34. For other references, see Enderwitz's above cited article in the new edition of the *Encyclopaedia of Islam*, pp. 515-516.

14. I shall not take up the Shu'ubiyya of the West since my aim is to draw conclusions from the study of one case, and the Eastern Shu'ubiyya provides ample material for that study.

15. According to their opponents or to literary historians, the Shu'ubis wrote books on the vices of Arabs or on despicable groups among them. Thus, for example, the famous philologist Abu 'Ubayda (d. 209/824) wrote a book on vices (*al-Mathalib*), a book on the vices of a particular Arab tribe (*Mathalib bahila*), and another book on Arab robbers (*Lusus al-'arab*); and the chronicler al-Haytham b. 'Adi (d.

207/822) wrote three books on vices (*al-Mathalib, al-Mathalib alikabir*, and *al-Mathalib al-saghir*), a book entitled *The Vices of the Arabs(Mathalib al-'arab*), a book on the vices of a particular Arab tribe (*Mathalib rabi'a*), and a book on the names of the whores of the Quraysh in pre-Islam and their children (*Asthma' baghaya quraysh fi l-jahiliyya wa asma' man waladna*); see Ibn al-Nadim, *al-Fihrist*, ed. Rida Tajaddud, Teheran, [1970], 59, p. 112. Some Shu'ubis chose to write books on the virtues of the non-Arabs. Thus, the above-mentioned Abu 'Ubayda wrote a book on the virtues of the Persians (*Fada'il al-furs*), and Sa'id b. Humyad al-Bakhtakan (d. 240/854) authored *The Superiority of the Persians over the Arabs and their Boasting About That* (*Fadl al-'ajam 'ala l-'arab wa iftikharuha*); see ibid., 59, p. 137. Other Shu'ubis compiled works in which they mixed extolling the Persians with denigrating the Arabs. This is what the litterateur Sahl b. Harun (d. 245/859) did: he had very strong Shu'ubi leanings and "composed many books and treatises" on the subject (ibid., p. 133); it seems to be also what the fourth/tenth century Samanid administrator al-Jayhani (see below, n. p. 17) did in a book that Tawhidi refuted (*Imta'*, I, p. 78).

16. Ibn Qutayba, *'Arab*, p. 344.

17. The sources mention two Jayhanis. The first is Muhammad b. Ahmad b. Nasr, who was a poet and major figure in the Samanid administration in Bukhara at the beginning of the fourth/tenth century (Yaq,ut l-'Hamawi, *Mu'jam al-udaba'*, ed. D. S. Margoliouth, Cairo, 1930, VI, pp. 293-294); Ibn al-Nadim (in *al-Fihrist*, 401) lists his name among "the leaders of the Manichean theologians who adhere to Islam in appearance but are in reality heretics" (*min ru'asa'ihim al-mutakallimin alladhina yuzhirun al-islam wa yubtinun al-zandaqa*). The second is Ahmad b. Muhammad b. Nasr, who was a wazir of the Samanids in the latter half of the fourth/tenth century and authored a number of books, including *Kitab al-ayin* (Ibn al-Nadim, 153; Yaq,t, II, pp. 59-60). Margoliouth suggested (in *Islamica* 2 [1934], pp. 389-390) that the second was the Shu'ubi meant by Tawhidi, whereas the editors of the *Imta'* (I, p. 86) believed that the first was the more likely one.

18. Tawhidi, *Imta'*, I, pp. 86-87.

19. Tawhidi, *Imta'*, I, p. 89.

20. Ibn Qutayba, *'Arab*, p. 344.

21. On this subject, see the article by Enderwitz mentioned above.

22. al-Jahiz, "Dhamm," p. 193.

23. al-Jahiz, "Dhamm," pp. 191-192.

24. al-Jahiz, "Dhamm," pp. 194-196.

25. al-Jahiz, "Dhamm," pp. 191, 192-193, 195.

26. Some of the Shu'ubis, such as the poet Bashshar b. Burd, wished to portray Shu'ubism as a harmless literary fashion (see Norris, p. 35). But this does not seem to be the way their contemporaries viewed the Shu'ubiyya.

27. Ibn Qutayba, *'Arab*, p. 344.

28. al-Jahiz, *Kitab al-Hayawan*, ed. 'Abd al-Salam Muhammad Harun, Cairo: Maktabat wa Maba'at 'Isa l-Babi l-Halabi, 1938-1945, VII, p. 220 (translated in Norris, pp. 35-6).

29. Gibb, p. 69.

30. The works refuting the Shu'ubis' claims are numerous, and some have been used above in reconstructing those claims, the main ones being al-Jahiz's treatise on the vices of the secretaries, Ibn Qutayba's *Kitab al'arab*, and a section of Tawhidi's *Imta'*. Other works are a large section of al-Jahiz's book *al-Bayan wa l-tabyin* (ed. 'Abd al-Salam Muhammad Harun, Cairo: Maktabat al-Khanji, fourth edition, 1975), III, *passim*, and a section of Ibn 'Abd Rabbih's *al-'Iqd al-farid* (ed. Ahmad Amin, Ahmad al-Zayn and Ibrahim al-Ibyari, Cairo: Lajnat al-Ta'lif wa l-Tarjama wa l-Nashr, 1953-1965, III, pp. 403-417). As Norris noted (p. 44), they also wrote books on the etymology of Arabic tribal names such as Ibn Durayd's (d. 321/933) *Ishtiqaq* and Ibn Faris' (d. 395/1004) *al-Sahibi fi fiqh al-lugha*. Norris adds, "By the time al-Zamakhshari (d. 538/1143), himself a Persian by descent, wrote his *Mufassal,* the debate was nearing its close; an unconsious identification of Islam with (linguistic) Arabism had taken root in the conscience of believers, and Zamakhshari was able to thank his Maker for ordaining his preoccupation with philology in order to fight the Lord's battles against the party of slander and mockery. Centuries before him, *Jahiz,* in *Kitab al-Bayan*, had expressed similar sentiments."

31. So that no language is comparable to it (Tawhidi, *Imta'*, I, pp. 77-78).

32. See Tawhidi, *Imta'*, I, pp. 83-85.

33. According to Tawhidi, the nature of the land and its topography certainly affects lifestyles (e.g., that of the pre-Islamic Arabs), so that if Chosoroes and Caesar were to live in such forbidding terrain as that of Arabia, they would have ended up behaving exactly like the pre-Islamic Arabs or even worse; this is to be noted in those Arabians' achievements in high culture when rain fell and their land became fertile (Tawhidi, *Imta'* I, pp. 79-81). The Tawhidi, *Imta'* roots of the idea are in Ibn Qutayba, *'Arab*, pp. 365-370).

34. Tawhidi, *Imta'*, I, pp. 87-88.

35. Tawhidi, *Imta'*, I, pp. 82-83; Abu Sulayman al-Mantiqi also thought the Arabs had purer minds; ibid., pp. 88-89), and are, according to Tawhidi, better and purer than those of the dishonest, conniving, deceitful city-dwellers (ibid, pp. 82-83).

36. Ibn Qutayba, *'Arab*, pp. 361-4, 370.

37. Tawhidi, *Imta'*, I, pp. 89-90.

38. Ibn Qutayba, *'Arab*, p. 373.

39. Ibn Qutayba, *'Arab*, pp. 353-4.

40. Ibn Qutayba, *'Arab*, p. 346.

41. Ibn Qutayba, *'Arab*, p. 346.

42. Ibn Qutayba, *'Arab*, p. 344.

43. Ibn Qutayba, *'Arab*, p. 348.

44. Jahiz, *Rasa'il*, IV, p. 20.

45. Ibn Qutayba, *'Arab*, p. 348.

46. Ibn Qutayba, *'Arab*, pp. 351-2.

47. Ibn Qutayba, *'Arab*, pp. 352-3.

48. Tawhidi, *Imta'* I, pp. 91 and 92.

49. Ibn Qutayba, *'Arab*, p. 349.

50. Ibn Qutayba, *'Arab*, p. 344.

51. Ibn Qutayba, *'Arab*, p. 350.

52. Ibn Qutayba, *'Arab*, p. 352.

53. Ibn Qutayba, *'Arab*, p. 344.

54. Ibn Qutayba, *'Arab*, p. 344. See also Tawhidi's deriding of the Shu'ubiyya for their unfairness (*fa-l-yastahi l-Jayhani ...min al-qadh' wa l-safah al-ladhayn hasha bihima kitabahu; Imta'*, I, p. 85), and his accusing them of "asabiyya," fanatical factionalism (ibid., pp. 86, 88) and prejudice (ibid., p. 88).

55. Tawhidi, *Imta'*, I, p. 88.

56. So said Abu-Hamid al-Marwarrudhi; see Tawhidi, *Imta'*, I, p. 90; also Ibn Qutayba, *'Arab*, p. 372.

57. This according to Tawhidi; *Imta'*, I, pp. 91-92.

58. This according to Abu l-Hasan al-Ansari; see Tawhidi, *Imta'*, I, pp. 93-94.

59. This according to Abu Sulayman al-Mantiqi; see Tawhidi, *Imta'*, I, p. 95.

60. Ibn Qutayba, *'Arab*, p. 345.61. Jahiz, *Rasa'il*, IV, p. 301.

62. Ibn Qutayba, *'Arab*, pp. 350-51.

63. Ibn Qutayba, *'Arab*, p. 354.

64. Ibn Qutayba, *'Arab*, p. 352.

65. Ibn Qutayba, *'Arab*, p. 377.

66. Some modern scholars have explained the conciliatory attitude of the Shu'ubis' opponents as an attempt at wooing the Persians, specifically in the case of Ibn Qutayba; see Mottahedeh, p. 180, where he says that Ibn Qutayba believed that the new Arab ruling class and the older Iranian ruling class could indeed have a shared genealogical prejudice against their subordinates, who had no ties of kinship; see also Norris, p. 37.

67. Ibn Qutayba, *'Arab*, p. 346. Abu 'Ubayda authored several books on Qur'an and Hadith; see Ibn al-Nadim, *al-Fihrist*, p. 59.

68. Tawhidi, *Imta'*, I, pp. 85-86.

69. Ibn Qutayba, *'Arab,* pp. 357-60.

70. Tawhidi, *Imta'* I, pp. 85-86.

71. Ibn Qutayba, *'Arab*, pp. 351 and 364.

72. Tawhidi, *Imta'* I, p. 75.

73. Tawhidi, *Imta'* I, p. 75.

74. Tawhidi, *Imta'* I, p. 70.

75. Ibn Qutayba, *'Arab*, p. 350.

76. Tawhidi, *Imta'* I, pp. 75-77, 81-82, 85; roots of the idea are in Ibn Qutayba, *'Arab*, pp. 370, 373.

77. Tawhidi, *Imta'* I, p. 81.

78. Pellat (in *Le Milieu basrien* [Paris: Librairie d'Amérique et d'Orient, 1953], pp. 220-221) argued that *zandaqa* is an extreme manifestation of sentiment arising in the first instance from a sense of worldly superiority and only thereafter spilling into spiritual matters.

79. Norris, pp. 41-42, states, "Among the Shu'ubis there were undoubtedly some whose private religious convictions placed them completely outside orthodox Islam. Most of them were believers or dabblers in Manichaeism or in a Zoroastrian dualism, and were dubbed *zanadiqah*, . . . a word which in Muslim law denotes any heretic who is

a danger to the state. To the *zindiqs*, the claims of the Arabs, as Muslims and as Arabs, were totally unacceptable. Ibn al-Nadim . . . mentions a certain Muhammad b. al-Husayn, nicknamed Daydan, who was a secretary to the governor of Isfahan in the second/eighth century and was sympathetic to those who sought a restoration of Sasanian power. He was a philosopher and astrologer, belonging to the *Shu'ubiyyah*, and he was bitter against the Islamic government. He believed with certainty in [such neo-Platonic and un-Islamic-or Ismaili-abstractions as] the Universal Soul (*al-Nafs*), the Intelligence (*al-'Aql*), Time (*al-Zaman*), Space (*al-Makan*) and Matter (*al-Hayula*). He also supposed that the stars exercised control and spiritual action over the world and that they predicted a return to Persian rule and to the religion of the Magi. Such beliefs, which were allied to academic snobbery and to deprecation of Arabism, were widespread in certain circles in Baghdad and Basra. Among their best-known manifestations is a poem attributed to Abu Nuwas . . . and quoted by Jahiz. . . :

> I said, "Glory to God" and he said, "Glory to Mani"
> I said, "Jesus is an apostle" and he said, "of the Devil";
> I said, "Moses is the interlocutor of the Benevolent Watcher";
> He said, "Your Lord, then, has an eyeball and a tongue?
> His very essence brought Him into being; if not, who did?"
> "I rose up there and then offended by an infidel to be shunned,
> Who argues by denying any belief in Him, the Lord most Merciful."

80. See J. L. Kraemer, "Heresy Versus the State in Medieval Islam," in *Studies in Judaica, Karaitica and Islamica*, ed. Sheldon Brunswick, Bar-Ilan University Press, 1982, pp. 167-180. Kraemer's thesis in this paper is that the heretics "in the world of Islam who were truly heretics, not merely libertine poets, mystic visionaries or cultured secretaries, were objectively enemies of religion and Islam and a real danger to the state and social order. Hence, their persecution and suppression were the natural reaction of the state authorities." (pp. 167-168).

Chapter 6

1. However, a good deal of research has been carried out on twentieth-century Islam, mainly in political and anthropological contexts. See Dru C. Gladney, *Muslim Chinese: Ethnic Nationalism in the People's Republic* (Cambridge: Harvard University Press, 1991).

2. For more details on the Chinese intellectual tradition, along with the translation of two early texts, see Murata, *Chinese Gleams of Persian Light: Sufi Texts in Chinese* (Albany: SUNY Press, forthcoming).

3. See, for example, Donald Leslie, *Islamic Literature in Chinese* (Canberra: Canberra College of Advanced Education, 1981); idem, *Islam in Traditional China* (Canberra: Canberra College of Advanced Education, 1986).

4. In the Buddhist context, they are usually translated into English as the "world of forms" and the "formless world."

5. Wing Tsit-Chan, *A Source Book in Chinese Philosophy*, (Princeton: Princeton University Press, 1973), p. 85. He continues by saying, "No other Confucian Classic has presented this idea so clearly and so forcefully."

6. For a great deal of documentation on the Islamic view of cosmic balance, see my *Tao of Islam: A Sourcebook on Gender Relationships in Islamic Thought* (Albany: SUNY Press, 1992).

7. The whole text of The Great Learning of the Pure and Real is translated in my *Chinese Gleams of Persian Light.*

Chapter 7

1. As cited in *The Oxford Dictionary of Quotations*, (2nd ed.; London: Oxford University Press, 1955), p. 557.

2. Jamal A. Badawi, "Muslims, Jews, and the Abrahamic Connection," in *Muslims and Christians, Muslims and Jews: A Common Past, a Hopeful Future*, ed. Marilyn Robinson Waldman (Columbus, Ohio: Islamic Foundation of Central Ohio, Catholic Diocese of Columbus, Congregation Tifereth Israel, 1992), p. 24. Emphasis added.

3. One might note as one example among many the recent discussion of the need for genetic diversity in apples in Michael Pollan, "The Call of the Wild," Apple, *New York Times*, 5 November 1998.

4. See Nathan Glazer & Daniel P. Moynihan, *Beyond the Melting Pot* (2nd ed.; Cambridge: MIT Press, 1970).

5. Peter N. Stearns, *The Industrial Revolution in World History* (2nd ed.; Boulder: Westview Press, 1998), pp. 136-137.

6. Peter Manuel, *Cassette Culture, Popular Music and Technology in North India* (Chicago: University of Chicago Press, 1993), p. 2.

7. Arthur M. Schlesinger, Jr., *The Disuniting of America: Reflections on a Multicultural Society* (New York: Norton, 1992), see the title of the book and p. 119.

8. Daniel Patrick Moynihan, *Pandemonium: Ethnicity in International Politics* (New York: Oxford University Press, 1993). The phrase is the title of the final chapter in the book.

9. See, for example, the analysis in Roland Robertson and JoAnn Chirico, "Humanity, Globalization, and Worldwide Religious Resurgence: A Theoretical Exploration," *Sociological Analysis* 46, No. 3 (1985).

10. Benjamin R. Barber, *Jihad vs. McWorld: How Globalism and Tribalism are Reshaping the World* (New York: Ballantine Books, 1996).

11. Barber, *Jihad vs. McWorld*, p. 5.

12. See, for example, Roland Robertson, "Globalization: Time-Space and Homogeneity-Heterogeneity," in *Global Modernities*, ed. Mike Featherstone, Scott Lash, and Roland Robertson (London: Sage, 1995).

13. Terence E. Fretheim, "The Book of Genesis: Introduction, Commentary, and Reflections," *The New Interpreter's Bible*, I (Nashville: Abingdon Press, 1994): pp. 413-414.

14. Farid Esack, *Qur'an, Liberation, and Pluralism* (Oxford: Oneworld, 1997), p. 172.

15. This terminology is from Ira M. Lapidus, *A History of Islamic Societies* (Cambridge: Cambridge University Press, 1988), p. 237.

16. See, for such usages Robert Wuthnow, *Communities of Discourse* (Cambridge, MA: Harvard University Press, 1989) and John Obert Voll, "Islam as a Special World-System," *Journal of World History* 5,

No. 2 (1994).

17. See, for example, John O. Voll, "Renewal and Reform in Islamic History: *Tajdid* and *Islah*," in *Voices of Resurgent Islam*, ed. John L. Esposito (New York: Oxford University Press, 1983).

18. A discussion of *ikhtilaf* in the context of modern Muslim political thought can be found in John L. Esposito and John O. Voll, *Islam and Democracy* (New York: Oxford University Press, 1996), pp. 44-46.

19. Yusuf al-Qaradawi, *Islamic Awakening between Rejection and Extremism*, Issues of Islamic Thought Series No. 2 (Herndon, VA: International Institute of Islamic Thought, 1401/ 1981), p. 82. See also the citation of Abu Hanifah, the prominent eighth century legal scholar, in J. Schacht, "Ikhtilaf," *The Encyclopedia of Islam* (new ed.): 3:1061.

20. Translation in Michel Chodkiewicz, *The Spiritual Writings of Amir 'Abd al-Kader* (trans. James Chrestensen and Tom Manning; Albany: State University of New York Press, 1995), p. 19.

21. Chodkiewicz, *Spiritual Writings*, p. 19.

22. Chodkiewicz, *Spiritual Writings*, p. 126.

23. The translations are from Ahmed Ali, *Al-Qur'an* (Princeton: Princeton University Press, 1984). The final translation is taken from the cover sheet for the notebook of materials distributed for the conference on "Cultural Diversity and Islam," at American University in Washington, DC, on 20 November 1998.

24. See, for example, the analysis in Issa J. Boullata, "Fa-stabiqu 'l-khayrat: A Qur'anic Principle of Interfaith Relations," in *Christian Muslim Encounters*, ed. Yvonne Yazbeck Haddad and Wadi Zaidan Haddad (Gainesville: University Press of Florida, 1995), pp. 43-53.

25. Aimen Mir, "Issa Boullata's Elements of Qur'anic Pluralism and the Debate over Exclusivism and Pluralism in the Qur'an," unpublished paper submitted in "Muslim-Christian Relations in World History" (Georgetown University INAF 441), April 1998. This paper provides a thorough analysis of the views of a number of Qur'anic commentators, both medieval and modern. I am grateful to Aimen Mir for permission to cite his paper in this presentation.

Chapter 8

1. See Nietzsche's article in *The Critical Dictionary of Theology*, s.d. De Jean-Yves Lacoste, P.U.F. 1998.

2. See the very dense monograph of Jamal al-Amrani: J. Vrin, p. 199.

3. See what I have said on this in *Min Faysal al-tafriqa ila fasl al-maqal: Ayna huwa-l-fikr al-isamiyy al-muasir*, Dar al-Saqi, Beirut, 1993.

4. I am anxious to mark this differentiation to introduce a critical history of the methods and reception levels and/or of rejection of modernity and modernization in Islamic contexts since the 19th century. It is certain that the negative face of modernity that accompanied the colonial domination widely nourished a reaction of global rejection leaving little place for discernment work between the emancipators of intellectual modernity and the imperialist instrumentalization of sciences and techniques for the expansion of the capitalist exploiter.

5. On this paragraph, see G. Makdisi: *Ibn 'Aqil*, Molla Sadra in EI.

6. Title of a stimulating work of Christian Jambet that finely analyzes *The Forms of Liberty in Shi'ite Islam* (subtitle), Verdier 1990.

7. See the recent work of P. Crone et al.

8. See R. Jamous, *Honor and Baraka*.

9. I will be returning to this terminology in the following chapters; thus I put some places by successive keys in different contexts of appropriation, a conceptual device destined to nourish a thought dynamic oriented method at once towards descriptive appropriateness and explanatory appropriateness.

10. The proper classical epistemology such as I described it in 1976 (see my *Critic of Islamic Reason*, 1984), continues to be practiced by several authors of today. See Jean Claude Vadet, author of several studies on Islam: *The Moral Ideas in Islam*, P.U.F. 1995. The book is published in the collection *Islamics* launched recently by Janine and Dominique Sourdel, Francois Deroches. See my reports in *Arabica* where I give precise examples referring to some very different authors;

but that have for a common trait the implicit adhesion closed to the dogma of a *homo islamicus* such as camped recently by my thinker friend Louis Gardet and that has just confirmed the very laymen and very learned J. Cl. Vadet. One can also consult the contributions of concerning Islam to the diverse dictionaries and encyclopedias recently published; I will cite notably the *Dictionary of Ethics and of Moral Philosophy*, under the direction of Monique Canto-Sperber, P.U.F. 1996.

11. For more details on the compared practice of the *ijthad* to the Imamiens and the Sunnites, see Devin J. Stewart: *Islamic Legal Orthodoxy*, op.cit.

12. In his thesis of *Truth and History* not yet published, A. Cheddadi has analyzed well the literary fracture of "first developments of historiographic Muslim" presented to the fair title like "a founded history" to the strong mythical dominance of Islam like true religion. There remains to pull the theological consequences of this conclusion on the mythical statute built not only of the true religion, but of Qur'anic discourses themselves whose historiography is a mytio-literary expansion. *Living Consciously Within a True Myth.* (John Hick, *The Fifth Dimension*).

13. How to insert this multi-dimensional problem made religious and of the true religion troubling the young kamikaze Palestinians? How to explain the Jews rejecting these crazy ones of God as vulgar terrorists while they give their life of the same manner for the sacred cause of the promised Earth? How to interpret nonchalantly or too hurt everywhere the fall of the innocent in the name of "valor," "dignity," "justice," "truth" the silence of believers and nonbelievers in front of a phenomena so complex, this launched a challenge to the conscience of our time of which one does not know how any more how to speak? How to realize the slap of modern said reason in front of this functioning contemporary society for that, in the saturated Temple-Mosque of the sacred one, the same actor who is a martyr, a terrorist passable of the all the lynchanges for the others? The governments responsible are the first to rid themselves of these questions because they must manage the urgency. And who in the academic world censures these questions so that they are not kept as scientific research objects and philosophical investigation?

14. Halbwachs, Maurice: *La Topograhie Legendaire des Evangiles en Terre Sainte.Etude de memoire collective*, Paris 1941.

15. The ancient thesis of A. Bouhdiba in *Sexuality and Islam*, PUF 1975, has for a long time filled the void in the bibliography of this immense void: despite her notorious insufficiencies, notably her conservatism on the *shari'a*, she remains an obligatory reference because the emptiness exists despite the production campaigning successes on the emancipation of women in Muslim environments.

Chapter 9

1. The official publication of the party, Mardom, is the prime and official example. Many memoirs of the party cadre, although written after the demise of the party indicate the same genre of thinking. See for example, Noor al-Din Kiyanoori, *Khaterat¸* Tehran, 1992/3; Iraj Eskandari, *Khaterat-e Siyasi¸* Tehran, 1988/9; Anvar Khame'ii, *Khaterat-e Siyasi: Panjah-o-Seh Nafar*, Tehran, 1993/4.

2. Ali Shari'ati, *Tashayyo'-e Alavi, Sashays'-e Safavi*, various editions.

3. Pahlavi, Shah Mohammad Reza, *Majmu'ah-ye Ta'lifat, Notgh-ha, Payam-ha, Mosahabah-ha va Bayanat-e A'ala-Hazrat Homayoon Mohammad Reza Shah Pahlavi Arya-Mehr, Shahanshah–e Iran*, 9 vols., np., nd. See also the leftist terminology in the official reports of a cabinet secretary who was executed after the Revolution. "Arezoo-ha-ye Payan na-Pazir: Tahlil bar Zendegi va Shakhsiyat-e Doktor Manoochehr Azmoon", in *Motale'at-e Siyasi¸*vol. 2, Autumn 1993, pp. 145-190. The above article consists of a partial file on Azmoon, collected by the SAVAK.

4.Franz Fanon, *The Wretched of the Earth¸* London, 1985; Marx and Engels, *The Communist Manifesto*, Various editions.

5. For an analysis of Soroosh's writings see Valla Vakili, *Debating Religion and Politics in Iran: The Political Thought of Abdolkarim Soroush¸* New York, 1996.

6. For what Khatami stood for, see Eric Hooglund, "Khatami's Iran," *Current History*, February 1999; Shaul Bakhash, "Iran's Unlikely President," *The New York Review of Books¸* November 5, 1998.

Khatami's own writings, *Bim-e Moj*, Tehran, 1993 and *Az Donya-ye Shahr ta Shahr-e Donya*, Tehran, 1995 indicate respect for and some understanding of Western philosophy.

7. See Khatami's interview with the feminist journal *Zanan*, May 13, 1997, p.63; See also other interviews and reports in *Ettela'at*, April 1999 and in *Asr-e Ma*, April 14, 1997. The most complete accounts of statements by Khatami are collected in *Didgah*. Ironically, the president's public statements are published for select circulation only.

8. Much of the following is based on personal observation during the winter of 2001.

9. Christopher de Bellaigue, "The Struggle for Iran", *New York Review of Books*, 16 December 1999, pp. 51, 57-59.

10. Ibid., p. 56.

11. Masood Mohajer, "Cheh Asan Roohiyeh-ha Mimirand", IRAN, 22 February 2001.

12. Faramarz Rafipoor, "Arzesh-ha-ye Mazhabi, Arzesh-ha-ye Maddii", *Nameh-ye Pazhoohesh*, Vol. 14, Nos. 14-15, Autumn-Winter, 1999-2000, p. 226.

13. Ibid., pp. 199-200.

14. Sayyed Reza Naghib al-Sadat, "Tahlil-e Film-ha-ye Por-Masraf-e Vidio-i dar Sal-e 1374", *Nameh-Ye Pazhuhesh*, pp 229-237.

15. *Ham-Bastegi*, March 12, 2001.

16. *Ham-Bastegi*, June 17, 2001.

Chapter 10

1. In a challenging essay, Salem challenges conventional notions of Western approaches to conflict resolution and points out that its "theorists and practitioners operate within a macro-political context that they may overlook, but which colors their attitudes and values. This seems remarkably striking from an outsider's point of view and is

largely related to the West's dominant position in the world. All successful empires" develop an inherent interest in peace. The ideology of peace reinforces a status quo that is favorable to the dominant power. The Romans, for example, preached a *Pax Romana,* the British favoured a *Pax Britannica,* and the Americans today pursue, consciously or not, a *Pax Americana.* Conflict and bellicosity is useful, indeed essential, in building empires, but an ideology of peace and conflict resolution is clearly more appropriate for its maintenance."

2. The concept of Muslim minorities is not without its complexities; in Mogul India, while they were in a numerical minority, they could hardly be described as a religious minority with the usual connotations of marginalization. In other countries such as Ethiopia and Tanzania, they may be a numerical majority while being on the political margins of society.

3. According to the 1991 population census, 166,609 and 157,801 Indians and Coloreds respectively indicated that they were Muslim. 9,048 Blacks and 1,697 whites also listed Islam as their religion. The total population for that year was 38,012,000. The 1996 census records 553,585 Muslims out of a total population of 39,806,598, which makes for about 1.3 percent of the population.

4. The ministers of justice, constitutional affairs, and of water affairs, the chief justice, deputy speaker of the Upper House, secretary for safety and security, director general for the state treasury, the chairpersons of several parliamentary select committees, and about 10 percent of all members of parliament are Muslims. At one stage during the uprisings of the 1980s, 16 percent of all the detainees in the Western Cape and 14 percent of all the participants in the constitutional negotiations during the early nineties were Muslims. (Personal calculations).

5. In this context, the term *Malay* is probably of linguistic rather than national derivation. Malayu was the common trading language of the Indonesian Archipelago from where many of the first Muslims in the Cape hailed.

6. Where both communities live in roughly equal numbers in the same city such as Kimberly in the Northern Cape, a combination of local consultation on issues such as the sighting of the moon and cultural allegiances, such as in the settling of divorces, will determine the

outcome of the issue at hand—for example, the council to assist in the mediation of disputes and ignore the (Indian) *Jami'atul 'Ulama*.

7. Many of these problems were the immediate products of the socioeconomic policies of the apartheid regime, which had its own illicit drug-dealing operations to generate income for their struggle against "terrorism." Yet those bereft of political insight find it convenient to blame democracy and posit simplistic solutions—termed "Islamic"—of chopping off hands, castrating rapists, and hanging murderers.

8. Samuels, Sardien, and Shefer narrate an interesting account of an exercise whereby participants were asked to bring along something of symbolic value to them and explain that value to the rest of the participants. One woman participant had brought a blanket along, which was draped over her knees. She spoke of the blanket in the following manner: "This blanket was given to me by my mother-in-law, who lives in a rural area, when I got married. When I visit my family, I wear the blanket around my body, and it becomes a symbol of my status as a married mature woman. But when I am here, in the urban areas, mostly I use this blanket over my legs to keep me warm." (1997, 41) In the varying functions of her blanket are reflected the different layers of her identity.

9. Ahmed speaks about how Muslims had "consciously to define and redefine themselves in terms of Islam" and how Islam easily incorporated local pre-Islamic cultures. "In Indonesia the Wayang or shadow theatre, the cyclic of plays in the rural areas adapted from stories from the Hindu epics of the Ramayana and Mahabarata, continues with the introduction of new Islamic characters. Hamza, the Prophet's uncle, was a favorite character. While Islamic characters were introduced in traditional plays, pre-Islamic heroes were updated and adjusted in Islam. Tradition among the Yennger of east Java has Ajisaka, famous for his wisdom and beauty, visiting the prophet in Makkah to obtain his spiritual knowledge. But Ajisaka does not become a Muslim. Indeed impressed by Ajisaka's ability to make himself invisible, the Prophet declares, 'You will be my equal.' Another example of the influence of Islam is provided by the popular dance. Although the traditional forms of dancing remained on the Indonesian islands, now after Islam, the legs are neither kicked high nor wide open as shown in the sculptures of Hindu Borobudur." (Ahmad, 1988, p. 109)

10. The term *ummah* occurs nine times in the Meccan context and forty-seven times in that understood to be Medinan. It is used to refer exclusively to the socio-historical community of Muslims (Q. 2:143; 3:110), to "a group of people" (from among the Muslims in Q. 3:104 and from among the Christians in Q. 5:66), community in the broad sense (Q. 6:108; 7:34; 10.47), and to an individual (Q.16:120-1). In the verse cited in the text above, it refers to the communities of all the Prophets. For much of the Medinan period the term was used to describe "the totality of individuals bound to one another irrespective of their colour, race or social status, by the doctrine of submission to one God." (Ahmad 1979, pp. 38-9) Looking at the way the term *ummah* has today acquired an exclusivist meaning, Ahmad says, "The main difficulty in dealing with the history of ideas is that terms are more permanent than their definitions" (ibid. 1979, p. 39).

11. In many ways this dilemma is reflected in the developed world, where many progressive Christian bodies and liberal churches are opening their doors to Muslims in the spirit of theological dialogue and solidarity against racism, xenophobia, and so on. Little do these Muslims realize that a part of this opening up also extends to gender, sexually marginalized groups, and environmental concerns.

12. Tibi is, in fact, explicit about this essentialization when he says, "In my view, scholars who exclusively stress the diversity of Islam fail to see that Muslims, be they in the Middle East, South Asia or black Africa, share a virtually consistent common worldview" (1992:11). This kind of reasoning has the effect, even if unintended, of placing those Muslims committed to pluralism outside the realm of the faithful.

13. Loy cites UNDP statistics that indicate that in 1960 countries of the North were about twenty times richer than those of the South. In 1990- after vast amounts of aid, trade, loans, and catch-up industrialization by the South, North countries had become fifty times richer. The richest 20 percent of the world's population now have an income about 150 times than that of the poorest 20 percent, a gap that continues to grow. According to the UN Development Report for 1996, the world's 358 billionaires are wealthier than the combined annual income of countries with 45 percent of the world's people. As a result, a quarter million children die of malnutrition or infection every week, while hundreds of millions more survive in a limbo of hunger and deteriorating health (n.d.:1,2).

Chapter 12

1. Even the figure of Muslim population in Thai society is not unproblematic. See my brief discussion of the politics of contending figures of Muslims in Thailand in Chaiwat Satha-Anand, "Bangkok Muslims and the Tourist Trade," in Mohamed Ariff (ed.), *The Muslim Private Sector in Southeast Asia*. (Singapore: Institute of Southeast Asian Studies, 1991), pp. 96-97.

2. Ashis Nandy, "The Twilight of Certitudes: Secularism, Hindu Nationalism, and Other Masks of Deculturation," *Alternatives*. 22 (1997), p. 160.

3. Ibid., p.160.

4. See Kumar Suresh Singh, *People of India: An Introduction*. (New Delhi: Anthropological Survey of India, 1992), Vol.I, as quoted in Nandy, "The Twilight of Certitudes," fn. 13, p. 174.

5. All these figures are from Pasuk Phongpaichit, Sungsidh Piriyarangsan and Nualnoi Treerat, *Guns, Girls, Gambling, Ganja: Thailand's Illegal Economy and Public Policy*. (Chiang Mai: Silkworm Books, 1998), pp. 86-111.

6. It is possible to find such collaborations elsewhere in the region. See for example, Alfred W.McCoy. *The Politics of Heroin in Southeast Asia*. (New York: Harper and Row, 1972).

7. Ampa Santimetaneedol, "Villagers find courage to drive out drug dealers," *Bangkok Post*. June 8, 1998.

8. Situation in Thai Society, 1997: A Summary. (Bangkok: Thai Development Support Committee, February 1998), p. 60. (In Thai)

9. See a critical view of mainstream development in Saneh Chamarik, *Development and Democracy: A Cultural Perspective*. (Bangkok: Local Development Institute, 1993).

10. These figures are those of National Housing Authority. See *Situation of Thai Society 1997: A Summary*, p. 27. (In Thai)

11. Seksan Prasertkul, "Ban Krua Ban Krai" in *Manager's Daily*. April 25, 1994. (In Thai)

12. Muslims in Thai society are not monolithic. There are, in fact, at least six lineages of Muslims in the country: Chinese, Persian, Indian/Pakistani, Arab, Cambodian and Malay Muslims. See Chaiwat Satha-Anand, "Bangkok Muslims and the Tourist Trade," pp. 96-97.

13. See account of this particular protest in *Managers' Daily*. April 22, 1994. (In Thai)

14. Kaewsan Atipothi, "Mob 'Ban Krua': Flash of Democracy in front of the Government House?" in *Managers' Daily*. May 3, 1994. (In Thai)

15. *Managers' Daily*. April 25, 1994; April 22, 1994; and May 3, 1994. (In Thai)

16. Chalida Tajaroensuk, *Protesting Process of Ban-Krua Community on 2nd Stage Expressway System Project (Collector-Distributor Road)*. Master's Degree Thesis, Faculty of Social Development, National Institute of Development Administration (NIDA), 1996, p. 86 (In Thai). This thesis also underscores the use of nonviolent actions by the Ban-Krua community.

17. *Lessons of Non-Government Organizations on Resources and Environment in the South.* (A seminar document prepared for "Thai Non-Government Organizations: Looking Back and Ahead: A Seminar to commemorate the first decade of Non-Government Organization Coordinating Committee", January 28-29, 1997, pp. 1-2.

18. Supara Janchitfah, "Charting their own course," *Bangkok Post*. (Outlook Section), July 16, 1998.

19. For 198 methods of nonviolent action, see Gene Sharp, *The Politics of Nonviolent Action (Part Two): The Methods of Nonviolent Action.* (Boston: Porter Sargent, 1973).

20. For the politics of wearing *hijab* in Thai society see Chaiwat Satha-Anand, *"Hijab* and Moments of Legitimation: Islamic Resurgence in Thai Society," in Charles F.Keyes, Laurel Kendall and Helen Hardacre (eds.), *Asian Visions of Authority: Religion and the Modern States of*

East and Southeast Asia.(Honolulu: University of Hawaii Press, 1994), pp. 279-300.

21. Supara Janchitfah, "Charting Their Own Course."

22. Sanitsuda Ekachai, "Reform before it is too late," *Bangkok Post* (Commentary), September 24, 1998.

23. But number alone may not be enough. Compare also Gustavo Gutierrez, *The Power of the Poor in History.* Robert R.Barr (Trans.) (Quezon City, Philippines: Claretian Publications, 1985).

24. See a reporter's photograph in the *Bangkok Post*, June 8, 1998.

25. *The Glorious Qur'an* (Trans. and Commentary by A.Yusuf Ali) (U.S.: The Muslim Students' Association, 1977), V: 174, p. 168.

26. Robert Burrowes, *The Strategy of Nonviolent Defense.* (New York: State University of New York Press, 1996). But see also my critique of the possible exclusivity of these dimensions in Chaiwat Satha-Anand, "'Nonviolenza Pragmatica' e 'Nonviolenza Per Principio': Una Contrapposizione Illusoria" (Overcoming Illusory Division: Between Nonviolence as a Pragmatic Strategy and a Way of Life) in my *Islam e Nonviolenza* (Torino: Edizioni Gruppo Abele, 1997), pp. 64-84. (In Italian)

27. See my "Introduction: Exploring the Frontiers," in Chaiwat Satha-Anand and Michael True (eds.), *The Frontiers of Nonviolence.* (IPRA's Nonviolence Commission; Honolulu: Center for Global Nonviolence; and Bangkok: Peace Information Center, 1998), pp. 2-3. See also Michael True, "Since 1989: The Concept of Global Nonviolence and Its Implications for Peace Research," in *Social Alternatives.* Vol.16 No.2 (April 1997), pp. 8-11.

28. See a somewhat similar analysis of another concept related to nonviolence, forgiveness, in my "The Politics of Forgiveness" in Robert Herr and Judy Zimmerman Herr (eds.), *Transforming Violence: Linking Local and Global Peacemaking.* (Scotdale, Pennsylvania: Herald Press, 1998), pp. 68-78.

29. Gene Sharp, "Nonviolent Action in Acute Interethnic Conflicts," in Eugene Weiner (ed.) *The Handbook of Interethnic Coexistence.* (New

York: Continuum Publishing Company, 1998), pp. 371-381. The quote is on p. 381.

30. Samuel P. Huntington. *The Clash of Civilizations and the Remaking of World Order.* (New York: Simon & Schuster, 1996), p. 263.

31. For example, see Edward Said, *Covering Islam: How the Media and the Experts Determine How We See the Rest of the World.* (New York: Pantheon Books, 1981); and Daya Kishan Thussu et al., "The Mechanics of Demonisation: The Role of the Media," in *Terrorising the Truth: The Shaping of Contemporary Images of Islam and Muslims in Media, Politics and Culture.* A Report on the International Workshop organized by Just World Trust, 7-9 October, 1995, Prepared by Farish A.Noor (Penang: Just World Trust, 1997), pp. 28-35.

32. See for example, Bruce B. Lawrence, *Shattering the Myth: Islam Beyond Violence.* (Princeton, New Jersey: Princeton University Press, 1998).

33. See my "The Nonviolent Crescent," in Glenn Paige, Chaiwat Satha-Anand and Sarah Gilliatt (eds.) *Islam and Nonviolence.* (Honolulu: Center for Global Nonviolence Planning Project, Spark Matsunaga Peace Institute, 1993), pp. 7-26.

Editors' Biographical Sketches

Abdul Aziz Said is Professor of International Peace and Conflict Resolution at American University's School of International Service in Washington DC. Said currently occupies the Mohammed Farsi Islamic Peace Chair, and is the Director of the Center for Global Peace. Said has a Ph.D. in International Relations from American University. Since 1957, Said has been teaching on the subject of international relations, human rights, democracy in world politics, ethnicity, peace and conflict resolution, spirituality, and Islamic peace. He has served as a member of the White House Committee on the Islamic World, Consultant to the United Nations Development Program, Consultant to USIA and the Department of State. Said's books include: *Concepts of International Politics in Global Perspective, Human Rights and World Order, Ethnicity and U.S. Foreign Policy,* and *Minding the Heart* (forthcoming).

Meena Sharify-Funk is a Ph.D. Candidate in International Relations at American University's School of International Service. Her areas of specialization are International Peace and Conflict Resolution and Islamic Studies with a particular focus on the status of women in the Islamic world. She also has coordinated two international conferences in Washington, DC on the subjects of Muslim-Christian relations and Islamic responses to cultural diversity.